CHURCH AND RELIGION
IN RURAL ENGLAND

CHURCH AND RELIGION IN RURAL ENGLAND

Douglas Davies, Charles Watkins,
Michael Winter,
Caroline Pack, Susanne Seymour,
Christopher Short

T&T CLARK
EDINBURGH

T&T CLARK
59 GEORGE STREET
EDINBURGH EH2 2LQ
SCOTLAND

First Published 1991

ISBN 0 567 29201 X

Typeset by Type Aligne, Edinburgh
Printed and bound in Great Britain by Billing & Sons Ltd, Worcester

Contents

Acknowledgements

Our principal acknowledgement must be to the clergy of the five dioceses and the residents of the parishes studied in this book without whose help and assistance this research could not have been carried out. We would also like to thank the Leverhulme Trust for providing the funding for the clergy study, and the Archbishops' Commission on Rural Areas for supplying additional funds to extend the study to Durham. Other people who have provided help and advice at different stages of the project include: Andrew Bowden, Elizabeth Brooker, John Clark, Grace Davie, Adrian Gregory, Ewan Harper, Chris Lewis, Jan MacLaran, Jeremy Martineau, Celia Richardson, Alan Rogers, Andrew Stocks, Debbie Whatmough and Philip Wheeler. The staff of various county record offices and electoral roll officers for the parishes provided help in finding relevant documentary material. The Diocesan Bishops, Secretaries and staff of the five dioceses were of great help in providing background support while the surveys were being carried out. Finally we must especially acknowledge the support and encouragement of our publishers.

1

Introduction:
The Rural Church Project

In 1988 an unlikely, and probably unique, partnership was forged between a department of theology and an agricultural college. The University of Nottingham Theology department linked up with the Centre for Rural Studies at the Royal Agricultural College at Cirencester, to found the Rural Church Project. With funding from the Leverhulme Trust and the Archbishops' Commission the first phase of the Project started with a detailed study of five English dioceses (Durham, Gloucester, Lincoln, Southwell and Truro). This book is a report of the findings from those five dioceses.

In September 1990 *Faith in the Countryside*, the report of the Archbishops' Commission on Rural Areas (ACORA) was published. By that time the bulk of this book was already written, and we awaited the ACORA report with considerable anticipation and not a little apprehension. The apprehension was based on the fact that while ACORA had received a considerable body of evidence from our own work in the 'Rural Church Project', we did not know until the publication of the Commission's report how that evidence had been utilised, and therefore whether there would be any overlap between the report and our own book. In the event our fears were entirely unfounded. Although *Faith in the Countryside* makes considerable use of our data, there is very little overlap in terms of substantive findings or approach. The ACORA report draws from different sources and is primarily concerned with making recommendations for the attention of both government and the church.

We make few policy recommendations, rather we report on one of the most comprehensive empirical studies of religion that has ever been carried out in England. It is not our intention to provide a statistical

1

commentary on *Faith in the Countryside*. Indeed we have already published an extensive report, in four volumes, which summarises the data generated by the Rural Church Project (Davies et al 1990). Rather we want to consider and reflect upon the facts of faith in the English countryside today.

This is a book which touches on many worlds, and necessarily draws from many disciplines, but is not a reference book or a text book. We hope that it will be of interest to sociologists of religion, to geographers and rural planners, to historians and theologians, but above all it aims to present to the general reader what we have found out about the organisation and operation of the Church of England today, especially in rural areas. In other words the audience we have had in mind is a general one rather than a group of specialist theologians or academics. But nor have we insulted the intelligence of our so called 'lay' readers by 'popularising' or 'simplifying' what we have to say. Religious issues are complex and demand serious reflection. Our book is fully referenced and deals with a number of difficult issues of theology and sociology. But we try to explain our terms and to avoid the use of jargon. We do not shy away from admissions of uncertainty and perplexity in the interpretation of some of our findings. Our belief is that any project as large and ambitious as this one will inevitably throw up new questions as well as providing answers. On occasions, then, our data raise all sorts of fresh issues or prompt further questions. *Church and Religion in Rural England* is not the last word on the rural church, both in the sense of reaching firm and final conclusions on all the aspects we have covered and, more literally, in saying all that can be said about certain issues. Our own investigations are continuing, particularly in the realm of other denominations in rural England (which are hardly touched upon in this book).

When the project was conceived we were struck by the paucity of social science literature covering contemporary mainstream church life in Britain. In particular we became increasingly conscious of the neglect of a key group of 'professionals' resident and active in rural areas. In view of the ubiquitous nature of church and clergy, even in these post-Sheffield days, it seemed extraordinary how little attention had been focused on the church by the plethora of rural planners, geographers, sociologists, and so forth, who had catalogued and lamented the decline in educational, transport and welfare services in the post-war period. The clergy remain numerically significant in the countryside and they have a role which has never been defined exclusively in religious terms. Indeed the parochial organisation of the church and the numerical strength of the clergy (even after several decades of decline) mean that many rural dwellers in special need are more likely to have access to a local clergyman than to a social worker, a solicitor, or even a branch of the Citizens Advice Bureau. Yet the role of the clergy has been routinely neglected by social geographers and others interested in rural service provision.

The research for the Rural Church Project was conducted between October 1st 1988 and January 1990. Two main investigations were carried out and the results of these provide the basis for this book. The first was a study of the church itself, its deployment of resources and personnel, particularly the clergy, and the work and views of the clergy. This was a three phase process involving appropriate contextual research of an historical and geographical nature to provide the background to the changing nature of the rural church in recent decades, a postal survey of the Church of England clergy in five dioceses, and in-depth interviews with a sub-sample of clergy in each of the five dioceses. The second part of the study was an interview survey of parishioners - both church attenders and otherwise - carried out in a sample of parishes in the five dioceses.

The book is based on postal survey returns from 572 clergy in the five dioceses, representing a response rate of 66%, 101 face-to-face interviews with rural clergy, and 489 interviews with parishioners, a 67% response rate. There was little variation in response rate by diocese. Although the methodological details of the surveys are set out in an appendix to this book, a few comments are necessary here to set the scene for what follows. First, the postal survey was of all incumbent clergy in the five dioceses. This phase of the survey, therefore, covered both urban and rural clergy and allows comparisons between the two. By contrast the interview surveys of both clergy and parishioners were all conducted in rural parishes, carefully selected to represent different kinds of rural community and parochial organisation.

We are conscious that there are difficulties with the questionnaire approach, and two criticisms are commonly levelled at such surveys. First they are seen as biased due to sampling difficulties, and secondly they are sometimes seen as providing a mere snapshot in time with attendant dangers of ignoring dynamic processes of social change. We were conscious of both dangers in the design of the research. The first problem was largely overcome by the more than satisfactory level of response we received from both clergy and people. In the case of the clergy, in particular, we were impressed by their enthusiasm to participate in the survey and we experienced none of the problems of bias brought about by an inadequate response rate. Moreover we received far more information than we had expected, both on the postal returns where many clergy had given us much additional comment as well as answering the specific questions, and in interviews all of which lasted at least two hours, with many taking three, four or even over five hours to complete.

In order to avoid a static picture emerging from the questionnaire survey we attempted to introduce dynamic elements in two ways. First, we included retrospective and dynamic elements in the questionnaires, especially the interviews. For example, we asked clergy to reflect on their own ministry over time. Thus we were able to build up a picture not only of clergy work in the Summer of 1989 but of changes and processes over time. Secondly, we undertook additional contextual work throughout the project. We reviewed the changing organisational structure of the church and deployment of clergy in the five dioceses through use of diocesan records, and some interviews with key personnel such as archdeacons, diocesan secretaries and clergy of other denominations. In addition, although our primary methodology is firmly within an empirical social science method, we have, during the course of the project, read widely in the field of pastoral theology. Our reading of this literature prompted various questions and served to direct and re-direct our work as the project has progressed.

Above all this is a book in which we attempt to allow people to speak, both the parishioners we interviewed and, perhaps rather more, the clergy. It is important that at a time when the church is publicly concerned to help voice the needs of underprivileged groups its hierarchy should also be attentive to its own priests. We would not wish to dramatize this point, but it remains worth making. Our concern, therefore, is to describe and comment on what many people and clergy have said to us about their experiences, opinions, and beliefs connected with the Church of England.

Turning now to the contents of the book itself our aim has been to provide an overview of what we consider to be the main elements which together make up church and religion in the English countryside. Thus in Chapter 2 we start with the basic organisational principle of Anglicanism, the parish. We consider the way in which the parochial system lies at the heart of Anglicanism, in both theory and practice and the influence this has had on the way in which principles of ministry have been developed over the centuries. From the parish in ecclesiology we turn to the parish as a geographical unit in Chapter 3 which considers social and economic changes in rural parishes. As *Faith in the Countryside* has so well demonstrated, it is inappropriate to consider change in the church without attention to the widespread and rapid changes affecting rural England. Our dioceses were chosen to reflect some of the contrasting types of change experienced in England.

Chapter 4 turns from the parish to the parish priest with an examination of the central figure of the clergyman. We look at the work of the clergy and their views on the different aspects of their life and work. This is not a chapter on the theology of ministry, some of that is dealt with later, but a social analysis of clergy work, its content and meaning. Perhaps we should say at this point that because the vicar, as a priest, has historically been male we have used throughout this book masculine words to describe the clergy who participated in our survey.

In Chapter 5 we consider the question of church and sect. This may, at first sight, seem a rather curious jump, but in fact it is a logical extension of the themes of the preceding three chapters. What are the implications for a parochial and clerical religion of rapid rural social change? Can the Church still claim to be the church of rural England and does it exist for all the people or solely the members of its congregations? These are the questions addressed in this chapter. Chapter 6 turns to the deployment of staff, in particular changes over time and the role of the laity. Chapter 7 considers the organisation of the church in terms of views on its parochial structures and government, as well as buildings and financial affairs.

Chapter 8 deals with forms of worship, the nature of services on offer in rural churches and church attendance. As well as using the data provided by the clergy we utilise the findings of our survey of parishioners and examine the type of people who attend church at both regular Sunday services as well as at special services such as those associated with Christmas and Harvest. We also focus on some of the issues involved with holding services in rural churches, in particular the clergy's views on united benefice services and small congregations, and the levels of ecumenical development. Chapter 9 considers the varieties of religious belief and practice, as uncovered in the survey of parishioners, to gain some picture of rural religion today and to see how pastoral ministry has responded. The concluding Chapter 10 examines some of the theological implications of our studies.

2

Parishes Old and New

The Church of England functions as it does largely because of the way it has been historically formed. Parishes lie at the heart of that historical formation and nowhere is this more clearly seen than in rural areas.

As parish-based religion the Church of England is essentially local religion. While the diocesan bishop expresses something of the Anglican Church's ideal of a Universal Church reaching beyond local confines in both time and space, in practical terms, it is the local focus of the vicar that takes precedence. This is reflected in the emphasis upon the vicar or parish priest throughout this book.

The situation as we found it in our survey was largely concerned with the vicar in his parish, his geographical territory, with his parish church and his responsibility for those who live there as part and parcel of what the Church of England had meant historically and still means to many people today. In this book we describe ways in which clergy along with churchgoing and non-churchgoing people view this picture of the parish. These images vary to a considerable degree, yet often revolve around the idea of parish priest, church, and life. In describing these varied images we may perhaps help foster an understanding of the depth of commitment felt and also of attitudes to change in the contemporary rural Church of England.

Some clergy and regular churchgoers may hold a theological definition of the church and the Christian life and particularly of the place of the church in the parish which they see as inadequately held by others. One view is of the 'church' as the body of Christ visible in a gathered community of the faithful while another is of the vicar as a paid professional servicing the needs of those in his parish patch. This kind of stark alternative lies behind many ideas of modern religious life and

7

it reaches into the social and religious history of England in a profound way. It has been said that if more of the Lord's people were historians fewer would need to be prophets. There is some truth in this. The fact that for most of its history the Christian church has been present in Britain is significant. And for a thousand years of this history the faith has been organized in geographical areas of dioceses and parishes. The parish, parish priest, and parish church constitute a fundamental part of the very concept of Christianity as culturally present in Britain.

These social facts can sometimes appear far removed from theological discussion. When speaking theologically about the church we normally start with God. Moving from Christ as head of the Church Universal we move to bishops as guardians of the tradition who, in turn, share their pastoral care with representative priests. Just how theological considerations relate to popular outlooks is something we shall consider specifically in Chapters 9 and 10. For the moment we simply make the point that serious consideration must be given to historical and cultural facts of parish organization when moving into theological debate. It is the Christian church itself which helped form the parish structure of England and through its ideas of ministry and priesthood came to furnish parish priests serving people in geographical areas.

In terms of the history of religion the parish has been a very durable institution which has survived major changes of church policy and social upheaval. It is easy to take for granted the fact that the historical switch from Catholic to Reformed religion in England ultimately left parishes intact. Similarly the varied commitments within the Church of England as expressed in Anglo-Catholic, Evangelical, and Central outlooks have operated within the parochial system and under a variety of patronages. Perhaps even more importantly, the last hundred years have witnessed the growth and acceptance of a training system for priests based initially in theological colleges of distinctive churchmanship styles and now also involving part time training courses of a much more mixed outlook. But basic to the vast majority of these is the idea of the parish. Men were, and now men and women are, trained to serve within a parochial system. In more recent decades the rise of schemes to train people for work in 'secular' ministries as various forms of worker-priests has not been a tremendous success. Even when people have been trained for such a ministry outside the normal parochial systems of worship and ministry many have gravitated back to parochial involvement.

Some speak too of the appointment of people with very extensive parish experience to positions of dignity within the church as much more desirable than the appointment of individuals from more specialist areas. If, for example, academics are appointed to bishoprics, as was once not uncommon in the Church of England, the question of 'real' pastoral experience is likely to be raised. All in all this speaks of the durability and power of the parish as a vital concept in the pastoral theology of the Church of England. It is a concern also voiced when some parish clergy and laity ask what General Synod and 'higher' levels of church organization have to do with the parish, which is explored in Chapter 7.

One point that might be raised for discussion as a way of approaching local and national levels of Church life is to say that pastoral work typifies parochial Anglicanism while political involvement marks its national utterances. The question is not simple since theologically it is easy to argue that national political involvement is radically pastoral: the *Faith in The City* report could be cited as one major example. But that level of theological insight is not always present.

Church Local and National

Many have opinions about the Church of England. They like or dislike the local vicar, they were married in church or heard a priest take a funeral recently. Anecdotes abound and vicar jokes are not unknown, their appearance in television and poster advertisements stands as a mark of national recognition. So it is that local and personal knowledge is related to the national picture. The Church of England has also managed to retain a high public profile through media coverage. Bishops have expressed their views on politics and doctrine; lightning has struck York Minster. The Falklands and Gulf War Commemoration Services raised issues of patriotism and Christian identity while the church-state link has also been questioned in connection with the appointment of bishops and archbishops, and in Parliament's voice over doctrine. An Archbishop of Canterbury has even had an envoy taken as a political hostage.

While in some ways it is true to say that pastoral ministry makes the Church of England local while political matters make it national it may also be that national disasters and televised commemorative religious services have linked local knowledge of pastoral care with the national scene. At least these are issues that should not be ignored. If anything they will have raised the profile of ministers in their parishes rather than weakened them, almost irrespective of the level of faith among the people. Whether or not senior clergy appearing on television are identified with politicians is another interesting issue. These are speculative thoughts of background interest when we consider the detail of popular and clerical opinion later in this book.

They do, however, raise the topic of power and allow us to draw attention to the much less newsworthy yet fundamental fact of parish life where priests look at their own situation in the light of church hierarchy and social visibility. What the church means to a vicar who serves solely on the edge of a large rural diocese far from his own cathedral centre is not the same as for a priest much involved in General Synod or committees at Church House Westminster. For most priests and people the church is the parish church. As individuals we may applaud this as right and proper for pastoral care and evangelism or see it more negatively as the root of narrow minded parochialism. Certainly sharp distinctions between the one and the other need not be over accentuated but, similarly, the continuum needs to be remembered.

We have emphasized these points on national and local levels of church life in this discussion of parishes simply because when we interviewed clergy many were very glad of the opportunity to speak their mind. They were pleased to know that someone, albeit a researcher, was asking them what *they* thought. Some felt far removed, distant both geographically and in terms of identity, from the official media picture of the church.

It is already obvious that throughout the extensive research lying behind this book the parish was a dominant factor. We visited priests in their parish and talked to them at length about their life and work in their present parishes. They often spoke about their earlier parochial experience and the kind of parish they would like next. Their family life was parish influenced. The place of the parish in their outlook was fundamental, validating in a radical way their title of parish priest. So too with many of the lay people interviewed, whether churchgoers or not. They lived in parishes and were very often aware of parish facilities. This is not at all surprising given the place of parishes in English history, and the physical centrality of many churches in village communities. As we have already said the vicar and the church building are closely related in popular opinion. It is no accident that the expression 'going into the church' has been widely used to describe ordination. The fact that many active churchpeople dislike this phrase should not distract us from the truth expressed by it: that for many the vicar and the church are so closely related as to be indistinguishable.

Parish, Priest, and Pastor

The parish is, then, the distinctive feature of the post-Reformation Church of England. It is a key to subsequent Anglican development, especially in terms of the ministry and pastoral care. In general it is more important than bishops or the churchmanship of priests. In particular it was the rural parish which came to constitute an ideal which was later adapted for urban and general use. Christianity may well have been a city based religion in its infancy in the Mediterranean world but in England it took shape as a rural phenomenon. The nature of settlement and demography ensured that this was so.

Although by the twelfth century a network of parishes covered the country the weight of historical research suggests that it was only in the post-Reformation clergy that a 'single-minded devotion to the parochial ministry' emerged as a style of pastoral care on a wide front (Collinson, 1982:97). This period also witnessed a remarkable growth in the graduate status of the clergy. By about 1625 more than three quarters of the clergy were graduates. This fact may serve as a broad background for our sketched outline of the historical development of pastoral theology in the Church of England which is necessary to show how the parish, its parson and people became a pastoral unit.

George Herbert's *Country Parson* of 1652 set out an explicit model of ministry which would be influential for at least the next two centuries. The 'country parson' who features in the subtitle of Herbert's *Priest to the Temple* is set in contrast to priests who live in universities or great houses. The contrast is, obviously, not between rural and urban clergy. The priest is an immediate representative of Christ and is spoken of as such. He is not viewed as a representative of a bishop, indeed the prelates of the church are specifically not addressed.

Herbert's twenty second chapter on the life of the priest is entitled 'The Parson's Completeness'. In many respects this summarizes Herbert's entire concern for the representative churchman who is all in all to his people. He is able to give advice on the law as well as on basic cures for physical ills. This image of the omnicompetent priest is in many respects one from which later generations have sought escape. Historically and culturally, it marks a simple society with a relatively low level of total information and is certainly far removed from the modern world. As with other writers of the seventeenth and eighteenth centuries the major emphasis is upon an orderly personal and ecclesiastical life whose sincerity will impress and assist the spiritual life of congregations. Human need is perceived as basic and shared by priest and people alike.

The pastoral functions of the clergy, so evident in Herbert, parallel the contemporary concern expressed in the Ordinal of the *Book of Common Prayer*. Following the medieval problems of reduced populations in the Black Death, of earlier absentee priests and of monastic and Papal interference, the parochial system was in need of a dedicated workforce. So it was that a distinctive feature of the English Reformation was a commitment to pastoral obligation at the parish level.

The parish came to be the pragmatic focus of the English Reformation ideal. New vision and energy was brought to the pre-existing parochial structure of the land. The sixteenth and seventeenth centuries present a period when practice was brought into line with theology. George Herbert's country priest is the practical example of the model enshrined in the Ordinal of the Reformation *Book of Common Prayer*.

This interplay of theology and practice worked to the extent that the parish became what it still is in many respects, a fundamental entity prized by the Church of England with the parish priest viewed as the primary model of consecrated ministry. This is an important feature when we go on to look at the later development of non-stipendiary and work-focused ministries which are, perhaps, viewed with some suspicion in several quarters of the church precisely because they involve ministry outside normal parish concerns.

An important episcopal concern of the sixteenth and seventeenth centuries was to educate the clergy and to provide them with edifying material for their parishes and not just for their 'congregations'. The option of a gathered and eclectic congregation was not chosen by the English Reformers. For them 'Common Prayer' and a religion of the people at large was the ideal which the ministry and the law of the land tried to produce. For the Church of England the existence of parishes and the existence of an ordained ministry were two distinct yet interrelated facts of some importance at this time. Richard Hooker reminded the readers of his *Ecclesiastical Polity* that parishes were initially created in England in the seventh century and followed on from the original urban divisions created in the early church. While he saw such divisions as a wise form of church organization he argues against those who would so stress parochial structure as to limit the nature of the ministry itself.

Hooker stressed the nature of the ministry as an ordination to the wide service of God and not to a restricted place. 'Presbyters and deacons are not by ordination consecrated unto places but unto functions' (V.1iii.7.6). By doing this Hooker reaffirmed both the nature of parish organization and the nature of the ordained ministry. They were separate yet related entities which allowed a degree of freedom for ministers who could be used for wider purposes than direct parish life as need might arise. The minister was not created by an eclectic congregation even though he was set to serve a particular group of people. He was always a minister of the wider church who happened to serve in a particular place.

Yet the heyday of the parish ideal in practice was in fact very short, lasting from the Elizabethan religious settlement to the development of limited religious toleration under the Commonwealth. The Restoration re-established Anglican worship as normative, but it proved impossible not to give some breathing space for dissenting congregations. Although they suffered numerous legal penalties, dissenters were allowed to worship outside the Church of England by the Act of Toleration of 1689.

Other Churches and Secular Moves

The impact of religious 'competition' varied. Areas of domestic industry, towns, mining communities, and scattered settlements, in fact any area where the traditional order was weak, were more likely to have a Nonconformist presence. But overall, it seems likely that by 1700 a majority of parishes had some inhabitants who had a religious allegiance to a denomination other than the Church of England. Even so the church did not relinquish many of its privileges regarding these people in registering births, conducting burials and demanding tithes until the 1830s. The fifty years between the Act of Toleration and the rise of Methodism was a period of general decline in religious activity. Both the Anglicans and the Dissenters suffered a fall in attendance. Even the Catholic sub-culture was affected. Toleration was increasingly seen as covering indifference; not obliged to attend church many likewise did not attend chapel. The situation was alarming those who increasingly viewed churchgoing in terms of its social role in supporting good order. A gulf was developing between a highly cerebral theology grounded in scientific rationalism, suspicious of that enthusiasm which had been associated with rapidly expanding urban life and the social change of industrialization, and the need for a religion which could have meaning for the common people.

Pastoral activity was honoured in theory but was practically neglected to an astonishing degree throughout the eighteenth century as pluralism and absenteeism removed clergy from their parishioners. To an extent, the church failed to respond to the challenge of urbanization and industrialization, it even appears not to have even held its ground in the countryside where population was still increasing. Perhaps the most significant result of this was the rise of Methodism and with it a more extensive emergence than earlier dissenters had produced of a model of religious life based in a gathered community of the faithful.

One important reason for Methodism's birth within Anglicanism was an evangelistic attempt to restore the masses to the church. The revivalist programme aimed to provide dedicated laymen who would assist the regular clergy in reaching those lapsed into indifference. The Methodist discipline was designed to provide an underpinning for these new recruits. Methodists were to be a leaven to the whole church. But Methodism could not be contained within the eighteenth century established church. The clergy could not tolerate 'irregular clergy' drawn from the lower orders, considering them a threat to their position in the parishes. Voluntary associations were seen as incompatible with the universal parish ideal. Here pastoral care and evangelistic ideals were not at all seen as identical. For their part Methodists were frequently very critical of the sincerity and effectiveness of the regular clergy. Growing rapidly, Methodists set examples in revivalism for other Dissenters, especially Baptists. In addition, from about the 1780s, Irish immigration reached significant proportions reaching a climax in the 1840s. This brought about a revival of Catholicism in England as a numerically significant although largely urban force.

The Anglican claims to universality and the parochial ideal were shattered by Horace Mann's religious census of 1851 which showed that Anglicans were no longer a majority of the actively religious. Nominal allegiance was still high but participation weak. In most areas the Church of England had to compete as a denomination against other bodies which had emerged from sects and groups arising from Methodist Dissent and the rapid social change of the Industrial Revolution. The emergence and development of Methodism and dissent led to competition between churches which involved an increase in church building and extension during the second half of the nineteenth century. Robin Gill's preliminary researches suggest that rural church decline may have been linked with excessive competition between churches (1989:81). Investment in church extension at a time of decreasing rural population was a recipe for empty pews and a hostage to fortune as the secularisation debate was to prove after the nineteen sixties.

But the Victorian Church of England also had to compete with indifference and irreligion in the cities. No longer was the Church of England, in practice, an Ecclesia, a universal church within its national boundaries. No longer was it a church largely of rural areas and market towns. The later eighteenth and early nineteenth century witnessed the most significant shift in the social history of Britain that the church had ever had to face: the urbanization of an increased population largely devoted to industrialized life.

The nineteenth century saw the church attempting to adapt itself in at least two ways. Firstly that of theological revival. From the 1780s evangelicals within the church adopted some of the Methodist techniques of evangelism. Sunday schools, mission activity, and tract distribution, were some examples. In the 1830s the very different approach of the Oxford Movement also began to take effect. This stemmed initially from concern about the diminishing role of the Church of England and the need to reassert its centrality in the fact of Catholic emancipation and nonconformist pressure. The Oxford Movement began by claiming that the Church of England was the true Catholic Church of England and as such should be protected by the State. It failed in its attempt, weakened as it was by defections of prominent men to Rome, yet it established the centrality of the sacraments, the importance of congregations, and of the pastoral ministry.

Secondly, there was administrative reform. Absenteeism was eliminated by the 1850s, while the newly founded theological colleges improved the training of clergy and generally dispelled the image of the amateur 'gentry' replacing it with the newly emerging and numerically stronger clerical profession. Clergy numbers increased from some 15,000 in 1831 to around 24,000 in 1901; not enough to keep pace with a rising population but enough to fill neglected parishes and found new ones in the cities. The fact that old parishes were divided to form new ones should not be overlooked as a fact of history for it marks the importance of the parish organization of Anglican religion.

Urban Ministry After Rural Models

George Herbert's ideal pastor lived in quite another world from that of the industrial city. From the nineteenth century onwards the Church of England was to have a major focus of its work in urban contexts. In response to this many developments in theology and practice were to take place and a number of these will be discussed in subsequent chapters. One important feature of this changing church life concerns the ideal image of the priest.

One interesting and important shift in pastoral theology from the time of the *Book of Common Prayer* in 1662 to the *Alternative Service Book* of 1980 reflects an increasing focus on urban life as the dominant context of parish work. Within the urban context Anglican life has, perhaps inevitably, stressed the significance of those who constitute the regular worshipping congregation. The sheer number of residents within a town has made it impossible for clergy to think of themselves as closely involved in the lives of their geographically located parishioners. If one difference between the seventeenth and nineteenth centuries was the emergence of the Church of England as a strong urban presence, one of the more recent developments following the decline in the number of full time clergy during the twentieth century has been the application of urban pastoral models to rural situations. This may, initially, sound odd, but refers particularly to the fact that clerical training became a more formal and precise art at the time when urban ministry was strong.

One specific historical example of pastoral theological change will illustrate this rural – urban shift in pastoral theology. We draw it from John Gott's lectures and book of the same title *The Parish Priest of the Town* first published in 1888. Here we find the Bishop of Truro, John Gott, speaking enthusiastically of the dynamism and sense of change of the age itself, a dynamism coming to sharpest focus in town life, 'where four-fifths of England has gathered itself' (1906:9). He spoke as one who had already ministered for thirty years in urban contexts. At the outset of his lectures he established some major differences between the town priest and the village priest. In towns there was much more organization which added pressure to the minister's activity. Conscience was more difficult because of many social problems, and lastly there was the problem of unbelief focused in active agencies of opposition. As far as he was concerned in the country there were but few people who were the social equal of the parson. The few who did exist, neighbouring squires for example, afforded more by way of recreation than an opportunity for ministry. The basic idea conveyed is that rural ministry is a given pattern which involves little difficulty. It is the new urban context which challenges and excites. There is little concern over rural problems such as the agricultural depression of the late nineteenth century.

Setting Gott's comments in perspective we might say that the period 1830-1920 was one in which the church consolidated its position in the countryside where the social situation was more conducive to parochial revival and pastoral concern. The idea of the countryside as the bastion of the Church of England seems not inappropriate to the late nineteenth century.

The very success of the church in this respect was taken for granted. It had, after all, been a century of unparalleled growth in the number of clergy very many of whom were youthful. Yet in terms of the general population the long agricultural depression of the 1870s, 80s, and 90s, witnessed a flight from the land that seemed to show rural England in terminal decline. The success of the church in rural areas seemed insignificant compared with its failure in the cities. Perhaps it was a rural success that came a little too late for the way English populations were now developing. It was no wonder that Gott saw the cities as the focus of challenge, a theme that many pursued into the first two decades or so of the twentieth century.

Town and Country Pastoral Theology 1900-1950

Writing in 1912 Clement Rogers argued that there was a 'permanent contrast between the forms of social life in town and country' (1912:189). Part of the difference lay in the feudal and traditional nature of the country while the town enabled church life to be more exploratory and innovative, whether in music or Christian education. He saw a flow of churchpeople from the country to the towns and a smaller corresponding return as innovations passed back to rural parishes.

His major criticism was that urban pastoral methods were largely those of the country used in town but without any suitable adaptation. He thought that such pastoral work had some effect, but ultimately failed to embrace the complex life of towns. Rogers saw the industrial revolution and its consequences as having been largely avoided in clerical thinking. He wanted a a clear commitment to sociology as a Christian means of clarifying social issues within a theological analysis.

Rogers, himself, was a lecturer in pastoral theology at King's College London during the first two decades of the twentieth century. That strong urban context lent great weight to his analysis of town and country links. What is certain is that he saw the priest as a central figure in whose life the divine is brought to many kinds of individuals irrespective of location.

A different and interesting emphasis began in the nineteen thirties as the Parish Communion movement became increasingly active. From this time the Church of England began a new phase of sacramental and eucharistic renewal. This needs some exploration because it involves the significant issues of personnel deployment both in towns and especially in the country. C.E. Osborne's lectures in pastoral theology delivered at Durham in 1933 argued that England was entering a new and exciting period as far as the rise of a central eucharistic service was concerned. He stressed the fact that pastoral care was the one attractive feature of priestly work as far as the public was concerned and, although concentrating largely on industrial-urban settings, he emphasized the fact that when parishes come to be focused on the eucharist, care must be taken lest a narrowness of the communicant circle emerges as a danger to broader Christian service (1933:64). This issue of the eucharist as a barrier to church involvement especially in rural areas we consider in Chapter 8.

A.G. Hebert's edited collection of 1937 on *The Parish Communion* firmly fixes this concern over the centrality of the eucharist and also strikes a prophetic chord. Arguing that it might take twenty years to establish the eucharist as the main Sunday service, Hebert still expresses his hope that this would come about and do much to heal internal church divisions and party politics. Certainly by the nineteen sixties that was increasingly the case and now, in the nineteen nineties, the eucharist as the central service is as close to normative as Hebert could possibly have wished. He saw the Parish Communion as the means by which the Church of England might come to a true self-understanding. Such issues were within the wider Liturgical Movement. Fairbairn and Downton, in the Hebert volume, write 'from a country village' that conditions in country parishes are not what they were. Surpliced choirs, long fought over and defended as not being of Romish practice, were difficult to sustain but social factors of change were their main concern. They were worried about the isolation of villages being broken by transport bringing bed and breakfast visitors who would keep people from church; industrial occupations taking men away only to return at night; children being bussed to school outside their villages, while the radio had raised people's expectations at many levels. In addition they saw a growing sense of individualism in religion.

They conceive of the priest's task in liturgical terms. He must say the offices and be the man of prayer in the area of his charge. He may well feel himself 'cut-off' from his neighbouring clergy and in this he differs from town priests. Accordingly village priests should meet in their rural chapters to worship and support each other. We shall see the accuracy of this view when we explore the lives of present day rural priests in Chapter 4. A major feature of the Parish Communion for Hebert and his co-authors was the corporate breakfast shared after the service. They assume fasting before the eucharist. One obvious feature of the ideal of Parish Communion is the need for priests to celebrate. This is not a problem as long as priests are locally in good supply but, inevitably, becomes problematic if their number falls below the number of congregations requiring services within restricted times such as 8.0 and 11.0 a.m.

Ten years after Hebert, Charles Forder published *The Parish Priest at Work* in 1947. This was a thorough and detailed blueprint for parish organization and ministry. Of his twenty nine chapters the penultimate is devoted to 'The Country Specialist'. Forder drew heavily on *The Church in Country Parishes* of 1940 and on the church report on *Training for Ministry* of 1944. The overriding sense conveyed is of the country parson possessing leisure in a low-key occupation. He thought that in the church at large country ministry was rated lower than that in towns. This needed correcting, he said, and mentioned the suggestion that perhaps one theological college should be set aside for the training of country clergy. Other suggestions are that young clergy should be encouraged into the country to help counterbalance the trend for country clergy to be older and perhaps less able people.

This negative evaluation was simply reported by Forder. Yet when he came to give his own analysis of rural and urban differences he began with a description of 'the rural mind' as slow, long to carry grievances, and generally non-committal. Forder encouraged the priest to take interest in many aspects of rural organization, especially housing, education, farming and the recreational and social elements in village life.

Realizing that personnel shortages might make groupings of parishes inevitable he worried about the complete lack of clerical training in group practice. He also feared that different villages would not wish to be socially united through having to share clergy. This idea is evaluated in Chapter 6 below, in the light of clergy experience of shared ministry between villages today.

Town Church as Gathered Church

In Forder's comprehensive study of Anglican pastoral practice we can see the basic assumption that the parish priest is primarily a town focused individual. More than this, there is a clear acknowledgement that in towns the church is more congregational than parochial (1947:91). It is eclectic and gathered rather than open to all in a regular way. One major attitudinal difference we might observe from the position of the nineteen eighties compared with Forder's forties is the new high technology of the farming industry. The notion of slow witted labourers, a travesty then, has certainly now given way to skilled people who use very expensive and complex machinery.

Practically ten years later Martin Thornton's *Pastoral Theology* creatively argued for a parochial theology of three concentric circles (1956). At the centre lay the eucharistic community which expressed the 'remnant concept of the faithful'. Around them were occasional church members. On the outside was everyone else. The pastoral task lay in the direction of souls such that they might progress in their knowledge of God. Thornton saw the parish as a place in which the mystical body of Christ comes to expression.

For him the difference between rural or urban was inappropriate. His sacramental theology stressed the incarnation and makes 'place' vitally significant. 'Parish-plus-cure of souls' constitutes the sacramental whole, an 'integrated organism' (1964 Edition, p.18). In this book we have an extremely clear example of Anglican thought fully flourishing as a eucharist focused community theology. His idea of the remnant led to a discussion of exclusive membership principles as the truly faithful were separated from the worldly masses. This highlighted the Anglican paradox of being a state church fully accepting of inborn members and with responsibility towards all within a parish boundary and a Christian church requiring some degree of active commitment on the part of its members. What is obvious is the total acceptance of the parish as a vital concept, so much so that Thornton wished to see more bishops appointed so that dioceses might become smaller and approximate more to the more ancient ideal of episcopal urban-region ministry. Thus for much of the twentieth century the great issue for pastoral theology has been numerical. How can relatively few clergy minister to increasingly numerous populations?

Thornton's answer lay in the remnant. The priest should foster a small group in the parish which would be the worshipping 'remnant' whose spirituality he should develop by spiritual direction, worship, and teaching. 'Nine-tenths of the work of pastoral-priesthood, seeking to bring all to Christ, is the training and direction of the remnant' (1964:42). Thornton believed that the parochial remnant emerged naturally and directly from the monastic remnant. For centuries monasteries had been the focus of faith and with their dissolution the centre of gravity passed to the parish. The mistake which Thornton perhaps makes is to place too much stress upon the lay aspect of this assumed mantle. It is certainly easier to see the new parish priests of the English Reformation as leading a new style of spirituality rather than a newly constituted nuclear group of parishioners. Historical matters apart, Thornton's advocacy of a parish remnant is one answer to the reality of large modern populations. It is a scheme to which we return in Chapter 5 when considering gathered congregations and open parish communities. For the moment we mention Thornton to stress the fact that the parish as a worshipping community and as an arena of spiritual direction has retained its power in this scheme of pastoral theology related to the modern urban situation.

This strength of the parish has been emphasized by many. Roger Lloyd, for example, spoke of the parish up until 1914 as 'very much its own monarch ... self-sufficient and haughtily independent even of diocesan organisations' (1946:166). He also spoke of the dominant ideal of efficiency and activity in urban parishes spawning many clubs and meetings. Lloyd saw rural parishes as 'both the heart and backbone of English religion' (1946:177). Yet he had relatively little to say about them except that their priests were as dogged by small congregations as urban priests were by immense numbers. Perhaps the significant point is that urban parishes were increasingly active as internally complex institutions with an extensive life of their own, while rural parishes were more inextricably linked with the ongoing life of a wider community. In his second volume on *The Church of England in the Twentieth Century*, Lloyd gave more attention to the rural Church and to the numerous reports and analyses of rural Anglicanism in the period between 1918 and 1939. The burden of much of this analysis was that the old form of village life was undergoing rapid change. In terms of pastoral theology a major shift was noted and it is one which will be very significant for several later chapters in this book. Historically, Lloyd points out that ministry in the rural church meant the ministry of the vicar, but now with parishes being joined together and manpower decreasing the idea of ministry was being broadened to involve other people most especially the reader (1950:193).

Church, Rurality, and Postmodernity 1960-1990

There are some further background issues involving parishes, ministry, and rural contexts which we now want to pinpoint for the period 1960 to 1990. Many readers will already be familiar with Adrian Hastings' splendid *History of English Christianity 1920-1985* (1986) and will read that for broad church and social history. In addition we would highlight the issue of the mass media in contemporary society and church life because it has influenced the place of the church and its ministry in rural areas and the church in the nation.

Many church issues and personalities have more recently become familiar both to churchgoers and the population at large. This is particularly important in the light of attitudes and outlooks which have been called 'postmodern', a term used as a hall-mark of recent decades. 'Postmodern' culture is supposedly dominated by image, style, and individualist perspectives amidst a media realm of mass communication and is devoid of any underlying and unifying interpretation of reality. The church can be seen as both part of this stance and as an opponent set against it. Increasingly, for example, the church has stressed the place of community over against the lone individual. This has come to a very clear focus in the ACORA Report *Faith in the Countryside* (1990:18). Similarly a commitment to the past has been tempered by the perceived need to communicate in ways appropriate to the church's public as witnessed by the introduction of the *Alternative Service Book* and the many discussions it engendered (Fenn, 1987). Through television and international relations the Church of England has sought a pastoral and ethical perspective with a vision of a unified community of well-being. It is as though the ordinary parochial attitude has been elevated to a national and international stance with the aid of the media.

On a theological and liturgical front the Holy Spirit has come into the centre of discussion and of liturgical reform even to the point where the Father as first person of the Holy Trinity has taken a subsidiary position within the 'structure of feeling' of religion over this period in Britain (Harvey 1989:41,42). Liturgically, for example, the centrally placed communion table and Minister sets the scene for saying 'The Lord is here, His Spirit is with us'. This shared community utterance differs from the east facing altar with the back of the priest to the people, and prayers addressing the Lord who is somewhat distant.

In terms of political theology we have numerous examples of Christian commitment in India, South America, South Africa, and in eastern Europe. All have fed into the British social and political focus of the gospel so that the very issue of religion and politics has become a key concern. The media world has enhanced the theological idea of the Church Universal. This too has had its impact on rural church life. Parochialism in the introverted sense of absorbed self concern is less possible where television and interpreting clergy exist.

More specifically in theological terms the nineteen sixties was a period of explicit theological preoccupation with secularization and its consequences for traditional theology and church life. Even if bishop John Robinson's *Honest to God* (1963) was only a reflection of the established existential theology of Paul Tillich, it involved an extensive popularization. Throughout the nineteen seventies and eighties the Cambridge cleric Don Cupitt pursued a more atheistic version of existentialism, while David Jenkins as Bishop of Durham advocated an individual responsibility in theological thought which some read as atheism, or at least as an unfaithfulness to the established tradition. Here the power of the mass media came into its own. But that kind of instant comment which it so favours showed itself incompatible with the kind of interpersonal discussion vital if theological ideas are to be understood and acted upon.

In ecclesiastical and institutional terms this period was one of increased centralization and apparent democratization of the Church of England. Yet some saw the growth of Synodical Government as making it easier for interest groups to capture the public eye through the media and to advocate, for example, the ordination of women, the politically sensitive issue of dealing with inner-city deprivation, and the morality of the clergy in relation to homosexuality. The increased profile of the church on a national level may have helped alienate some clergy who viewed themselves and their parishioners as far removed from the interests and centre of power represented by General Synod in its London base. Most especially is this the case in more socially isolated rural areas.

In terms of spirituality the decades of the nineteen sixties to nineties spanned a time when, despite an overall decline in church attendance, the Charismatic movement emerged within mainline denominations mirroring house-church or restorationist movements outside formal church organization. Initially this was largely a middle class phenomenon. As such it has been interpreted as a religious movement within post-industrial society in which personalized authenticity within communal fellowships flourished within an authoritarian context (Davies:1984 b).

In a more traditional manner evangelical streams of the church were flowing fast and expanding. Great concern over evangelical identity coincided with this increase in members, not least amongst ordinands with the consequent flourishing of the respective theological colleges. At the national level Anglican Evangelicals met at Keele in 1967 and at Nottingham ten years later. The ensuing reports stressed, amongst other ecclesiastical commitments, the vital nature of the eucharist. In the Keele Report, *Keele '67*, Evangelicals acknowledged that they had tended to make the eucharist peripheral and that this was a mistake. Ten years later *The Nottingham Statement* (1977:24) was not quite so sure of this issue and admitted that as evangelicals they were 'equally divided' on the point but still pressed the significance of the eucharist.

Perhaps it ought to be mentioned that while the nineteen fifties had seen a growth in the parish communion movement, sixties secularism counteracted this to some degree. When the stress on the eucharist reasserted itself in the later sixties and throughout the seventies it was an emphasis grounded in ideas of church-focused piety rather than the Christian-sociology outlook underlying Gabriel Hebert's earlier influential 'Liturgy and Society'.

Throughout this period there was a rapidly developing movement to train both men and women for non-stipendiary ministry within the church. By the nineteen seventies the entire country was covered by this training network. Many intended to retain their jobs and exercise their ministry within them. Some of these later switched to parochial service, whilst others were trained for full time ministry through part-time schemes. From about the mid-nineteen eighties there were occasional complaints about the non-stipendiary ministry especially as to their overall competence in fulfilling parochial ministry. But, as yet, this form of training remains a firm feature in Anglican life. When Mark Hodge produced a study for the Advisory Council for the Church's Ministry

(ACCM) on *Patterns of Ministerial Training* in 1987 it was subtitled 'in the theological colleges and courses'. This firmly indicated the Anglican commitment as much to the new course pattern as to the established pattern of theological colleges.

One important aspect of non-stipendiary ministry lay in the servicing of rural communities, especially those in relative proximity to urban centres. Such activity is linked to the question of furnishing priests to celebrate eucharists and thus assumes the centrality of the eucharist in the parishes concerned, and in turn relates to the deployment of lay-readers. All these issues will be discussed in depth later in this book.

Significantly, within the training courses the issue of churchmanship took a form different from that in the theological colleges. While many of the colleges represented party positions, or even explicitly middle ground, the courses often fostered a broad Anglican sacramentalism lacking party spirit as such. This fostering of an inclusivist ethos may yet prove to be a major turning point in Anglican history.

The parish continued its strength as a key Anglican concept and this is illustrated by the fact that increasing numbers of bishops were drawn from the ranks of parochially tested and experienced individuals. It is interesting to see the very experienced urban-industrial priest Canon Gordon Hopkins of Durham write in a 1974 ACCM booklet on 'Ministry' that young clergy should beware 'the enemy within', those within the church who deride and attack the parish system. It is even more interesting to see him say that he does not know quite what that system is apart from being a geographical area (1974:4).

In terms of inter-church activity this period also witnessed extensive discussions on church unity and union. Frustrated schemes of Anglican-Methodist Union ran alongside dialogue between Anglicans and Roman Catholics as fruitfully expressed in *The Anglican-Roman Catholic International Commission (ARCIC) 1 Final Report* of 1981. The extent to which such committee-focused activity actually represented parochial interests has often enough been questioned. It had been argued in the nineteen sixties by sociologist B.R. Wilson that ecumenism was a form of retrenchment movement on the part of churches in the face of increased secularization (1969). It is interesting to see that the Charismatic movement had a degree of ecumenism within it arising from a shared religious experience amongst people of different church traditions, and not because of a formal doctrinal policy. Nonetheless, the house church movement was not prone to ecumenical ideas and favoured an authoritarian local base antagonistic to ecumenism which tends to possess a liberal perspective.

In 1983 John Tiller produced an influential report entitled *A Strategy for the Church's Ministry*. Of its hundred and sixty or so pages, seven are devoted to rural ministry. He argued that in the future it would be impossible to retain an extensive clerical presence in each parish so that some form of team ministry or shared ministry involving laity was inevitable. It was assumed that country populations were largely immigrant, comprising people in search of authenticity and identity. This element of escapism was to be opposed as the church reminded its members of their worldwide church commitments. Tiller argued that the greatest strength of the parochial system in the Church of England lay in the availability of individual pastoral care (p.32). He concluded with a formula recommending that each rural parish be kept as a basic unit of pastoral care but that group ministries be organised to share pastoral resources. The suggestion was that the rural deanery be that unit of pastoral resource. Here Tiller followed on from a discussion of Leslie Paul's work in 1964 on the deployment of the clergy with its suggestion of larger parish groupings for more efficient use of manpower.

One of Tiller's assertions can be seriously questioned. It is that country clergy are themselves recruited from urban populations and do not understand the mentality of 'country folk'. There is something of a contradiction here since he also argues that many rural dwellers are immigrants from the town. If that is the case and if it is also the case that rural clergy are themselves townsfolk then there should not be such a discrepancy between priest and people.

From our perspective Tiller's acceptance of the parish as the great strength of the Church of England should not be left to rest just at the level of pastoral concern. It should be seen as the manifestation of the Anglican Reformation ideal which we mentioned at the outset. It is easy to debate the nature of Anglicanism in terms of a three-fold order of ministry set amidst Prayer Book, the place of reason in interpreting scripture, and church tradition. A better way of characterizing the church, however, might be in its parish organization and ethos. The parochial system constitutes the Church of England. It is the parish not the diocese, the priest and not the bishop, which forms the centre of gravity of Anglicanism. The apparent theology and the actual practice run in opposite directions. If this is true we may expect parish ideals to determine the identity of priests. We need to ask about the place of the parish, the diversity of its work, and so forth in constituting priestly identity as, indeed, we do in subsequent chapters.

Parishes, Community and Society

The role of the ordained ministry has increasingly come to the fore in recent years. In 1989 the Advisory Council for the Church's Ministry published a report on Vocation and Ministry entitled *Call to Order*. Towards the end of this document the authors 'emphasise the importance of parishes as centres of shared worship, discernment and mission' (1989:71). Parishes seem to be interpreted as focused congregations. In a similarly interesting way, the word 'community' is used throughout the report to refer to the active congregation. Parish has thus become associated with congregational community. At one point clear reference is made to the Church of England as the established church of the land and as such it is said to possess the 'double role' including a 'wider ministry to society' as well as to the church congregation (1989:40). The mention of 'society' here, however, seems to imply the national level of church involvement and raises interesting questions about local society, or the more immediate 'community' of the parish. Just how clergy and people classify 'parish', 'community', and 'church' will be discussed in Chapters 4 and 5.

Call to Order is one example of the change that has occurred in implicit attitudes towards the ministry, parish, congregation, and broader community under the influence of the urban experience of the Church of England and those who speak officially for it. Perhaps in part because of the realization that an urban ethos has come to dominate church policy, the Archbishops of Canterbury and York set up their Commission on Rural Areas. It was timely that following the *Faith in the City Report* the countryside should not be ignored. But in terms of society itself, this focus of attention was also demanded by the fact that from the nineteen sixties onward the countryside has been increasingly repopulated to a significant degree by middle class and professional people, commuters or the retired. Many of these bridge the social worlds of town and country, had experience of urban churches or else wished to be involved in church life now that they identified themselves as villagers. This significant group could not be ignored. It was also true that the theological commitment of the church to social welfare and political issues which had been so evident in the *Faith in the City* report now began to direct its attention to social problems experienced by rural populations who were not well off and who suffered because of reductions in public services in rural areas. Accordingly, *Faith in the Countryside* also had its policy statements on these issues of local and national politics.

Throughout these reports and the discussion of them parish life remains of vital importance. In this book we shall explore many areas of concern and present our findings as they came to us from clergy and people living in rural areas. In one sense this book can be read as a study of parishes as much as a study of its official ministers; as such it will serve a useful purpose within the task of theological construction in the contemporary church. It is a complex area where financial concerns of clergy deployment and building maintenance interlink with ethical and theological concerns.

3

Villagers Old and New:
Social Change in Rural England

In England, one of the most urbanised and industrialised countries in the world, the tendency in this century has been to revere the tradition and the stability of rural life and to see change as negative. The rural clergy bask in this reflected cultural glory. At best the country parson personifies rural tradition and permanence as community leader and preserver of quintessential English rural life. At worst, he is quaint, ineffectual and eccentric, characterisics which may not be entirely unappealing to urban onlookers.

It is impossible to consider the changing role of the church and clergy in the countryside without looking in some detail at the wholesale social changes which have taken place in rural areas in post-war Britain. The massive restructuring of parochial organisation during this period has been accompanied by a rural transformation as the place of the countryside in the economic and social framework of Britain has changed out of all recognition. This chapter examines social and economic change in rural England, incorporating examples from the five surveyed dioceses, to provide the context for our consideration of church and clergy.

One reason why we set out to study the rural church was precisely because many church people and authorities speak of rural churches in a way that assumes they differ from their urban counterparts, and it is often assumed that rural areas provide a benchmark of stability and resistance to change in a changing and urban-dominated world. In fact, rural areas are far from this, so much so that one of the main objectives of this chapter is to point out that different rural localities are areas of great contrast and may be places of great change.

Of course, the real issues with regard to rurality have little to do with

29

watertight definitions, but much to do with perception, symbolism and ideology. The words 'rural' and, in particular, 'countryside' conjure up powerful cultural images. The same can be said of 'community', and in Chapter 5 we take a more detailed look at how the notion of community may be invoked within theology. There is a profound link between rurality and community in the popular imagination, and the church may play a key role in this expression of rural community. Its physical presence at the heart of many village communities makes this almost inevitable.

Ideologies are subject to change and traditions may be 'invented' (Hobsbawm 1983). Thus the largely positive views of rural life which emerged in nineteenth century England, and which have survived so strongly, were forged to counter earlier negative views. Alongside the 'invention' of an English country house tradition were the 'revival' of English folk song and dance (Lloyd 1969), the reinterpretation of mountainous landscapes, even the discovery of an English peasantry (Dewey 1974, Reed 1986). The 'back to the land' movement and embryonic environmental interest groups have their origins in the closing decades of the last century (Lowe and Goyder 1983, Marsh 1982, Wiener 1981).

Perceptions of the role of the church in this ideological reinterpretation of England's past are largely uncatalogued and are as complex as the notion of rurality itself. The church has not been immune from the need to invent traditions. In many ways parochial ministry too was 'rediscovered' in the eighteenth century. Indeed, as indicated in Chapter 1, before the Reformation 'the clergy formed an estate rather than a profession', membership of which did not necessarily entail parochial ministry (O'Day 1988: 187). It is possible to portray the emergence of the country parson as one of the pillars of rural continuity and a symbol of community cohesion and English good sense during the nineteenth century. But this was a position which had to be earned. The clergy's place in the rural idyll was by no means assured as Hardy's novels demonstrate. The contrast between the father and the sons of the clerical Clare family in *Tess of the d'Urbervilles* is a case in point. While the father is a low churchman and, although somewhat narrow, respected by, and loving towards, his parishioners, his high church Oxbridge sons are boorish and culturally at odds with country parishioners. While this may say as much about Hardy's ecclesiastical prejudices as it does about any real Puseyite inadequacies, it nevertheless encapsulates one of the tensions in the church as part of the rural idyll. Generally, Hardy's clergy are either harbingers of damaging change or are entirely ineffectual. Church fashions – doctrinal, ecclesiastical, liturgical – are not static. So the church as preserver of rural continuity and solidity may also be the church as harbinger of change and the destroyer of tradition. It is this interplay between religious change and social change in the countryside which lies at the heart of this book.

The remainder of this chapter is devoted to describing the main aspects of social change in rural areas. These provide the backcloth against which religious change is played out. Because our overview is necessarily brief we have provided full bibliographic detail throughout, both for rural social change generally and the special circumstances of the five selected dioceses in particular. The reader requiring extra details is advised to look at some of the key references, as in the useful broad-brush reviews of social change in the English countryside provided by Howard Newby (1979), David Phillips and Alan Williams (1984), Anthony Russell (1986) and Tony Champion and Charles Watkins (1991).

The Five Dioceses

In recognition of the importance of contrasting rural communities, one of the main objectives of the Rural Church Project was to examine five very different dioceses. The dioceses were selected to represent different types of rural area from Truro in the far south west of England to Durham in the north east. In between lie Gloucester, Southwell and Lincoln. It would have been impossible to make a selection of dioceses which would be fully representative of rural England in all its various guises. However, the five do provide some fascinating contrasts and between them cover a diverse range of rural localities. The locations of the dioceses are shown in Figure 1.

The diocese of Truro is almost entirely coterminous with the county of Cornwall[1]. Cornwall itself is a county of variation and in a number of ways, it is untypical of southern England. Its historical economic dependence on mining, quarrying and fishing has forged this distinctive character. Of the three, the quarrying of china clay remains the only industry of continuing major economic significance. In recent decades the role of tourism in the county's economy would be hard to exaggerate. Cornwall also stands apart from the rest of the south of England in three other crucial respects.

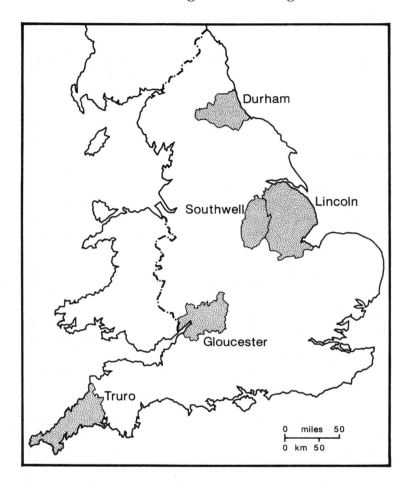

Figure 1: The five dioceses included in the Rural Church Project.

First, Truro is a diocese in which the Church of England was, for many years, rather weak compared to Methodism. In the 1851 religious census Cornwall had the lowest proportionate Anglican attendance of all English counties (Everitt 1972). Recently, though, Methodism has gone into sharp decline and it can no longer claim the pre-eminent position it once held (Winter 1991). Secondly, it has a strong sense of separate cultural and even ethnic identity (Hamilton Jenkin 1945). Attempts have been made to revive its ancient Celtic language, and powerful pleas have been made to find a distinctive Cornish path for economic and social development which respects the special character of Cornwall and its people (Deacon et al 1988). While some of the peculiarities of Cornish culture may themselves have been invented to satisfy the tastes of tourists and middle class incomers, it is undoubtdly the case that an indigenous and distinctive regional culture does exist in Cornwall in a way which is absent from most of the rest of southern England. Thirdly, its settlement pattern provides a contrast to that of the nucleated villages of Anglo-Saxon England. Many Cornish parishes comprise a number of hamlets and dispersed farmsteads often with no one village dominating. The shop and chapel may be in one settlement area, a pub in another, and the church in a third. This can give the false impression of a sparsely populated county but, compared to elsewhere in the west country, Cornwall, especially to the west, is relatively well populated. It was not until comparatively recently that Truro assumed the role of a dominant 'county' town, vis-a-vis the claims of various other settlements such as Penzance, Redruth, and Bodmin. The decision in the last century to build the cathedral church of the newly established diocese in Truro (Brown 1977) was one of several moves which led to Truro's current attraction as the growth centre of Cornwall.

To travel nearly 500 miles from Truro to Durham is to move to a diocese with a number of similarities. Durham diocese covers County Durham and parts of Tyne and Wear to the north and Cleveland to the south. Like Truro, Durham has a mining legacy, of coal rather than tin, and like Truro it has many of the economic problems associated with remoteness from metropolitan England. Unlike Cornwall, though, it has not experienced rapid population growth, has a relatively limited tourism industry (although there is considerable potential), and the diocese is one of the oldest in the country. Although it has a measure of regional identity, this is not vested in Durham *per se*. Its cultural distinctiveness is harder to pin down than in Cornwall and there has been some debate on what might constitute a north-eastern region and north-eastern identity (Townsend and Taylor 1975, Cornish et al 1977). A more fruitful approach to regional or local cultural distinctiveness might be to focus on the sociology of the mining villages which are so important in County Durham (Bulmer 1978, House and Knight 1967). As in Cornwall, Methodism has been a powerful force historically, although its strength lies in Primitive Methodism based both in the Dales mining and farming villages and in the East Durham coalfield (Moore 1974) rather than the Wesleyan and Bible Christian Methodism of Cornwall. Inland from the Durham coalfield the diocese contains a large area of remote Dales upland. Its former lead mines are now derelict and the area is sparsely populated, with some of the most difficult land for agriculture in the country, although in central and south Durham there is a large area of productive arable land. The diocese also includes the commuter belt for major centres such as Middlesborough and Newcastle.

Further south Lincoln provides us with the most purely agricultural of our five dioceses. With the exception of an area which falls within the influence of Humberside, it is a diocese in which industrial-urban commuting is relatively limited, although Grantham to the south is now only an hour's rail journey from London. Agricultural and allied employment remains important. The diocese covers all of Lincolnshire, most of South Humberside, and part of South Yorkshire. The population density is low, tourism potential somewhat limited (notwithstanding the attractions of Lincoln itself and coastal resorts such as Skegness) and economic activity rather restricted. It has some of the typical features of a remote agricultural area with declining rural services, and a slow growth in alternative employment opportunities (Wright 1983). Nonetheless, in common with many English rural counties, it has shared in the population growth of recent years, after losing population until the 1970s. As far as the Church of England is concerned, Lincoln diocese provides some of the earliest examples of experiments in team ministry and multi-parish benefices. Its free church heritage should not be forgotten. One of the most original and exciting pieces of work on nineteenth century rural religion focused on part of the county (Obelkevich 1976).

Southwell, immediately to the west of Lincoln, is a relatively compact diocese almost exactly identical with Nottinghamshire. Like Truro, Southwell is a recent diocese created in 1884 out of the dioceses of Lincoln and Lichfield to furnish a diocese for the East Midlands. It contains many growing villages dominated by commuting to Nottingham, Mansfield, Worksop and Newark. It also contains a number of mining villages in the locality known as the Dukeries. These communities were relative latecomers to mining and thus Southwell contains villages which have been transformed by mining during the current century. Communities, such as Bilsthorpe, Clipstone and Ollerton grew, between 1921 and 1931, from agricultural settlements with populations of just a few hundred to mining villages of between two and four thousand people (Waller 1983). The results perhaps reveal some of the more recent social changes induced in rural areas by counterurbanisation:

> Although the aristocrats who still owned most of the land themselves reluctantly accepted the coming of mining to the Dukeries because of the financial attractions of coal royalties, there was an undercurrent of fear and dislike on the part of the 'old villagers' who resented the 'swamping' of their quiet culture by heavy industry and its workers. This resentment was still apparent after fifty years (Waller 1983 289-90)

In contrast to Southwell, Gloucester is what many people might think of as a quintessential English rural diocese. The diocese covers all of Gloucestershire and small parts of Herefordshire, Worcestershire, Warwickshire, Wiltshire and Avon. From the high Cotswolds to the lush pastures of the Severn Valley, to the heavily wooded Forest of Dean, it is a scenically attractive area. The beauty of the varied landscapes in the area is matched by the attractions of many of the smaller towns and villages. Those built in the famous Cotswold stone provide some of the most architecturally appealing settlements in 'olde' England. Nonetheless the diocese has its industrial centres too, at Gloucester and, historically, in the old mining settlements of the Forest of Dean. The Cotswolds themselves have changed much since the early years of the century when a remote, and almost feudal, community near Stroud was immortalised in Laurie Lee's 'Cider with Rosie'. No longer are the squire and the vicar the sole representatives of wealth and privilege in a community dominated by farming and small-scale trade. On the contrary, Gloucester provides an example of how communites can be revolutionised through 'quiet' processes of social change. Nowadays, stations like Kemble near Cirencester take high-income commuters to London in just over an hour. Even for those who do not travel to London there are the fast growing centres of Cheltenham, Gloucester and Swindon all of which have been at the forefront of the recent out-of-London growth in high-technology and financial enterprises (Cooke, 1989; Harloe, et al, 1990).

Demography and Economics: Centrifugal Tendencies

In a paper presented to the Royal Society of Arts in 1990 Howard Newby, the doyen of the renaissance of rural sociological research in Britain, drew an analogy from physics when he described recent changes affecting rural society as 'centrifugal tendencies'. That centripetal forces have been replaced by centrifugal forces is an undeniable conclusion from the data on the relocation of economic activities and populations in post-war Britain, especially during the last two to three decades. This only gradually dawned upon the social science community, and yet the evidence for a reversal in well-established theories concerning the location of both economic activity and population can be traced back to the nineteen sixties[2].

As Newby points out, the decentralisation of economic activities and peoples has not been accompanied by a decentralisation of power and control. On the contrary, many would argue that the nation-state has grown in influence alongside the economic power-brokers represented by 'the city'. In other words, counter-urban processes are only partial, and, indeed, are only possible as an outcome of an economy in which power is located centrally. It is central financial and political power which allows the organisation of a complex society in such a way that the flows of people and of capital, which define counter-urbanisation, are both politically and physically feasible. In a sense these processes actually refer to the urbanisation of the countryside, socially and economically. But as the land use is 'rural', contrasts between town and country retain ideological and cultural significance. Yet in all other ways that contrast has been minimised. It is thus possible to reject on historical, economic and sociological grounds the notion of post-industrial society whilst retaining a firm grasp of the highly symbolic importance of the countryside within a transformed economy and society.

What then do these centrifugal tendencies mean for the rural areas with which we are concerned? Rural depopulation was rife throughout many areas of England until the nineteen sixties, see for example the lengthy discussion of the declining villages of County Durham in Edwards (1971), and even into the nineteen seventies. In the immediate post-war period it remained one of the perennial concerns of social analysts such as John Saville:

> Rural depopulation has occurred in the past century and a half, and will continue in the future, because of declining employment

opportunities in the countryside. .... in the absence of a rural economy that can provide economic opportunities for a greater part of the natural increase of its population than occurs at the present time, the depopulation of our rural areas will not be reversed (1957)

However, since then there has been a remarkable turnaround in rural fortunes. Most rural areas, but not such remote ones as parts of County Durham, have experienced a recovery of population levels and often quite severe population pressure upon the existing housing stock. In all but Durham diocese population increased between 1981 and 1987, and the increases have been substantial, with Truro showing the most marked growth of more than 15% in the eastern section of the diocese. Gloucester showed solid gains outside Cheltenham and the city of Gloucester itself which both declined slightly. Durham, although experiencing slight increases in some districts, saw decline in many mining and farming communities. Lincoln experienced solid gains in spite of the problems faced by some of its more remote agricultural communities. Southwell commuter villages grew substantially.

It is likely that the 1991 census will show virtually no rural districts in England to have been immune from population increase. The revolution in population trends which this signifies, together with a profound social and economic transformation, has spawned a voluminous academic debate. The causes of counter-urbanisation take us into many different areas of enquiry. Many of the accounts stress the importance of macro-economic factors and the national, and even international, re-organisation of industrial production, but social survey work among migrants has shown that not all have moved to satisfy purely economic objectives (Champion 1989). Of course, of crucial importance has been the extension of car ownership and improvements in communications generally.

In Cornwall there is a paradox in that population has been shifting to an area which has experienced relatively low levels of economic performance and high unemployment. Some of the migrants are retired but many more, of working age, have opted to move to the county for social and environmental reasons (Perry 1987, Perry et al 1986). As well as the social and economic motivations of those individuals questioned in survey investigations are the complex cultural factors, which surround the rural (and seaside) idyll. Whilst not denying the importance of 'rational' socio-economic decisions, the attractiveness of Cornwall to in-migrants probably rests as much on a heady mixture of Daphne du Maurier, John Betjeman, the pastoral arcadia of television advertisements for Cornish cream and butter, and hazy memories of rugged cliffs and sheltered coves of childhood seaside holidays. In this sense Cornwall is very much a special case exercising a nation-wide pull and, as a result, experiencing large population changes.

Between 1860 and 1960 the population of Cornwall was almost static. In fact the century showed a small decline of about eight per cent (Perry 1987). But since then the county's population has increased by a third. It grew by 13.3% in the nineteen seventies compared to just 0.8% in England as a whole, and by 6.2% between 1981 and 1987. In an extensive social survey in Cornwall in the early nineteen eighties it emerged that the typical in-migrant was a skilled worker between 30 and 40 (Dean et al 1984). Semi-skilled and unskilled workers continue to leave the county and are replaced by supervisory, skilled, and managerial/professional workers (Perry 1987). Perhaps a quarter of these migrants are native Cornish returning to the county. The bulk of the remainder come from London, the west Midlands or the north-west of England. If these trends continue, the native Cornish will soon be a minority in the county. Indeed Ronald Perry, extrapolating from current trends, has estimated that the Cornish born and bred will comprise only 36% of the county's population in the year 2010 compared to nearly 70% in 1960.

Cornwall may be a special case but many of the same trends can be observed in less exaggerated forms elsewhere. An early study of rural re-population and its social consequences was conducted in Nottinghamshire in the mid nineteen sixties, where David Thorns (1968) observed the growing tendency for higher income families in Nottingham to move to villages in the south of the county. A decade later Parsons (c1978) examined the same processes, comparing the experiences of Nottinghamshire and Norfolk. Clearly, in the case of Southwell diocese, much of the population movement is over a relatively short distance and reflects the important economic role of Nottingham. The story in Lincoln is rather different, for Lincolnshire is a county with neither the scenic attractions of Cornwall nor the economic strengths of Nottinghamshire. Yet its growth has been steady. To some extent undoubtedly it benefits from the increasing distances that commuters have been prepared to travel, not least as a consequence of cheap fuel prices in the nineteen eighties. The city of Lincoln itself is just forty miles from Nottingham and eighty from Hull, and is now just about within commuting distance of London.

The population of Gloucestershire has grown steadily in recent decades, although this has been limited in many of the rural parishes by severe restrictions on new development by local authority planning controls. These measures are based on the need to protect the special architectural and environmental qualities of many settlements (Cloke and Little 1987). This brings us to one of the curious paradoxes of the current trends. The data used tend to be analysed at the district level, and therefore include agglomerations of medium and small towns and larger and smaller villages. In reality, population increases are likely to be confined to certain communities, often the larger ones. Where planning policies have protected settlements from new development then population levels are likely to have continued to fall, as shown by Weekley (1988) in Leicestershire, not least due to the declining average size of households. The pressure for development in these villages may be intense and the demand for vacant properties even more so, but the actual population levels are static or even in decline. The same phenomenon was observed for the north Cotswolds more than twenty years ago (Jackson 1968). Thus, general district-wide increases in absolute population levels mask much more complex patterns of in and out migration and changes in the economic functions of rural areas.

Moreover, not all villages are attractive either to developers or to 'incomers'. In many of the declining mining villages we visited in County Durham, for example, there were no such pressures. Even in the attractive Dales many villages are so remote from major centres of population and wealth that they have continued to lose population. However, there are signs of the beginnings of rural population recovery even in Durham and the 1991 census results will need to be examined very carefully indeed. Similarly in Cornwall the rapid increases in population do not extend to all communities. Some of the old tin communities as well as existing china clay villages are not the kind of settlement to attract many incomers. Moreover, such settlements may suffer from a continued loss of young local people leaving the rural areas in search of work. Thus, although counterurbanisation is now such a well attested population trend we should not conclude that population loss is no longer a cause of concern for rural areas. Indeed the effects of in-migration on house prices may even exacerbate the difficulties faced by locals wishing to continue living in a rural location. Such population decline may be masked in the aggregate increases recorded for a district as a whole but is none the less real for the inhabitants concerned.

Contrary to popular mythology, counterurbanisation is not solely to do with the settlement of elderly and retired people in the countryside. For example, almost a third of net migration to the south-west region, which includes both Gloucester and Truro, is from those in the 25-44 age group (Court and Boddy 1989). A recent detailed study of migration to the Exmoor community of South Molton in Devon found a wide diversity - in terms of both age and occupational background - of in-migrants (Bolton and Chalkley 1990). This confirms the earlier findings of a large-scale study of population change in Cornwall (Dean et al 1984, Perry et al 1986, Perry 1987). Between 1981 and 1987 the population of Cornwall grew by more than 5% while Durham's population fell by more than 3%. Gloucestershire, Nottinghamshire and Lincolnshire all experienced slight population increases.

Economic Change

Population shifts are associated with, although not necessarily solely caused by, economic changes. The last two decades have witnessed wholesale changes in both the UK and the world economies. The implications for rural areas are profound. Many places in southern Britain have experienced a rejuvenation of manufacturing employment at a time when the traditional urban heartlands of manufacturing, in the north and midlands, have suffered recession. The service sector has grown, often dramatically, but primary industries, such as agriculture, mining and fishing have declined or, at best, experienced mixed fortunes.

The reasons for these changes are complex and have prompted voluminous discussion amongst sociologists, economists and geographers (eg. Green 1989, Urry 1984). Amongst the factors cited are the attractiveness of 'greenfield' locations for new businesses and the low levels of unionisation of labour in many rural locations. In reality, however, many of the changes have as much to do with regional shifts of economic activity as with shifts from urban to rural locations *per se*. In Cornwall, for example, growth has been concentrated upon Truro with surrounding villages feeling the pull of the new activity most strongly. Remoter villages in the far west of the county or in north Cornwall have benefitted less from new economic activities, although their populations are likely to have increased as part of the overall upturn in the fortunes of rural areas. The point is, though, that it is misleading to see restructuring as entirely to do with *rural* relocation if much of the new enterprise is located around Plymouth, Truro, Cheltenham, Lincoln, or wherever. Yet, the characteristics of rural settlements within a wide radius of such centres are profoundly affected.

The five dioceses chosen for this study embrace the breadth of experience during these years of economic restructuring. Durham, in both its rural and urban localities, has experienced some of the greatest changes with relatively little compensatory growth in new sectors. Mining and manufacturing employment has declined although the service sector has grown, albeit somewhat slowly. Southwell and Lincoln have also witnessed radical changes in the manufacturing sector (and in mining in the case of Southwell) and rapid increases in the service sector.

Agriculture remains an important but declining part of the economy in our dioceses. It now accounts for less than 10% of the working population of Cornwall (the figure for fishing is only 1%). Farming is, however, the single most important sphere of economic activity and in some rural parishes may still be the only significant local source of employment. This was brought home to us in our social survey work carried out in five rural parishes in each diocese. Overall, just under 20% of the general sample were employed either in agriculture or other land-based activities such as forestry and gardening, including approximately one quarter of those interviewed in Durham, Truro, Lincoln and Southwell, but just 11% of those in Gloucester. Moreover, farming may provide a strong component in a county's sense of identity. This is certainly true of Cornwall and Lincolnshire, and is not without its importance in Gloucestershire, where such a small proportion of the working population are employed on the land.

But what of the new forms of employment and of economic activity? These are characterised more by their diversity than anything else. The rejuvenation of economic activity in many rural areas embraces new high-tech firms, small craft industries, small manufacturing companies, the relocation of firms involved in finance, and the leisure and tourism boom. The motives for moving to a rural location vary enormously:

> Established local entrepreneurs tended to show satisfying rather than optimising behaviour and to be people- rather than profit-oriented. New local entrepreneurs were craft- rather than

market-oriented. Owner-managers of incoming complete transfers, attracted by a combination of regional aid in a pleasant environment, were not strongly growth-oriented, and were the group most conscious of capital-transfer problems on retirement. The new incoming entrepreneurs came closest to the stereotype of a profit-maximising entrepreneur, but even this group contained many redundant or disenchanted executives from larger corporations, strongly attracted to Cornwall by the environment. (Perry 1978: 19)

These results of a survey of new firms in Cornwall should be borne in mind in discussions of macro-economic trends: rural restructuring is based on the decisions and motivations of individuals as well as on wider processes.

Many of the new manufacturing jobs in rural areas are in small firms. For example a study in 1980 showed that 50% of manufacturing jobs in the Horncastle Employment Office Area in Lincolnshire in 1980 were in units of less than ten people compared to 46% in Lincolnshire as a whole but just 3% in Great Britain (Wright 1983: 250). In a study of rural labour markets Bradley has demonstrated the 'dependence upon local, petit-bourgeois capital' suggesting 'the existence of local (rural) class divisions - between indigenous capital and labour' (1985: 48). In Cornwall, manufacturing employment rose by more than 50% between 1960 and 1975, with most of the increase being in the small firm sector. Two-thirds of this new employment was in branch-plants with headquarters based elsewhere in the country or abroad rather than in locally based companies. About 60% of the employment is female and much is low-paid unskilled work (Massey 1983).

In addition to new sectors of activity, many long-established economic areas have experienced internal changes which parallel the restructuring in the economy as a whole. For example, tourism has been an important element in the Cornish economy since the last century (Bennett 1949, Gilligan 1987). It is, however, now experiencing considerable change. The number of tourists visiting the county is static or declining. After peaking at nearly 3.5 million in the late 1970s, the number of annual visitors is now down to below 3.25 million. At the same time the visitors who do come are opting for a different type of holiday. Hotels and bed & breakfast have seen their market share in accommodation decline at the expense of self-catering accommodation and caravan and camp sites.

Such accommodation provides less employment in the economy, and this is a serious factor in assessing the positive or negative aspects of tourism in Cornwall (Shaw and Williams 1988). Against this declining economic significance has to be placed another factor which might be increasing the impact on the local economy. What visitors are less inclined to spend on basic accommodation costs they are more likely to spend on eating out - the catering sector - and in visiting tourist attractions as opposed to spending all their time on the coast. As a result total employment in the tourist sector seems to be creeping upwards. Much of this employment is seasonal and much is part-time lowly paid work. The research by Shaw and Williams (1988) has shown that there is a rapid turnover of tourist businesses, many being run for short periods by in-migrants from London and the south-east. Few tourist operators have formal training in tourism or indeed business studies, and many experience considerable difficulty as a result.

It has already been hinted that economic growth may not necessarily be reflected in higher wages or the elimination of unemployment. There are many reasons for this, but quite clearly one of them is that the relocation of economic activities is, in part, determined by the presence of a low wage economy, high levels of unemployment and weakly developed trades union activity. This is not to say that these are the only factors determining the location of activities but they do tend to be more important for those industries requiring relatively low levels of skills. In Cornwall, Lincolnshire and Durham these are likely to be important factors, but less so in Nottinghamshire and Gloucestershire. Thus economic change may reinforce pre-existing inequalities even while transforming patterns of economic activity. For example, Cornwall remains a low wage economy despite its changed economic and demographic status, while the infusion of high-tech and financial companies to the Gloucestershire economy allows its relative prosperity to remain intact.

Table 1 shows the average income figures for each of the five main counties of the dioceses in 1987, and Table 2 shows the unemployment rate in the five localities. Average earnings in County Durham, Cornwall, and Nottinghamshire are substantially below those of the UK as a whole. Those in Lincolnshire approach the norm, while Gloucestershire is above the average. A slightly different pattern emerges with regard to the rate of unemployment. Nottinghamshire and Lincolnshire come close to the national average, while County Durham and Cornwall have

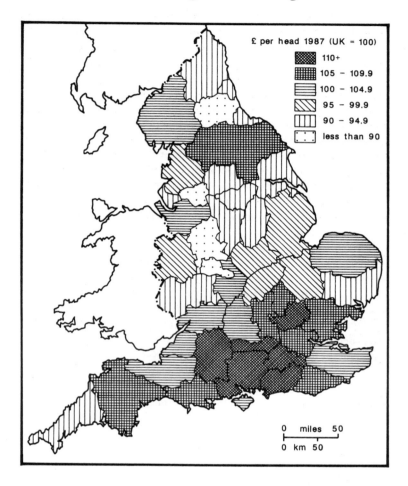

£ per head 1987 (UK = 100)

110+
105 – 109.9
100 – 104.9
95 – 99.9
90 – 94.9
less than 90

0   miles   50
0   km   50

Figure 2: Household disposable income (£ per head, 1987). Source *Economic Trends*, April 1990.

substantialy higher unemployment rates. Gloucestershire has a very low rate of unemployment.

Of course, averages tell us nothing about the range of income or unemployment levels, and it has certainly been claimed that some rural areas, especially in the prosperous south of England, are characterised by the presence of a high-income elite which lifts the mean figure so masking the true extent of particularly low wages (Deacon 1987). Certainly it is the southern shire counties which tend towards the highest incomes as the map in Figure 2 shows, although there are some notable exceptions. For example, Herefordshire and Worcestershire, which lie immediately adjacent to Gloucestershire, have lower mean wages than Cornwall. Cumbria, on the other hand, which abuts Durham, has higher incomes than the national average. The figures belie any simple assumptions about rural-urban or north-south divisions. Moreover, as far as rural areas are concerned Tony Bradley (1984, 1985) has convincingly demonstrated that relative inequalities in earnings are far greater within rural localities than in the nation as a whole.

TABLE 1. *Household Disposable Income £ per head, 1987*

	£ per head	£ per head (UK = 100)
Cornwall	4,397	94.4
County Durham	4,106	88.1
Gloucestershire	4,855	104.2
Lincolnshire	4,524	97.1
Nottinghamshire	4,419	94.9
UK	4,658	100.0

Source: Economic Trends, April 1990.

Social Change in Rural Areas

In this section we examine social change in the countryside. The broad characteristics should already be clear: fewer people working in agriculture, and more in the services sector; an influx of new residents and the departure of some indigenous rural dwellers; and a greater representation of the middle-class in the class structure. Commentators on rural societies have been quick to sieze upon the implications of these changes. Thus, for Howard Newby (1990) "rural Britain, which was once agricultural Britain, has now become middle-class Britain". Similarly Anthony Russell, in his book *The Country Parish* (1986), devotes a chapter to each of three groups in contemporary villages: the

TABLE 2. *Unemployment Rate (%)*

	November 1981	April 1990
Cornwall	16.3	9.0
County Durham	15.5	9.3
Gloucestershire	8.7	3.7
Lincolnshire	11.4	6.9
Nottinghamshire	11.2	7.2
UK	12.2	6.6

Source: Regional Trends.

Note. The derivation of the figures changed in a number of ways between 1981 and 1990, and care should be taken with the use of these comparative data.

farmers, the old villagers and the new villagers. There seems to be a general agreement that the first two groups are decreasing as the last group attain ascendancy. As a result the class composition of villages is changing. Of course there has always been considerable variation between villages, but it is generally true to say that the working class was predominant in the villages of the last century. Many 'closed' vilages were occupational communities in which the only people who were not employed as hired workers on the land were the farmers themselves, the parson, the teacher, the squire and a few people engaged in trade. Other more 'open' villages had a stronger representation of tradesemen and artisans as well as smaller non–employing farmers (Mills 1980; Reed 1986). The old villagers of today are often descended from this last group rather than from agricultural workers. The farm workers were a much more mobile group in any case, while the artisans were more fixed through ties of petty property ownership. In some ways the artisans and farmers formed a middle class, but of a very different nature and scale to the salariat of the twentieth century.

While we would not dispute the general tenor of these arguments we do wish to stress that the details of these processes and the consequences for rural social change require a more subtle analysis than broad generalisations would suggest. Three observations are particularly pertinent. First, the processes are more deeply rooted and historically well established in some areas than others. Secondly, the precise impact of change is clearly mediated by the very different social, economic and spatial structures which already exist. Thirdly, change is not necessarily imposed from outside and, therefore, any account of rural social change has to take into consideration the dynamic of change within communities as well as the impact of outside forces. Let us consider each of these aspects in turn.

Clearly, few would deny that the rate of social change in rural areas varies. It is clear in the works of Newby, Russell and others that change is more advanced in the south of the country, with remoter rural communities in the north and west still to experience the full impact of change in the village. But Russell, in particular, tends to see change as really a rather recent phenomenon. His discussion of the impact of new villagers presupposes a resistant and very different kind of old villager. For Russell, newcomers are either 'here today and gone tomorrow' with no intrinsic interest in the village, or else when seeking to become involved in village activities they find "the local community difficult to get to know, clannish and distinctly unlike the warm acccepting community portrayed in rural 'soap operas'" (1986:172). Either way the distinction between old and new villagers is stark and suggests sharp divisions.

In reality the relationships are infinitely more diverse. It has to be remembered that in many areas of the country the middle-class have long had a highly visible presence. We have already commented on the work of Thorns in rural Nottinghamshire in the mid 1960s. The impact of middle-class newcomers in rural Hertfordshire was examined by Ray Pahl (1965a, 1965b) in the early 1960s. Gerald Wibberley in the very first issue of the journal of the European Society for Rural Sociology in 1960 took the opportunity to stress the radical sociological changes now confronting villages. Equally telling are the images of popular literature. Scores of light 'rural' novels have poured from the pen of 'Miss Read' since 1955, and the overwhelming impression of her villagers is that they are resolutely middle-class. A village provides an admirable backcloth for the 'William' stories of Richmal Crompton. Her first story was published in 1922, and the village is peopled with retired colonels, the wealthy and not so wealthy middle-class (many of them single women which presumably reflects the loss of eligible men in the 1914-1918 war), and commuters to 'town'. It is the servants, the prevalence of houses to let, and the setting of a depressed agricultural landscape which remind us that the book refers to a village of seventy years ago. The villages of several of Agatha Christie's novels are similarly middle-class. Turning to more serious literature E.M. Forster's *Howards End* provides another example of middle class village England and John Cowper Powys' small Dorset and Somerset towns have an equally middle class stamp. Even D.H. Lawrence's Midlands working villages are not without their middle-class representatives.

Many attractive villages in the Home Counties and also those within easy reach of main centres of population elsewhere have probably had a strong middle-class presence since the inter-war years, and certainly a rapidly growing one since the 1950s. In such communities the distinction between old and new villagers is likely either to be attenuated or else an abbreviation, with only limited foundation in the realities of longevity of residence, for class conflict. Marilyn Strathern (1981) has convincingly demonstrated how conceptions of community may, in fact, have little to do with any meaningful residential criteria but a great deal to do with other criteria of 'belonging'. In some circumstances, for example where a recent housing development has taken place, lines of cleavage may reflect neither class nor localism, but the occupation of particular housing.

Some villages, therefore, have a long history of middle-class occupancy. The divisions between new and old villagers, whilst not entirely irrelevant, will be far less clear cut than in the popular characterisation of rural change. The opposite side of this coin is clearly that some villages have only recently experienced the arrival of newcomers and some of the tensions referred to by Russell may well be starker in such villages. This brings us to the second point. The impact of demographic change clearly varies according to the nature of the communities receiving the population influx. This is very much a two-way process. The impact of incomers is mediated by the existing characteristics of the 'host' settlement, but by the same token those characteristics influence the kind of people moving to a rural area.

Some of these differences are spelt out in Russell's fourfold classification of countryside which, he suggests, "form concentric rings around the principle metropolitan areas" (1986: 3). It is worth quoting his characterisation in some detail:

> The *urban shadow countryside* can be found in the immediate vicinity of urban areas. In this countryside, commuters tend to be predominant, and the villages often have the feeling of a

discontinuous suburb. The farming community, though present is not particularly evident, and, because of the proximity of an urban centre, the facilities and services in the village are often minimal. The *accessible countryside* frequently has better facilities as the urban centre is at a great distance. Commuters and the retired live in considerable numbers in these villages, but the farming community and the local resident group are more evident. ... The *less accessible countryside* (sometimes defined as that area beyond a travelling distance of one hour from a metropolitan centre) is characterized, in some areas by de-population. Commuters are less evident, though there are significant numbers of retired people ... The farming and local resident community is much more evident than in the previous two types. In the *remote or marginal countryside*, the local resident community and the farmers form a majority of the year-round population, although there are some retired people. (1986:3)

As a broad charicature of contrasting rural communities this has descriptive value, although clearly the impact of economic change and relocation will have profoundly altered the complexion of many communities in the less accessible countryside. But a far more serious concern with this spatial approach is that it ignores the great contrasts that are to be found within regions and counties. One of the problems is that the images of rurality tend to be based upon particular types of rural settlement, usually the village of thatched cottages, a green and a church. The contrasts in the mind's eye then have to do with those inhabiting the cottages. It is easy to conjure up a vision of a continuum from the rustics through the retireds to the middle-class commuters. The appearance of the thatched cottages, their gardens and outbuildings is slightly different in each case, encapsulating the nuances of class and status.

But let us take a rather different imaginative route. Picture three villages in Gloucestershire. The first, because of severe development control, has had few new houses since a dozen post-war council houses were built. The remaining fifty homes are all 'highly desirable' Cotswold residences. Many have been in middle-class ownership, although not necessarily by the same people, for half a century. Social change is relatively slow, not because the community is traditional in any sense, but because of the limitations on development and the relative immobility in the housing market. There are wide disparities in wealth but few overt incomer-local conflicts. Indeed many of the middle-class residents consider themselves every bit as 'rural' and 'local' as the council-house inhabitants, some of whom have recently moved in from the local town in any case.

The second village was until fifteen years ago very similar to the first, but then a major new development of fifty 2 to 4 bedroom houses took place. The estate on the edge of the village was much resented by most villagers, old and new, when first built. Much of the resentment remains, although some bridges have been built. At election time the middle-class of the 'two villages' are drawn together in common cause for the Conservative Party, with the exception of a few Liberal households. But politics tends to be far less important than the old-new village cleavage.

The third village is an 'overflow' village a few miles from Gloucester and with hardly any Cotswold cottages. It is rural in terms of population size and facilities, and it still has a couple of working farms close by. Its preponderance of new housing is inhabited by newcomers too, but few of them are there by choice. Some of the new houses are actually cheaper than in the towns and the village is thus a dormitory town for semi-skilled and unskilled workers.

In different parts of the country we could add several other 'types' to these mental pictures. Villages in areas dominated by family farming are very different from those where large scale capitalist farming dominates; villages with an industrial heritage are different from those with farming or fishing histories; some traditional estate villages still remain; and so on and so forth. We do not deny the overwhelming movement of the middle-class to the countryside or the pull of many outer rural areas for the retired, but to characterise social change in the rural areas entirely in terms of concentric rings of middle-class influence is to ignore the complexity and diversity of rural social change. In recent work the geographer, Sarah Harper (1987a, 1987b, 1990), has thrown considerable light on this diversity of reasons for migration and the variety of rural settlements to which migrants move even *within* areas normally considered monolithically middle-class; one of her study areas, for example, was Hampshire.

Thirdly, we turn to the question of indigenous change. Most accounts of rural social change tend to assume that the impetus comes from outside with new people imposing their ideas and life-style upon traditional rural dwellers. In reality, of course, society as a whole is changing, and it is almost impossible to separate out indigenous and exogenous causes of change. In those rural areas which have prospered in the post-war era, much new wealth has come to, and through, the entrepreneurs and farmers already living in the villages.

If we take agriculture, for example, we find an industry where a massive social change has taken place. Capital has replaced labour on the farms and the industry is influenced more than anything else by government or EC policies. And yet change does not occur without farmers themselves changing; they are not entirely unwitting victims of external circumstances. They have bought and sold land, adopted new technologies, diversified their businesses and some have benefitted from the influx of new people and new money. While some resent criticism from environmentalists others have forged alliances with the new middle-class on district and county councils. Yet in other ways farmers have become members of a socially closed and encapsulated sub-community (Newby et al 1978).

Moreover, there have been new entrants to the industry and a physical movement of farmers around the countryside. For example, in the immediate post-war decade a considerable number of farms changed hands. Some were bought by sitting tenants, others by farmers' sons and many by new farmers returning from war-time service. Any agricultural area contains a proportion of farmers, a quarter or more in most studies, who have moved in from outside, so that any notion of farmers as a homogeneous and permanent group within the community is seriously misplaced.

Turning now to some of the consequences of change in the village, it is inevitable that the protection of the countryside by planning control has led to a rapid increase in house prices combined with declining public sector services. Newcomers to rural areas tend to be less reliant on public services, particularly transport, and hence less dependent on local facilities. Moreover they are undoubtedly, on average, more wealthy than most indigenous rural dwellers. Thus the poor and the rich often live side by side in rural areas. To the outside observer this may suggest that relative deprivation will be experienced in a very real way in villages, especially if the richer newcomers assume positions of responsibility enabling them to make decisions concerning the allocation of goods and services which affect their neighbours.

The reality is probably more complex for some would argue that extremes of wealth and poverty have always been a feature of rural society and are less pronounced today than a century ago. Moreover, in today's countryside the source and extent of the wealth of the better-off are likely to be less apparent than they were when wealth derived from the land. Commuters whose home is in the village will inhabit a very different world of work in a city and will have kin and friendship networks on a national rather than a local basis. Thus different people within a village will inhabit contrasting, and often hidden, social and cultural milieu. It is ironic that many move to the countryside to find a close-knit community only to destroy the very foundation of such a community, if indeed it ever did exist, by their own way of life. This is not to deny that people may enjoy meaningful and fulfilling relationships within rural communities, but it is entirely mistaken to assume that these are based on the same principles that make for a sense of community.

If rural settlements have been altered out of all recognition through social change, they have also recently been subject to the consequences of a series of policies designed by the government in its pursuance of economic reform. The de-regulation of public transport may, in some instances, have led to a decline in rural services. The sale of council housing and the restrictions on new building have exacerbated an already grave rural housing problem. Those on low wages, face increasing difficulties in the housing market, not least because many rural areas have long been lacking in public sector housing compared to urban areas. Historically there has been a high level of private rented accommodation, but tourism and legislation on security of tenure have radically diminished the available stock. The relative availability of different types of housing tenure varies enormously from parish to parish in most rural districts. For all the recent talk about housing in rural areas, the decline of public transport, education, social services and so forth, it is widely recognised that the real issue is that of income. Low wages in rural areas appear to be endemic (Bradley 1984, 1985, 1987, Lowe et al 1987).

The Rural Class Structure

So far we have been using some rather broad brush notions of class when considering the social changes taking place in the countryside. We have also used, rather uncritically, the term 'indigenous', in many ways a short-hand term for a working class remnant in the countryside. The implication is that indigenous rural dwellers, 'old villagers' in Russell's terminology, comprise a category of people easily defined by reference to their place of birth or upbringing. In reality, as those whose attention has been exercised by the problem of 'local' housing need testify (Middleton 1988; Shucksmith 1981), the definition of 'local' is fraught with difficulty. Both class based and locality based distinctions are simplifications and this should be recognised in our discussions of rurality and locality.

In the population survey we sought information on both class and length of residence and it is worth considering the findings in some detail, not least because they illustrate the dangers of generalising too boldly on social change in rural areas. At its most basic a social class classification can refer merely to occupational categories graded primarily according to their income earning capacity. However classifications usually carry other connotations as well. In the sociological literature class position is usually seen as reflecting both market and work situations, in other words both income and economic security, and the location within systems of authority and power (Goldthorpe 1980). Our classification is a modification of the Goldthorpe index, identifying six main classes:

Class 1. All higher-grade professional and managerial occupations; higher-grade administrators; large proprietors. "What Class 1 positions have in common is that they afford their incumbents incomes which are high, generally secure, and likely to rise steadily over their lifetimes; and that they are positions which typically involve the exercise of authority, ... or at least ones which offer considerable autonomy and freedom from control by others" (Goldthorpe:40). Thus this group would include those large-scale owners of business, who might traditionally, have been seen as the 'upper' class alongside senior 'upper-middle' class members, such as lawyers, top civil servants and senior managers.

Class 2. Lower-grade professionals; higher-grade technicians; lower-grade administrators; small-scale managers. Typically "these positions guarantee income levels that rank directly below those of Class 1, and also carry 'staff' status and conditions of employment" (Goldthorpe: 40). This group might be termed the 'middle' class and is likely to consist of those whose educational attainments are close, if not equal in some instances, to those of Class 1. A classroom teacher would be located in Class 2, whereas a headteacher (of all but the smallest school) would be in Class 1. A doctor would be in Class 1 and a senior nurse in Class 2.

Class 3. Small proprietors, especially farmers; self-employed artisans; and all other own-account workers apart from the professionals and large business owners of Class 1. Incomes in this group will be variable but we can expect those in this class to own from small to quite large amounts of business capital. For want of a better expression in the English vocabulary we refer to this group as the 'petty bourgeoisie'. With the increase in self-employment status among some working class groups, for example farm workers, we were careful to allocate to this group only genuine own-account workers with a high degree of autonomy and business financial control.

Class 4. Lower-grade technicians whose work is to some extent of a manual character and supervisors/foremen. This was a small group in our sample and it is possible that some of Class 6 should have been allocated to this group. This is a working class group with close connections to the manual working class proper. They are separated from it only in so much as they are representatives of a "blue-collar elite" (Goldthorpe: 41) in terms of income and supervisory function.

Class 5. Routine non-manual workers in clerical, administrative, retail and commercial sectors. Although Goldthorpe tends to treat such workers as intermediate between 2 and 6, our feeling is that in our case they are really to be located alongside the manual working class in terms of income, security of employment, and work control. Indeed incomes, for both male and female workers in this group, are often below those of manual workers. Female workers in shops and offices were strongly represented in this group in our sample, and in many ways we see this as the female sector of the working class.

Class 6. Routine manual skilled and unskilled workers. These workers "sell their labour power in more or less discrete amounts ... in return for wages; ... they are, via the labour contract, placed in an entirely subordinate role, subject to the authority of their employer or his agents" (Goldthorpe: 41-2)

The allocation of a class position is relatively straightforward for those in work. It is less easy for those not currently employed. Moreover this problem raises a 'hornets' nest' in current sociological debate surrounding the allocation of women to class positions. We are very conscious of the criticisms that have been made of class classifications which determine the class position of women entirely according to the husband's occupation, criticisms that are rooted not just in feminist sensibility but also in empirical work on the experience of women themselves (eg. Abbott and Sapsford, 1987). Accordingly we have, where possible, allocated a class location to women on the basis of their own job rather than that of their husband. In the case of retired women we have referred back to their own previous occupation. Only in the case of housewives with no outside work have we relied on a location based on the husband's occupation.

Table 3 shows the distribution of classes according to diocese, and reveals some graphic contrasts which reflect the original reasons for chosing these particular dioceses as representative of quite distinct types of rural area. In the case of Gloucester the higher classes are particularly well represented, the two highest class groups comprising 40% of the general sample (See Appendix), compared to between 25% and 29% in Truro, Southwell and Durham, and only 14% in Lincoln. Manual workers are numerous in Lincoln and Durham (43% and 44% respectively) compared to approximately a quarter of the sample elsewhere. Truro has the highest proportion of Class 3 members, at 35%, reflecting Cornwall's long history both of small scale farming and small business generally.

TABLE 3. General Sample: Social Class by Diocese

Social class	Glos No	%	Truro No	%	Southwell No	%	Lincoln No	%	Durham No	%	Total No
Class 1	14	20	11	17	8	13	3	5	6	9	42
Class 2	14	20	5	8	11	16	6	9	12	18	48
Class 3	12	18	23	35	18	26	14	21	10	15	77
Class 4	1	1	-	-	1	1	3	5	2	2	7
Class 5	11	16	10	15	10	15	11	17	8	12	50
Class 6	17	25	17	25	20	29	28	43	29	44	111
Total	69	100	66	100	68	100	65	100	67	100	335

Turning now to length of residence, Table 4 shows the variation in length of residence by diocese. The main contrast is between Durham and the other dioceses. Durham had a much higher proportion of its population "born and bred" in the parish - 39% compared to less than a quarter in the other dioceses. Table 5 shows the relationship between length of residence and social class. The findings are striking: the manual members of the working class were far more likely to be indigenous to their parish of residence than other classes. Whereas 38% of the manual working class had always lived in the parish, this was the case for only two per cent of managerial and professional residents. By contrast, more than twice as many of the professional and managerial group had moved into the parish in the last five years, compared to the manual working class (38% and 17% respectively).

TABLE 4. *General Sample: Length of Residence in Parish by Diocese*

Years in parish	Glos No %	Truro No %	Southwell No %	Lincoln No %	Durham No %	Total No
1 - 5	19 27	22 33	19 28	18 26	18 26	96
6 - 10	9 13	8 12	19 28	10 15	9 13	55
11 - 20	12 17	11 17	10 15	12 17	4 6	49
21 +	16 23	15 23	13 19	14 21	11 16	69
Always	14 20	10 15	7 10	14 21	27 39	72
Total	70 100	66 100	68 100	68 100	69 100	341

TABLE 5. *General Sample: Length of Residence in Parish by Class*

	Social Class					
Years in parish	1 No %	2 No %	3 No %	4 No %	5 No %	6 No %
1 - 5	16 38	18 38	23 30	4 57	14 28	19 17
6 - 10	9 22	12 25	9 12	- -	10 20	15 14
11 - 20	8 19	10 21	12 15	- -	9 18	10 9
21 +	8 19	3 6	20 26	2 29	9 18	25 22
Always	1 2	5 10	13 17	1 14	8 16	42 38
Total(335)	42 100	48 100	77 100	7 100	50 100	111 100

What is Rural?

At the outset of this chapter we shamelessly adopted a loose and entirely pragmatic approach in talking about rural areas. This was quite deliberate because we remain convinced that the issue is essentially one of perception rather than objective definition. However, if that is the case then it is useful to establish more rigorous factors which might be associated with those areas which are perceived in our culture as 'rural'. At the very least we should review the attempts that have been made to define rurality, and indicate how our chosen dioceses fare according to these definitions. Our discussion so far has taken for granted that 'rural' places can be characterised and analysed relatively easily. Yet the changes we have discussed imply a blurring of social and economic distinctions between urban and rural areas. Rather, the differences are much more likely to lie between those places which have gained from change and those which have lost.

The simplest and probably most useful way of distinguishing between urban and rural areas is the relative proportion of open countryside found in an area. Wibberley (1972) regarded rural areas as essentially "those parts of a country which show unmistakeable signs of being dominated by extensive uses of land". This simple and commonsense functional definition unfortunately has inherent problems of scale. Is the small country town, with a population of perhaps 4,000 people, rural? How does one place the large housing estate associated with a military airport or the settlements associated with a holiday camp within this framework? On the assumption that we all have some notion of rurality which allows us to define and categorise places with a degree of ease as social actors, it is worth commenting on the sort of factors involved. The importance of landscape and rurality within English culture lies at the root of the separation we draw between town and country. It is partly a question of scale and appearance, but it is also strongly cultural and psychological, with deeply embedded expectations that rural settlements will exhibit certain characteristics to do with community dynamics and social cohesion.

In an effort to circumvent all this conceptual confusion a comprehensive rurality measurement has been devised by Cloke and Edwards (1986) to define district council areas on a scale of rurality. This is based strictly on information derived from the 1981 census, and follows on from a similar classification based on the 1971 census (Cloke 1977). Many of the individual factors brought into play by Cloke and

Edwards are not obviously rural but together they add up to a measure of rurality which seems to produce a good fit with our instinctive, or rather socially and culturally determined, notion of rurality. Without examining in detail the sixteen variables used by Cloke and Edwards, it is worth briefly commenting on some of them because of what they tell us about the assumptions which lie behind our everyday expectations of rurality. Ten of the variables directly concern population – its level, density, distribution, the distance from large centres of population and migration. The assumption is that the more sparse the population and the greater the distance from an urban centre, the more 'rural' a district. Other variables include occupation and amenities. The four categories of rurality thus derived are extreme rural, intermediate rural, intermediate non-rural, and extreme non-rural.

The rurality index is a useful means of delineating the broad pattern of rurality in England and Wales. It is of little use, however, in assessing the characteristics of areas at scales lower than the district level. Moreover, the index should be used with care. As Hoggart (1986) has pointed out, it would be mistaken to use the index, and hence the rurality it describes, as a way of *explaining* geographical variations in economic conditions. As Ray Pahl noted more than twenty years ago "any attempt to tie particular patterns of social relationships to specific geographical milieux is a singularly fruitless exercise" (Pahl 1968: 293). In other words rurality cannot be seen as a determining factor in sociology.

This is not to say, however, that rural areas no longer have special characteristics. The sparsely distributed populations characteristic of such areas do have an effect on the nature of social relations (Blacksell, Economides and Watkins 1991). While close-knit communities are no longer seen as peculiarly rural phenomonena certain attributes of many rural communities still give some distinctiveness, and certain sociological factors are useful in helping us to understand particular rural areas. These include a high proportion of petty-bourgeoisie businesses, the continuing importance of kin networks, relatively low use of social welfare services, relatively high attendance at church, and so forth. None of these defines a rural place. None is confined to rural areas. Indeed inner cities share some of these characteristics. Neither can any of these factors be divorced from underlying spatial, economic and geographical features. Moreover, crucially, all are 'threatened' by the impact of recent changes on the countryside. Together, though, they do help us to build up a picture of rurality.

Finally, in this section we turn to the index of rurality derived from the views of the clergy themselves as this is used in the book as one of the main ways to differentiate between different kinds of rural or non-rural areas. The postal survey sought respondents' perceptions of the 'locality' of their parishes. From these data a set of rurality variables, relating to benefices (and therefore clergy) rather than individual parishes, was defined, and five mutually-exclusive categories created, as follows:

(1) *Totally Rural*

This category labelled 'totally rural' comprises benefices in which *all* the parishes had been ticked or mentioned as rural, and *none* of which had been ticked or mentioned as anything else. Out of the whole sample, 188 benefices (33%) were defined as 'totally rural'.

(2) *Partly Rural*

This category comprises benefices which were rural plus some other definition, except small country town. It includes those benefices in which *at least one* parish had been ticked or mentioned as rural, and benefices in which all the parishes had been ticked or mentioned as rural, but some of which had also been labelled with other categories, and therefore were not included in the 'totally rural' category. For example, it would include a benefice of one rural parish and one suburban parish, or another of three parishes all described as a mixture of rural, commuter and fishing. Of the total sample, 84 benefices (15%) were defined as 'partly rural'.

(3) *Small Country Town*

This category comprises *all* benefices where *at least one* parish was ticked or mentioned as small country town, regardless of whether rural or urban was also mentioned. In total, 93 benefices (16%) were defined as 'small country town'.

(4) *Part Urban/Non Rural*

This category is the most mixed. It includes all those benefices where parishes were *not* described in any way as rural or as small country towns, except for those benefices in which all parishes were ticked or mentioned as urban (these are included in the 'urban' category). Examples of benefices included in this category are those with commuter, suburban, mining, estate and fishing labels where they were *not* combined with rural or small country town descriptions. A total of 68 (12%) of benefices fell into this category.

(5) *Urban*

This category comprises benefices in which *all* the parishes were ticked or mentioned as urban, and *none* of which was rural. Benefices are included where mention was made of estate, commuter, suburban, mining and any other category as long as all the parishes were also designated as urban. In total, 129 (22%) of benefices were defined as 'urban'.

The frequencies of the these rurality categories in the five dioceses are outlined in Table 6 below. Truro emerged as the most rural diocese, with 86% of clergy in the three rural categories, and the highest proportions of the totally rural and partly rural categories. There were, however, slightly fewer small country town benefices than in Lincoln (22%), the second most rural diocese. Despite the inclusion of the South Humberside conurbations, which contribute significantly to the classification of 21% of benefices as urban, Lincoln remains a strongly rural diocese. Gloucester was the third most rural diocese with 69% of benefices falling into rural categories. The large towns of Gloucester and Cheltenham reduce the overall level of rurality and contribute to the significant number of benefices classified as non-rural (27%). Whilst the proportion of benefices classed as totally rural is high, there was a low level of partly rural benefices (only ten per cent) which implies a relatively sharp division between the rural and non-rural areas. In Southwell, only 52% of benefices were classified as rural. Durham was the least rural diocese of the five, with only 36% of benefices classified as rural.

Rural Futures

Predicting the future is fraught with hazard, yet, this chapter would be incomplete without some attempt to speculate on the likely future course of change in rural areas. Indeed some measure of speculation is vital if the Church of England is to judge correctly its choice of policies on the deployment of staff and mission.

The first point to make is the need for the utmost caution in

TABLE 6. *Classification of Rurality by Diocese*

Diocese (% of clergy/benefices)

Category	ALL	Glos	Truro	Southwell	Lincoln	Durham
'RURAL'	64	69	86	52	79	36
Totally rural	33	41	46	26	40	15
Partly rural	15	10	18	13	15	16
Small co town	16	18	22	13	24	5
'NON-RURAL'	34	27	10	48	21	62
Pt.U/Non R	12	9	3	19	8	19
Urban	22	18	7	29	13	43
Missing	2	4	4	-	-	2

Nb. 'Rural' comprises categories of totally rural, partly rural and small country town.'Non-Rural' comprises categories of part urban/non rural and urban.

extrapolating from current trends or taking too seriously the pronouncements of policy makers and analysts. A lesson from very recent history provides an apposite example. During the 1950s and 1960s, when planning policy was still strongly influenced by worries concerning rural depopulation, key settlement policy emerged as a major way forward for the revitalisation of rural areas (Cloke 1979). It was reasoned, entirely inappropriately as it turned out, that the only way in which rural areas could survive, economically and socially, was if services and people were to be concentrated in a select few settlements. For the rest there would be benign neglect. Most denominations toyed with the implications of key settlement policy for their own strategies, but it was the Methodist Church which probably went further than any in allowing its own policies to be influenced. The extent of the closure of rural Methodist chapels, which proceeded apace in some, but not all, districts in the 1960s, is now recognised by many as a mistake consequent upon too literal an interpretation of planning policy and its likely long-term implications.

The planning of church deployment and activities must always be undertaken with due regard to a *range* of future options rather than an assumption that one particular pattern will prevail. Thus, while most commentators would agree that many of the changes affecting rural areas will continue into the next century, there are a number of factors which will influence the precise nature and extent of the changes. It is clear that much of the relocation which has occurred is dependent upon cheap and efficient transport systems. As pointed out earlier, the centrifugal forces at work in the British economy do not extend to power, either political or financial, which remains heavily centralised in London, (and to a great extent in Brussels, Paris, Bonn, Tokyo and New York). Within England the pull of London remains immensely strong. Many of the larger businesses which have been re-located in rural areas have head offices in London or depend for finance upon the London markets. Many smaller businesses are dependent upon London markets or expertise. The need to travel to London remains very real. Despite modest efforts to de-centralise, many government departments continue to be based in London, and despite programmes of privatisation the direct influence of government activities on the UK economy remains great.

Thus any change in the pricing or the quality of transport services might severely curtail the opportunities for rural living for many thousands of people, going beyond just those who commute to the metropolis each day. Moreover, the possibilities of this happening are very real. Already one consequence of the rapid economic change of the late 1980s has been congestion on the roads and increased awareness of some of the inadequacies in public transport. Many commuters, who moved to more distant rural locations in the 1970s and early 1980s, now find their journey times actually increasing. But a far more serious possibility is that of massive increases in fuel prices, possibly as a consequence of oil shortages as was once feared, but also as a response to the need to control carbon dioxide emissions. The 'greenhouse effect' has become a major focus for international concern, and there is increasing evidence that the only effective way to counter climate change is through the reduction of emissions. Controlling the use of motor cars is an obvious means of reducing emissions and the tax system a possible way in which this will be achieved.

Such a scenario might very seriously counter the outward movement of people and businesses, especially as far as the more remote rural areas are concerned. On the other hand, in some areas the process has probably gone too far for serious disruption to occur. It is hard to imagine new processes of centralization which would strip a county such as Gloucestershire of its continued potential for demographic and economic growth. Moroever, there are technological developments which would boost centrifugal forces. For instance, one response to increased fuel prices might be to step up the use of computer and telecommunication technologies which allow home-working. As further advances in technology occur it is not hard to imagine the numbers working from home increasing (Watkins 1989). If the number of cars were to be reduced a combination of homeworking and improved public transport might yet enable rural areas to retain the edge as 'desirable' places to live.

What these possibilities might mean to the poor in rural areas is worrying. The skills required by the new technologies are high and the traditional primary rural industries of agriculture and forestry are likely to continue to shed labour. Suggestions that new environmentally friendly or organic farming might take on more workers are entirely conjectural. The evidence is all to the contrary. Of course, much depends on future government policies. We have become used to policies of de-regulation and a return to the market place, and yet the policies required to control pollution are anything but laissez-faire. It is quite possible that the free market rhetoric will continue and, indeed, will operate in many areas. Exceptions may have to be made as far as certain environmental controls are concerned, but these will be grudging. Any notion of a long term strategy to cover environmental, economic and social objectives is likely to be resisted. Alternatively, the need for environmental controls might prompt the re-assimilation of intervention to achieve social and economic objectives, with positive policies to favour the housing and work needs of disadvantaged people in rural areas.

(1) None of the dioceses is entirely coterminous with the main county in which the cathedral city is located, but for the purpose of analysis in this chapter we have tended to equate the dioceses with their respective counties – Cornwall, Gloucestershire, Nottinghamshire, Lincolnshire and County Durham.

(2) In truth, the trends that are now so apparent challenge the very foundations of many of the assumptions of economics, geography and sociology regarding the centralisation and concentration of peoples and industry in a modern economy. This is plainly the case with regard to the many models developed to explain and examine the location of economic activity (amongst the most well known examples are Isard 1956 and Christaller 1966 German edition 1933). As Gregory (1978: 40) points out, many of these models were "little more than translations of neo-classical utility theory into a spatial context". They are thus wholly inadequate to explain complex social phenomena

in anything other than a highly idealized manner, and the evidence of current centrifugal tendencies throws this into sharp relief. It is as well to stress caution, however, for the nature of the claims regarding centrifugal tendencies should not be taken to imply some kind of rural renaissance in every sense, still less the rejection of industrial society *per se*.

4

The Vicar

In Chapter 2 we mentioned the identification of the incumbent clergyman with his parish, both as a focus of loyalty (or dissent) for the parishioners, and as the representative of the church in theological and organisational terms. In discussing the development of the parochial organisation of the church we found it impossible to avoid a consideration of the model of parochial ministry developed within the Church of England during the last two or more centuries. The central role of the parish priest may now be questioned in much contemporary reflection on ministry, but its legacy and its continued influence in practice is profound. In the same way that many of the ideas surrounding the work of the parish priest were developed long before the zenith of the parochial clergy in the nineteenth century, so contemporary developments in ecclesiology have to be considered in the light of the stubborn resistance of a clerically dominated church organisation, particularly, it would seem, in rural areas.

To talk of stubborn resistance is not to imply that support for a traditional pattern of parochial ministry is somehow 'wrong'. However we would argue, that there is a clear mismatch between the expectations for rural ministry born out of parochial reorganisation and the advocacy of an increasing role for the laity, and rural ministry in practice. Elsewhere in this book we demonstrate the limited development of lay ministry in rural areas and the great problems posed by parochial reorganisation. The centrality of the vicar is, in practice, beyond dispute. He remains at the heart of the Church of England's ministry and, alongside the church building, provides the essence of the church's cultural, social and visible identity. The church as both the body of Christ and a body of people may have been much espoused in ecclesiology (see for example Hanson and Hanson 1987), but in social practice it is but slowly assimilated.

This chapter focuses on the central figure of the clergyman through a detailed account of clerical work, views and attitudes. This is an ambitious task and involves summarising a considerable quantity of data assembled during the course of the Rural Church Project. Readers wishing to delve deeper into the statistics should consult two of the four separately published monographs which provide a comprehensive dataset (Davies et al 1990b and 1990d).

The study of clergy by social scientists is far from new, not least because of the need for evidence on two inter-related issues which concern the sociologist of religion. First, secularisation is one of those concepts which has intrigued and tantalised a generation of scholars (Wilson 1969; Martin 1978), and has necessarily involved a focus on the clergy as "guardians of the sacred" (Martin 1978), and their response to changes in society. Secondly, there is the whole debate about the professionalization of the clergy, consequent upon an increasingly differentiated and specialized 'secular' society (Dunstan 1967; Golner et al 1973; Hinings and Foster 1973; Jarvis 1975, 1976).

Two studies, in particular, have elaborated on these conceptual areas in the light of empirical evidence derived from sociological investigations of the clergy (Ranson et al 1977; Towler and Coxon 1979). Together these studies provide a useful picture of the educational background and social origins of the clergy, their belief systems, particularly their response to change, along with contrasts between those adhering to different churchmanship and theological persuasions. They have also reflected a preoccupation with their religious beliefs. This approach "draws attention to the cognitive dimension of religious activity, so that rituals and practices take second place" (Turner, 1983 p4). The content of religious belief is an important area, as shown in Chapter 9, but it is equally important to investigate religion as an element of social structure and social relations as we do in this chapter.

Thus, while these earlier works provided an excellent starting point for our own considerations we felt the need to consider the sociology of work and community as well as the sociology of religion. The focus of these works on professionalization directed attention towards the training, identity and beliefs of the clergy. Thus in Ranson et al, much attention is directed to the autonomy of the clergyman and his relations with others in the church hierarchy and with members of the laity. The empirical question of what the clergy actually do in their work is not directly addressed. In the case of Towler and Coxon the survey methodology, a survey of ordinands, prevents this. Ranson et al employed a lengthy postal questionnaire survey (106 questions) among parish priests, covering a wide range of topics such as authority and decision-making within the diocese, ecumenical questions, the role of the laity, and so forth. Although one question asks the respondent to rank in order of priority seven main tasks of the ministry, none seeks any information on what time and energy the priest devotes to particular tasks. One final point on these earlier studies is that they are now somewhat dated. Towler and Coxon's study of the clergy, although published in 1979, relies primarily on data collected in 1962 and 1966, whilst Ranson, Bryman and Hinings' 1977 book uses survey data assembled between 1970 and 1973.

In the remainder of this chapter we develop a social profile of the clergy as a distinctive occupational group in modern society. We consider their age, training and experience in an attempt to build up a composite picture of the clergy in the five dioceses we surveyed. We discuss their family and social life, and the content and nature of the work of the parson. Unless otherwise specified, the data are drawn from the postal survey and, therefore, refer to all clergy, both rural and urban.

Age, Training and Experience

Turning first to age, we find the average clergyman is on the elderly side, and for this tendency to be particularly pronounced in the totally rural benefices (Table 7). In totally rural and small country town benefices at least a quarter of clergy were aged 60 or more, compared to only 15% in urban areas. In totally rural benefices nine per cent of clergy were aged over 65. Only 12% of all clergy were under 40 years of age. This is a third of the figure recorded by Ranson et al (1977) for three dioceses in the early 1970s, and reflects the decline in young men coming forward for ordination in the intervening period. The interpretation to be placed upon this trend is not entirely clear, for there can be no absolute correlation between age and resourcefulness, ability and so forth. We should not necessarily be worried about an ageing clergy. Indeed there might be certain benefits for ministry if one of the reasons for a high average age is the late entry of men with useful life-experiences from outside the ordained ministry.

Nonetheless, the current age profile of the clergy does carry with it certain connotations. For the population as a whole it is generally accepted that opinions and beliefs are less likely to change as a person becomes older. Therefore, the formative training years of clergy are likely to have implications for current beliefs and practices, although it has to be said that some of our data show changes in outlook as a result of pastoral experience. It is no surprise, therefore, as shown in Chapter 8, that *Book of Common Prayer* services are far more common in rural areas under older priests than elsewhere. Churchmanship also is strongly influenced by age[1]. A mere seven per cent of clergy describing themselves as central churchmen were under forty years old compared to 19% of open evangelicals and 21% of modern catholics. Central churchmen and traditional catholics account for a sizeable majority of clergy over the age of sixty. Central clergy are more strongly represented in rural areas than elsewhere.

TABLE 7. Age of Clergy by Rurality, (%; No=572)

Age Group %	Totally rural	Partly rural	Small country town	Part urban non-rural	Urban	All
Under 40	8	18	6	19	17	12
40-49	21	31	25	41	29	28
50-59	42	33	44	30	39	39
60-65	20	17	24	10	13	17
Over 65	9	1	1	-	2	4
Total	100	100	100	100	100	100

Although the average age of ordination of those surveyed was thirty, nearly two thirds (63%) of the clergy were ordained before this age. It is interesting to note, though, that 20% of clergy in totally rural benefices were ordained at or after the age of forty compared to just 5% of those in urban areas. In other words four times as many clergy in totally rural benefices are likely to have experienced some form of secular work prior to ordination compared to those in urban parishes. A corollary of this is that a greater proportion of those ordained late in life receive their training on a part-time basis through a regional course of training. Whereas this applied to only 2% of those ordained under the age of forty, 43% of those ordained at forty or over were trained through a course.

Overall 90% of respondents were College trained, but in totally rural benefices the figure dropped to 84%, reflecting the higher proportion of late entrants.

Thus the rural parishes have a higher proportion of older clergy, a significant minority of whom were late entrants to the ministry and came via a training course rather than College. Central churchmanship is particularly well represented, a reflection of both the age profile and, speculatively, the non-party emphasis of many training schemes. Nearly all evangelicals (97%) attended theological college, compared to 83% of traditional catholics. Central clergy were the most likely to have attended courses (12%), compared to only two per cent of conservative evangelicals. This may reflect the strength of evangelical colleges in standing for their particular tradition, and the importance of this to candidates of evangelical persuasion. Courses are more likely to reflect a range of churchmanship, which may prove attractive to central ordinands.

There was some difference between dioceses on training with as many as 12% of clergy in Gloucester and Truro trained through courses, compared to only four per cent in Southwell and Durham. This perhaps reflects the contrasting class composition of the areas (see Chapter 3) with a tendency for members of the educated middle-class, well represented in Gloucester and Truro, to undertake mid-career training courses. Certainly, in the interview survey we came across a number of late entrants to the ministry who had given up high status and lucrative occupations. If this is so, and more work is required to confirm this, it denotes a change since the detailed studies of the recruitment and training of ordinands carried out in the 1960s by Towler and Coxon (1979). They found late entrants to be distinctive in having left school earlier and being more likely to come from a working class background.

Looking at the theological colleges in more detail, Table 8 lists the most frequently mentioned colleges. It essentially shows the great diversity of College backgrounds with only one College, Salisbury and Wells, accounting for more than 10% of all respondents.

Of course, there is much more to preparation for the rural ministry than formal theological training. Of particular importance to those now occupying incumbencies in rural areas is the nature of previous ministerial appointments, especially curacies. The postal survey respondents were asked to furnish details of up to four previous ministerial appointments. The findings showed quite a high degree of mobility, with 70% of the

TABLE 8. *Most Frequently Mentioned Theological Colleges*

College	Number of clergy	% of all resps	% of College trained resps
Salisbury and Wells	61	11	12
Lincoln	53	9	10
Warminster/Kings London	51	9	10
Cuddesdon/Ripon	45	8	9
Cranmer Hall, Durham	30	5	6
Trinity Bristol (incl. Tyndale/Clifton)	27	5	5
Oak Hill	25	4	5
St Johns Nottingham/ London Coll. Divinity	23	4	5
Mirfield	22	4	4
Total 'Top Nine'	337	59	66
Other★	170	30	34

★The other Colleges all scored less than 20 mentions each. They were in descending order of importance: Chichester (18), Wycliffe Hall Oxford (18), Queen's College Birmingham (16), Ridley Hall Cambridge (16), St. Stephen's House Oxford (14), Cheshunt (12), Westcott House Cambridge (12), Kelham (11), Ely (10), Lichfield (7), Edinburgh (6), Rochester (6), St. Aidan's Birkenhead (6), St. Chad's Durham (6), St David's College Lampeter (6), St Michael's College Llandaff (4), Bernard Gilpin Society (2), St Deiniol's Library Hawarden (1).

clergy having worked within more than one diocese. More than a half (54%) had been paid incumbents (including priests-in-charge) in their most recent appointment, and just over a quarter (26%) had been assistant clergy. Only seven per cent had worked in teams.

With regard to rural experience, the survey showed that more than a quarter of clergy currently working in totally rural benefices had had no previous rural experience, and nearly a third of those in partly rural benefices. Indeed, in rural benefices, more clergy had had exclusively urban experience than exclusively rural. Urban clergy were even less likely to have experienced working in a rural area. Although nearly two thirds (63%) of current rural clergy had had some rural experience in the past, less than half (46%) the urban or part urban clergy were in this position. In addition, even in rural areas, rural experience was by and large limited to one or two appointments - only eight per cent of rural clergy had held more than two past rural positions.

By contrast, 86% of all clergy had had at least some urban experience (compared to the 57% who had had rural experience). Urban and part urban clergy would appear to be considerably better prepared for their current posts than rural clergy - nearly all had had prior urban experience and nearly 30% had had three or four relevant previous appointments. Only three per cent of clergy currently in urban or part urban benefices had had no prior urban experience. This has much to do with the shortage of rural curacies. Just 22% of all the curacies mentioned by our respondents were in rural, partly rural or small country town benefices. But, if small country towns are excluded, just eight per cent of all curacies were located in totally rural or partly rural areas. Less than one third (31%) of clergy currently working in totally or partly rural areas had held rural curacies (including small country towns), and very few (two per cent) had held more than one. Clergy currently in small country towns were even less likely to have held a rural curacy - only a quarter had done so, the same proportion as in partly urban areas.

Thus, a majority of the current incumbents in rural areas assumed their incumbency with no or very minimal parochial experience in a rural parish. Those who had some rural experience were more likely to have received it as an incumbent of another parish rather than through a curacy. And even those who had held a rural curacy had in most cases done so in a small country town rather than in a more typically rural benefice. This clearly raises many questions on the applicability of current curacy provision and post-ordination training. Whilst we have no wish to raise spurious arguments about the special nature of 'rural' ministry, it is quite clear that certain aspects of rural work are very different from urban ministry. An incumbent coming to a rural benefice without appropriate experience is likely to face, for the first time, the problems of organising worship in a multi-parish setting. If his experience has been in suburbia the congregations may appear small and the expectations regarding style of worship somewhat traditional. Moreover, he will be coming to a community which may have faced quite distinctive recent demographic and social change and yet, in land use terms, still be dominated by agriculture with all the complexities of technology, politics and economics which that encompasses. At the very least some special knowledge and empathy is probably required.

The Clergy at Work

Although remarkably little attention has been focussed on the content of clergy work it is of the greatest importance to a full understanding of professionalisation and secularisation. Both topics require an understanding of the *social position* of the clergyman in society. The theoretical significance which is attached to the religious functionary in any analysis of the changing place of religion in society depends on a considerable body of assumptions about what the clergy actually do. Social position may be defined as "a social identity that carries with it a certain range of prerogatives and obligations that an actor who is accorded that identity (or is an 'incumbent' of that position) may activate or carry out" (Giddens 1979: 117). Clearly an understanding of social position depends upon a combination of societal expectations and the actions and beliefs of 'incumbents'. Our view is that while the beliefs of clergy are well understood their actions require far more attention.

Therefore, an important element of the Rural Church Project was to ground all consideration of the social position of the clergy in an investigation of the nature and content of clergy work. We wanted to find out not only what the clergy considered to be important and meaningful about their job but also how, in fact, they spent their time. Accordingly, one of the more complex and demanding sections of the postal survey asked respondents to provide estimates of the time spent on a range of twenty one different activities (with extra space for recording any others not listed) for one week, the 6th to the 12th November 1988. Inevitably some felt unable or unwilling to complete the schedule fully and in some instances the week in question was notably atypical due to illness, holidays or synodical commitments. When such situations were excluded we were left with 469 responses out of the 572 in the total sample. The following analysis is thus based on fully completed returns from those who described themselves as full-time parish clergy.

Not all the activities are necessarily 'work' in a strict sense, although in many instances the respondent's presence, *qua* clergyman, is likely to be of significance. This may be as true for church meetings where the clergyman attends as a church member rather than a leader (eg. lay led bible study groups) as for non-church community events. The total number of hours recorded in the week are not, therefore, strictly comparable to those occupations where work can be more discretely defined. The 60 hour a week clergyman should not automatically be seen as working a third as much again as the 40 hour a week factory or office worker who devotes most of his or her spare time to church activities. Nor, on the other hand, would we dispute the fact that many clergy feel permanently 'on call', in a manner which is not necessarily so in other occupational groups. Suffice it to say that many of the clergy are clearly very busy and fully occupied people and we are confident that it is legitimate, for the purposes of this exercise, to treat the hours recorded as 'work'. The average amount of time spent in work and related duties and activities is 56.6 hours per week. These figures mask quite a variation with a minimum of 18.5 hours and a maximum of 116.5 hours recorded by different individuals; however a large majority (74%) spent between 40 and 69 hours a week on the recorded activities.

Suggestions that multi-parish rural livings might make greater demands upon the time of the clergy or alternatively that rural livings still provide an easy option were not, on the whole, substantiated by the data. It is true that those working the longest hours tended to be located in urban or small country town parishes. Twenty per cent of priests in these livings recorded more than seventy hours a week, compared to 11% in totally rural benefices. Similarly 18% of single parish incumbents worked more than seventy hours a week compared to eight per cent of those with four or more parishes. However, in terms of average working weeks, the differences between contrasting locations are not that great, as shown in Table 9.

It is no longer the case, as the Paul Report (1964) concluded, that a third of clergy, mostly in rural areas, are underemployed. Indeed, our evidence might be taken to indicate that the Sheffield formula has to some extent righted this anomaly (if in fact the anomaly ever existed). However rurality and population size, particularly the latter, continue to have some bearing on the total number of hours spent in work and related activities. This should not be taken to indicate that the creation of multi-parish benefices has no influence upon the nature of clergy work. The nature of work and its effectiveness may vary even if amounts of time do not.

Of far greater importance than the total number of hours worked is the content of clergy work. Table 10 shows the summary results for all dioceses.

TABLE 9. *Average Total Number of Hours spent in Work and Related Activities*

	Average total hours
Clergy in:	
Totally rural parishes	54.8
Part rural parishes	56.3
Country town parishes	57.9
Part urban/non rural parishes	58.3
Urban parishes	56.9
Clergy with benefices of:	
1 Parish	57.1
2 Parishes	56.7
3 Parishes	53.1
4+ Parishes	54.7
Clergy with benefice populations of:	
< 1,000	55.7
1,000–1,999	53.6
2,000–4,999	55.3
5,000–9,999	58.5
10,000+	59.6

Looking first at absolute mean amounts it can be seen that the single most time-consuming activity is visiting which on average takes up just over seven hours for the week. This is followed closely by parish administration at nearly six hours and service and sermon preparation and attendance at regular Sunday services at between four and five hours each. No other single activity occupies more than four hours per week, an indication of the extreme variety of tasks which go to make up the working life of the clergy. When the activities are amalgamated into the seven main groupings we find that the time spent on sacerdotal tasks is 16 hours which, at 29% of total time, comprises the largest single group. If the time spent on private devotions and study is added to the sacerdotal activities we have figures of 23.3 hours and 41% for directly 'religious' activities.

TABLE 10. How the Clergy spend their Time (No=469)

Activity	Mean no of hrs	Mean proportion of time %
1) SACERDOTAL		
Service and sermon preparation	4.7	9
Attending services - regular Sunday	4.2	8
regular weekday	3.0	5
other (eg weddings)	1.7	3
Leading preparation classes	1.5	3
Bible study or prayer groups	1.3	2
Total 1	16.4	29
2) PASTORAL		
Visiting	7.1	12
Counselling at home	1.8	3
Chaplaincy	0.8	1
Work with schools	1.5	3
Other work with children or young people	0.9	2
Church social events	1.0	2
Total 2	13.1	23
3) ADMINISTRATION		
Parish administration	5.8	10
Parish meetings	2.6	5
Magazine preparation	1.7	3
Church fundraising	0.7	1
Total 3	10.8	19
4) PRIVATE DEVOTIONS & STUDY		
Private prayer	3.7	7
Private study	3.2	5
Total 4	6.9	12
5) DIOCESAN OR DEANERY DUTIES	2.6	5
6) TRAVEL BETWEEN ACTIVITIES	3.3	6
7) OTHER		
Non-church social/community	2.2	4
Other	1.3	2
Total 7	3.5	6
MEAN TOTAL	56.4	100

Pastoral work and administration are also both important categories, with administration accounting for nearly 11 hours of activity in the week, although this includes time spent on parish meetings which presumably have a wider organisational and strategic function than merely that of routine administration. The mean figures mask the fact that whilst all clergy perform tasks in each of the main groups, they are not necessarily involved in every activity within the group. There are clearly some core activities, such as attendance at Sunday services and visiting, which occupy virtually all of the clergy, but some activities, such as chaplaincy undertaken by 25% of the clergy, are minority pursuits only. A relatively high proportion of clergy were involved in weekday services (85.7%), work with schools (66.5%), and diocesan or deanery duties (61.6%). By contrast the number involved in church fundraising (26.1%), bible study or prayer groups (55.7%) and non-church social/community activities (56.8%) was relatively low.

The figures are consistent with the findings of Ranson et al (1977) when they asked their respondents to rank various ministerial roles according to their relative importance, not in terms of time, but as an imperative within ministry. Thus the most important role was that of 'pastor', followed closely by 'celebrant', 'preacher' and 'counsellor'. The roles of 'leader', 'administrator' and 'official/representative' were considered to be far less important.

As Ranson et al found some striking differences between the Anglican, Roman Catholic, and Methodist subjects of their survey we were interested to see whether churchmanship seemed to influence work patterns within our own sample. At first sight the allocation of time to pastoral work, administration, travel and other activities is remarkably constant across the different traditions of churchmanship. Diocesan and deanery duties tend to be carried out to a slightly greater extent by central churchmen and modern catholics. Private prayer and study is virtually identical for four of the five groups with traditional catholics standing apart with 15% of their time devoted to prayer and study compared to 11-12% for the others. Although the differences are relatively small, conservative and open evangelicals do appear to spend more time on sacerdotal activities than their central or catholic colleagues. This is rather a surprising finding, in view of the traditional commitment of many catholics to weekday communion services and liturgical worship generally. In fact the catholics do spend more time on weekday services than their evangelical colleagues, a quarter of their sacerdotal time compared to eight to nine per cent for evangelicals, but evangelicals score much more heavily on service and sermon preparation and in leading bible study and prayer groups. Open evangelicals devote 15% of their sacerdotal work to these activities compared to only five per cent for modern catholics.

In view of the striking differences in the composition of sacerdotal duties according to churchmanship we also considered the possible influence of commitment to a radical, liberal or charismatic orientation, but our evidence showed that these orientations had little apparent influence on the apportionment of time. Charismatics are slightly above the mean for the amount of time spent on sacerdotal duties and radicals slightly below. Radicals score rather highly on diocesan and deanery duties. But when sacerdotal work is divided into its component parts we find no great differences emerging, except for bible study and prayer groups which figure much more highly on the agenda of charismatics than either liberals or radicals. Thus contrasting traditions of churchmanship seem to have a greater influence upon the allocation of time amongst different sacerdotal duties than do charismatic, liberal or radical orientations.

Another possible source of variation is the age of the clergy. Our evidence showed that those over 65 years spend a greater amount of time, absolutely and proportionately, on private prayer and study than their younger colleagues – 20% of their time compared to between ten and 14% in the other age bands. They also spend significantly less time on pastoral duties and administration than other groups.

A number of commentators have emphasised how rural ministry has become very different in content and purpose in recent years. These views centre on the impact of parish reorganisation and rationalisation upon the time available for the clergy to perform specific functions. Put very simply it is sometimes assumed that the priest in a multi-parish benefice will find a greater proportion of his time taken up with administration, travel, and some sacerdotal duties to the detriment of both pastoral work and the quality of Sunday worship. The caricature is of the priest spending Sundays dashing from church to church to fulfil the needs of half a dozen parishes and the rest of the week in administration, for example contending with several different parochial church councils. Travel will eat into his time both on Sundays and in carrying out any pastoral work during the week. Visiting and involvement and leadership in community life are squeezed out with the priest assuming the more narrow role of religious professional or functionary. In contrast his single parish urban counterpart will have a relatively small number of Sunday services to perform, less routine administration, limited travelling, but more occasional offices – funerals, baptisms, weddings – some of which will be linked to pastoral work. Thus, for Anthony Russell,

> The need for rural clergy to service the largest possible number of churches on any particular Sunday, has led to a situation in which it is now normal for the clergyman to arrive from a previous service at the last minute, and sometimes to disappear during the last hymn (the singing of which is partly drowned by the roar of his departing car). (Russell 1986: 250)

Similarly, Leslie Francis describes the following experience of one of his team of ordinands when attending a church service as part of Francis' participant-observation exercise in a study of rural Anglicanism in Norfolk:

> As the clock struck ten, Nick was beginning to wonder why he had seen no signs of the vicar. Then, suddenly, the church door burst open and the vicar came rushing in. Nick says that the vicar then 'flew around the church putting things out'. .... The service began just seven minutes late. The vicar set off at a breathless pace, and none of the congregation could keep up. (Francis 1985: 138)

There are obvious and immediate practical grounds for these views – to do with the decline in clergy numbers and the radical parochial reorganisation of recent years. If the caricatures are true we would expect to find significant differences in clergy work patterns according to key variables such as rurality, size of benefice and the number of parishes in an incumbency. We may also discover contrasts based on the personal traits of the clergy, such as age and different traditions of churchmanship. In fact, the situation is far less clear cut than the caricatures imply, as is revealed by an examination of the influence of the three main variables of what we might term ecclesiastical geography: rurality, the number of parishes in a clergyman's charge; and the population of the benefice.

In practice the division of work is remarkably similar between urban and rural clergy and between those with differing numbers of parishes and people, especially regarding the time spent on administration and travel. Only the sacerdotal category seems to be a focus of consistent variation. The totally rural parson seems to spend less time on sacerdotal work than those in other localities, as does the multi-parish incumbent and those with benefices with low populations as shown in Tables 11, 12 and 13.

TABLE 11. Clergy Work by Rurality, All Dioceses Mean Proportion of Time (%)

	Totally rural	Part rural	Small country town	Part urban non rural	Urban
Sacerdotal	26	29	31	32	30
Pastoral	23	23	21	22	23
Administration	19	19	20	19	18
Private devotions/study	14	11	11	12	12
Diocesan or Deanery duties	6	4	3	3	4
Travel between activities	7	6	6	5	5
Other	5	7	7	7	6

TABLE 12. Clergy Work by Number of Parishes in Benefice, All Dioceses, Mean Proportion of Time (%)

	1 parish	2 parishes	3 parishes	4+ parishes
Sacerdotal	30	30	27	24
Pastoral	23	21	22	24
Administration	18	19	19	20
Private devotions/study	12	13	13	13
Diocesan or deanery duties	5	4	6	5
Travel between activities	5	7	7	7
Other	6	6	5	6

Contrasting Ministries

The average clergyman in a totally rural benefice spends 26% of his time on sacerdotal work compared to from 29 to 32% elsewhere. The time spent on pastoral and administrative duties is almost identical across

TABLE 13. *Clergy Work by Size of Benefice, All Dioceses, Mean Proportion of Time (%)*

	< 1,000	1,000– 1,999	2,000– 4,999	5,000– 9,999	10,000+
		Benefice Population			
Sacerdotal	26	26	30	31	31
Pastoral	21	23	23	23	21
Administration	19	18	19	18	21
Private devotions/study	15	13	12	11	10
Diocesan or deanery duties	8	6	4	3	5
Travel between activities	6	7	6	5	5
Other	5	6	6	7	6

the range of localities, although slightly more time is spent in small country towns on administration than elsewhere. The totally rural parson makes up for his lighter sacerdotal load by a higher involvement in both private prayer and study and in diocesan and deanery duties. In the case of prayer and study this would appear to be linked with the higher proportion of elderly clergy located in rural areas. Together these categories take up 20% of his time compared to 14–16% elsewhere. Although the amount of time spent on travel shows a slight downward gradation from totally rural to urban or non rural areas, it is very slight and does little to support the commonly held contention that travel consumes a disproportionate amount of the rural parson's time. The difference between travel in totally rural and totally urban benefices is recorded at only one hour per week. Administration and pastoral work are similarly constant.

The country parson, whether defined by the rurality index, number of parishes or size of benefice population, appears to allocate less time to sacerdotal duties than his urban counterpart or, indeed, his neighbour in the small country town. On administration, travel and pastoral work the allocations are roughly the same. These data require careful explanation for none are in accord with our initial expectations. In fact this closer examination of the evidence re-inforces our original view that rural and urban work is likely to be quite different, although not necessarily in all the ways we had anticipated. There are two strands to our argument: first, some of the categories need unpacking as they contain rather different elements; secondly, in each category we need to assess qualitative differences rather than merely concentrating on numeric data.

Thus the differences observed with regard to sacerdotal duties should not necessarily be taken as evidence which is entirely contrary to the caricatures we have cited. In reality, the situation is more complex but ultimately it can be used to support the contention that rural clergy, especially those with several parishes, have a difficult task in maintaining a pattern of worship acceptable to their parishioners. Tables 14 to 16 show the breakdown of sacerdotal duties. They reveal significant variations in the nature of the sacerdotal work undertaken. Although sacerdotal work tends to account for a greater proportion of a clergyman's time in urban benefices, this is largely due to the much greater incidence of weekday services and other church services such as occasional offices. The amount of time spent on service and sermon preparation does not vary greatly by rurality nor, even more surprisingly, does the time spent on Sunday services. Indeed incumbents of multi-parish benefices, if anything, spend slightly less time conducting Sunday worship than their single parish colleagues.

TABLE 14. Sacerdotal Duties by Rurality, Mean Number of Hours and Mean Proportion of Sacerdotal Time

	Totally rural	Part rural	Small country town	Part urban non rural	Urban
	%	%	%	%	%
Service/Sermon Preparation	4.7 (33)	4.5 (27)	5.0 (28)	5.3 (29)	4.2 (25)
Services – Regular Sunday	4.0 (28)	4.3 (26)	4.5 (25)	4.3 (24)	4.0 (23)
Regular weekday	1.9 (14)	3.0 (18)	3.4 (19)	3.3 (18)	3.9 (23)
Other	1.1 (8)	1.9 (11)	1.9 (11)	1.9 (11)	2.3 (13)
Leading classes	1.1 (8)	1.9 (11)	1.7 (10)	1.6 (9)	1.5 (9)
Bible study/prayer groups	1.2 (9)	1.2 (7)	1.3 (7)	1.7 (9)	1.2 (7)

The figures show, therefore, that the rural multi-parish clergyman, in contrast to his urban colleague, holds fewer weekday services and has fewer occasional offices to attend to. He also spends less time leading

TABLE 15. *Sacerdotal Duties by Number of Parishes in Benefice, Mean Number of Hours and Mean Proportion of Sacerdotal Time*

	1 parish %	2 parishes %	3 parishes %	4+ parishes %
Service/Sermon Preparation	4.8 (28)	4.3 (26)	4.8 (35)	4.7 (35)
Services – Regular Sunday	4.1 (24)	4.3 (26)	4.1 (30)	3.9 (29)
Regular weekday	3.4 (20)	2.9 (17)	1.8 (13)	1.6 (12)
Other	1.9 (11)	1.9 (11)	0.9 (6)	1.2 (9)
Leading classes	1.5 (9)	1.7 (10)	1.1 (8)	1.3 (10)
Bible study/prayer groups	1.3 (8)	1.6 (10)	1.1 (8)	0.8 (6)

TABLE 16. *Sacerdotal Duties by Size of Benefice, Mean Number of Hours and Mean Proportion of Sacerdotal Time*

	Benefice Population				
	< 1,000 %	1,000–1,999 %	2,000–4,999 %	5,000–9,999 %	10,000+ %
Service/sermon preparation	5.2 (37)	4.9 (36)	4.8 (30)	4.5 (25)	4.4 (23)
Services – Regular Sunday	3.8 (27)	4.0 (29)	4.1 (25)	4.2 (24)	4.5 (24)
Regular weekday	1.9 (13)	1.7 (12)	3.0 (19)	3.8 (21)	4.1 (22)
Other	1.2 (8)	1.1 (8)	1.4 (8)	2.3 (13)	2.6 (14)
Leading classes	0.8 (6)	1.1 (8)	1.6 (10)	1.7 (9)	1.8 (10)
Bible study/prayer groups	1.3 (9)	1.0 (7)	1.3 (8)	1.4 (8)	1.4 (7)

classes and slightly less time with bible study or prayer groups. All this is entirely consistent with both the practicalities of sacerdotal provision in rural areas, (fewer people meaning less rites of passage to perform) and some of our received assumptions regarding the nature of rural religion as less explicit and demonstrative. The picture for Sunday services, however, is somewhat surprising. What the figures seem to show, and this is supported by data in Chapter 8, is that few clergy attempt more than three full services on a Sunday or two short morning Communion services and two full services. The total of around about four hours in Sunday services is remarkably consistent across categories and entirely commensurate with the idea of a three to four service Sunday. However, there is a world of difference between conducting three services in one place and attending three or four different churches. We found that that those with several churches to attend on a Sunday felt under considerably greater pressure than their single parish colleagues.

When we asked clergy to specify sources of reward and problems in their ministry, several single parish clergy identified the positive side of having only one congregation to deal with. None cited having several congregations as a rewarding aspect of ministry, but several lamented the problems it caused. Moreover the concentration of non-stipendiary assistants, readers and so forth in single parish and urban benefices (see Chapter 6) means that an incumbent's role may be very different in services in rural and urban locations. An urban or small country town priest with three services in the one church may well receive considerable assistance even though he is present at the service. Indeed he may 'take a back seat' regularly when lay or ordained colleagues preach or celebrate. By contrast, the multi-parish priest is much more likely to officiate fully in all the services he attends, hence the feeling of greater pressure.

To sum up these differences in sacerdotal work let us consider the Sundays of two imaginary clergy. The Reverend John Smith has a four parish rural benefice, while Peter Brown has a single parish in the nearby market town. John's Sunday starts early with the quarter hour drive to his farthest flung church for eight o'clock Communion. The service lasts just half an hour but after talking to a few people briefly he has a bit of a rush to reach home again for a quick breakfast before the 9.30 Parish Communion in his home village. This is the largest congregation he will see today (30-40) and he is aided in the service by a lay person reading the epistle and by lay assistance in the administration of the chalice. It is the only lay assistance he will receive in the conduct of worship all day. This is also the only service of the day when he will see children; half a dozen attend for the first twenty minutes of the service before going off to Sunday School. The service finishes just after 10.30, but he has to skip coffee (a recent monthly innovation) to take a ten minute car journey to his smallest parish for eleven o'clock Matins. Matins complete, John takes something of a respite for lunch and the afternoon. Indeed he often feels that if only the services could be spread more evenly over the day the morning schedule would not seem so pressured. As it is, none of his PCCs will countenance an afternoon service and so he is at rest until the final service of the day – Sung Evensong at 6.30 in his fourth church. He has clocked up around four hours in church with quite a bit of travelling on top. He has preached three sermons.

Peter has a more leisurely start to the day. His early morning Communion service is at 8.15 and the church is two minutes walk away. In some ways the service is a hang-over from the days of his predecesssor, when it provided the only eucharistic worship on a normal Sunday. Now it is thinly attended and is celebrated by Peter's curate, with Peter reading the epistle and administering the chalice. Peter feels the service provides a good preparation for the day ahead. The main service of the day is the ten o'clock Parish Eucharist, which is attended by upwards of a hundred adults. Peter is in church making preparations a full half hour before the service starts. The service itself lasts an hour and a half, and includes the appearance of twenty Sunday School children half way through eager to perform a short piece of drama immediately prior to the Communion. Peter celebrates, but is assisted in the administration by his curate. The curate also reads the epistle and a lay person leads the intercessory prayers. The preacher is one of the two readers resident in the parish. The service is followed by coffee, which gives Peter a chance to catch up on parish news and make a number of pastoral enquiries. He leaves the church at twelve o'clock. Evensong is a much lower key affair lasting just under the hour. On this occasion Peter preaches, but the rest of the service is taken by the curate and the lessons read by two members of the congregation. Like John, Peter has spent four hours in church but he has preached only once and has been ably assisted by the laity and other clergy in each service. The garage doors have remained firmly shut.

It is worth staying with John and Peter to consider one more question, that of administration. The proportion of time spent on administration varies very little between different kinds of benefice. Once again, though, the quality and nature of the work varies. For John the main burden lies in maintaining the administrative and organisational framework for four parishes. This requires servicing four PCCs. For all intents and purposes his PCC secretaries are minutes secretaries only, but fortunately the parish affairs are relatively simple. PCC meetings are only once a quarter and there are no PCC sub-committees. John is acutely aware that much of his administration is merely passing information from a central point to the various PCCs resulting in no action. He sets aside a morning a week to go through the post and deal with other administrative tasks from his study. The main tools of this aspect of his work are the telephone, a single filing cabinet, and an elderly manual type-writer. Anything that needs to be passed on to the parishes he takes with him on a Sunday or while visiting. He feels much more could be done in considering some of the material that comes his way from the diocese, but is constrained by time and relatively inactive congregations. In some cases, though, he considers the diocesan information to be irrelevant to the needs of his four very small rural parishes. He receives little lay help, with the notable exception of the church accounts which are handled by a local retired accountant, as treasurer to the PCC.

Peter spends a similar proportion of his time on administration, but the work load is very different. He undertakes very little of the routine administration himself. The hub of his parish administration is in the church office converted from one of the back rooms of the church hall adjacent to the church. The office has two filing cabinets, photocopier and, the most recent addition, a word processor and printer. The PCC secretary, a retired civil servant, spends two or three mornings a week in the office and undertakes most of the parochial adminstration. He has regular meetings with the treasurer, and both meet with Peter fortnightly to keep him informed of matters that require his personal attention. PCC meetings are monthly but they are kept short. Much of the real work goes on in sub-committees dealing with such diverse topics as finance, worship, music and drama, youth work, and mission. The sub-committees are all chaired by members of the laity. Peter is an ex-officio member of each but he has no need routinely to attend every meeting. His administrative work tends to reflect particular projects of the moment and tasks which, he feels, require his input.

We found very few clergy were satisfied with their administrative role. Most felt it to be a distraction from their main pastoral and religious duties and begrudged the time and effort it demanded of them. This is entirely consistent with the low importance attached to administration in the Ranson et al study. Indeed they found administration to be given an equally low priority by Anglican, Methodist and Roman Catholic clergy alike:

> Religious functionaries seem to rank of low importance those tasks which derive from their possession of an office in a bureaucracy, even though these activities take up a good deal of their time: such tasks are perceived as mere drudgery which detract from their

central vocational tasks, rather than as means for the accomplishment
of these religious ends. (Ranson et al 1977: 64)

Many of the rural clergy we spoke to complained that administration
was becoming an increasingly burdensome part of their work, with
synodical government coming in for particular criticism (see Chapter 6).
But Ranson et al's work took place nearly twenty years ago, and they,
in their turn, pointed to similar findings from work in America in the
1950s and 1960s (Blizzard 1956, Jud et al 1970, Lauer 1973). Even in
1947 Charles Forder saw fit to commence his systematic pastoralia thus:

> At first sight it may appear that some apology is needed for the
> introduction of business methods into a parson's life, for a parson
> is, or should be, above all else, a man of prayer, a priest, a pastor,
> and a student.
>
> In spite of the necessity for order, there is a deplorable lack of
> business efficiency among the clergy as a whole. (Forder 1947: 3)

There is little new about clergy distaste for administration and the
efforts of others to remedy this.

On the question of travel we were somewhat surprised by our own
findings, as we fully expected rural and multi-parish incumbents to
spend a considerably higher proportion of their time on travel than their
urban or single parish counterparts. That this was not the case might be
explained by use of different modes of transport although this seems
unlikely. Clearly some urban priests will use public transport for hospital
visiting and the like and even do considerably more pastoral work on
foot. Rural clergy, on the other hand, may have developed a better
organisation of their time to maximise the efficiency of their travelling.
We also have to concede that travel may be such an integral and implicit
part of rural work that it has been under-recorded. Of one thing we are
certain, a number of the clergy we interviewed mentioned the cost of
travel as a significant factor in their finances. Financially the maintenance
of a car worthy of rural work is a far cry from use of bicycle, foot and
public transport in an urban area, even if the times spent on travel are
very similar.

Pastoral Work

The final key area for investigation is that of pastoral work. Tables 17,
18 and 19 show the variations in pastoral work. In fact the differences

are not great. Visiting, for example, takes up around 50% of the pastoral time across the board. Those in totally rural, partly rural and urban areas all spend nearly seven and a half hours a week in visiting, while six and a half hours is spent by those in the other two categories. Those with four or more parishes do more visiting than others but the difference is not great. Similarly there is very little difference according to size of the benefice, although in practice this clearly means that those in less populous benefices are more likely to receive a visit than those in more heavily populated locations. There are a few minor differences. Counselling at home, for example, is less common in rural and multi-parish circumstances.

TABLE 17. *Pastoral Duties by Rurality, Mean Number of Hours and Mean Proportion of Pastoral Time*

	Totally rural	Part rural	Small country town	Part urban non rural	Urban
	%	%	%	%	%
Visiting	7.3 (55)	7.3 (54)	6.6 (52)	6.4 (50)	7.4 (53)
Counselling at home	1.5 (12)	1.7 (13)	2.0 (16)	2.1 (16)	2.0 (15)
Chaplaincy	0.7 (5)	0.9 (7)	0.9 (7)	0.5 (4)	1.0 (7)
Work with schools	1.8 (14)	1.6 (12)	1.2 (9)	1.4 (11)	1.4 (10)
Children/youth	0.8 (6)	1.0 (7)	0.8 (6)	1.3 (10)	1.1 (8)
Church social events	1.1 (8)	0.9 (7)	1.2 (9)	1.1 (9)	1.0 (7)

Once again the real contrasts are qualitiative rather than quantitative. The nub of the issue here is the level of population served within each benefice. Charles Forder suggested that between two and four hundred house to house visits could be made a month, at a rate of ten to fifteen in an afternoon, based on an expectation that most women would not be out at work. Such figures suggest that even many urban benefices could be systematically visited in the course of just a year or two. In reality these figures are wildly optimistic. Certainly in rural areas, many of the clergy we interviewed felt three or four visits in an afternoon to be a good rate.

It was clear from the interviews that three main factors influenced the extent of visiting and its nature. First, where the population is high the possibilities for 'blanket' visiting are limited, notwithstanding Forder's

TABLE 18. *Pastoral Duties by Number of Parishes in Benefice, Mean Number of Hours and Mean Proportion of Pastoral Time*

	1 parish	2 parishes	3 parishes	4+ parishes
	%	%	%	%
Visiting	7.4 (55)	6.2 (50)	6.6 (57)	8.1 (57)
Counselling at home	1.9 (14)	1.9 (16)	1.5 (13)	1.5 (11)
Chaplaincy	0.8 (6)	0.8 (6)	0.5 (4)	0.4 (3)
Work with schools	1.3 (10)	1.8 (15)	1.3 (11)	1.9 (14)
Children/youth	1.0 (7)	0.8 (6)	0.8 (7)	1.0 (7)
Church social events	1.1 (8)	0.9 (7)	0.9 (8)	1.1 (8)

TABLE 19. *Pastoral Duties by Size of Benefice, Mean Number of Hours and Mean Proportion of Pastoral Time*

	Benefice Population				
	< 1,000	1,000–1,999	2,000–4,999	5,000–9,999	10,000+
	%	%	%	%	%
Visiting	6.9 (58)	6.9 (54)	7.3 (56)	7.3 (52)	6.8 (51)
Counselling at home	1.2 (11)	1.5 (12)	1.6 (12)	2.2 (16)	2.1 (16)
Chaplaincy	0.5 (4)	0.7 (6)	0.8 (6)	1.2 (8)	0.6 (4)
Work with schools	1.7 (14)	1.8 (14)	1.4 (11)	1.4 (10)	1.3 (10)
Children/youth	1.0 (8)	0.7 (6)	0.9 (7)	1.0 (7)	1.2 (9)
Church social events	0.6 (5)	1.1 (8)	1.0 (8)	1.0 (7)	1.4 (10)

expectations. Population levels clearly influence visiting policy. Secondly, clergy have very different views as to the efficacy and purpose of visiting which influence their aims and objectives in practice. Thirdly, visiting policy is influenced by the nature of the church in question and the demands placed upon the clergy by church duties and, indeed, by members of the congregation. As far as the rural clergy are concerned three broad patterns of visiting emerged from the interview survey. These can be loosely identified with three models of ministry: serving ministry, communal ministry, and associational ministry. Serving ministry refers to those whose sole focus for visiting is to serve those in particular need, especially the sick and the bereaved. In fact virtually all of those interviewed (97%) undertook such crisis visiting. However for some this was the core of their activity and they were unable or unwilling to go beyond this work. Thus those exercising a serving ministry of visitation had made a deliberate choice and usually questioned the efficacy of other types of visiting as the following quotations reveal:

> Ordinary visiting eased their (ie.the parishioners) consciences and kept people away from church. ... I refuse to compete with the television.
>
> I visit the sick of the parish. Having cups of tea with old ladies is not on the agenda.
>
> There needs to be some reason for visiting. It's not enough to turn up and say "I'm the parson".

A few even claimed that they would only undertake crisis visits by invitation and questioned whether visiting in other circumstances achieved anything worthwhile. But those with these views were in a minority. It was more common for a wider view of visiting to be employed. Those with a communal view accepted the centrality of crisis visiting but added to this the need to make other visits within the community. No less than 42% of those interviewed attempted to visit newcomers to the benefice and 21% sought to implement a programme of whole parish visiting, even if they failed to achieve this in practice:

> I'm interested in visiting. That is my priority. I said when I came I would try to visit all the people in six months. But I only achieved one half. I've done most here in T.. but not all in B..
>
> I can do eight a day. That's my number one priority. This is where we have failed miserably [as a church].

One of the most telling factors to emerge in this group was the recognition that visiting had become more of a problem not just because of larger groupings of parishes but as a result of more profound social changes in rural populations, particularly regarding mobility. A number lamented the fact that they were no longer able to pursue visiting in the same manner as in the earlier days of their ministry:

> I used to visit newcomers but now the turnover is so fast.
>
> When I came I visited every house in nine months. When I took on a third parish my work load doubled. The mathematics doesn't work out. I try to go to all the coffee mornings and functions. You can see a lot in half an hour, but you can only do one visit per afternoon.

Those adopting an associational style of visitation ministry had usually come to this position implicitly rather than through an explicit espousal of a particular pattern of ministry. In practice, some clergy, whilst not necessarily rejecting communal notions of ministry, found themselves confined to a combination of crisis visiting and serving the needs of their own congregation(s), through regularly visiting the faithful. Traditionally such an approach has been seen as a diversion from the real wider purposes of visiting. Charles Forder again,

> The sick and the weak, or possible backsliders, certainly need care, but the faithful often look for more attention than is their rightful due. As they get to know the clergy they expect fairly regular visits, and in fact the clergy are tempted to yield to this demand, for visiting these pillars of the church is very pleasant. But if visiting time is limited, these are the first visits to cut out. (Forder 1947: 264)

Nonetheless, some contemporary clergy, although but a few of our interview sample, consciously reject this view, arguing that the Church of England has neglected the spiritual needs of its own people. One of the claims of the modern house church or Restorationist movement is precisely this. Their system of 'shepherding' represents a highly organised system of pastoral care in which the visitation ministry exercised by church elders and leaders is primarily orientated towards the needs of the faithful (Walker 1985). A Pentecostal minister interviewed during the course of our researches was fully employed in the pastoral care of a congregation of just seventy. Although some Anglican ministers are closer to this associational model than others, its extremeness perhaps illustrates how distant the Church of England, in any of its manifestations, is from a 'pure' associational model of ministry. For the associationalists perhaps the only true focus for visiting outside the confines of the faithful is evangelism, and it is perhaps significant that only six per cent of those interviewed mentioned this factor when describing their visiting policy.

Whatever the views and policies expressed by the clergy, their parishioners consider visiting an important aspect of the work of the clergy. Forty two per cent of the general sample and 82% of the church sample had received clergy visits. Pastoral work was the single most important role ascribed to the clergy by parishioners, and an overwhelming majority considered it important for the vicar to visit his parishioners. There are, of course, more aspects to pastoral work than clergy visiting. One other dimension is work with schools. Of course, it has to be said that for many clergy their school activities revolve around the semi-official duties of management of church controlled or aided primary schools. To that extent this work falls within the purview of ecclesiastical work. Whatever their status, school governorships are now almost the only formal position of community responsibility commonly held by the clergy. With this exception the traditional model of the parson as a key local secular leader seems to have broken down almost entirely, as shown in Table 20. Only four were magistrates and twenty one held elected office as local government councillors. Two-thirds, however, were school governors.

TABLE 20. Clergy holding Positions of Responsibility Within the Community, All Dioceses

Position of responsibility	Number of Clergy (n = 572)	% of Clergy
Justice of the Peace	4	0.7
Parish Councillor	18	3.2
District/County Councillor	3	0.5
School Governor	372	65.3
Other position	78	13.7

Some held other forms of responsibility, such as membership of the management committee of the village hall or of a local charity, but even this was quite a small proportion, under 14% of the sample. One of our initial hypotheses was that the professionalisation model of the clergy, in which their role is reduced to that of guardianship of the sacred, might be less applicable in rural areas, where elements of a multi-faceted role for clergy could still be retained due to the absence of active caring professionals in the remoter countryside. Moreover, we also speculated that the uncertainties posed by the re-definition of the welfare state and the emphasis on self-help and voluntary community activities, under recent Conservative governments, might have led to a resurgence of a broader community leadership role for the clergy. However, we uncovered little evidence that the clergy were adopting leadership positions in new caring organisations. Whilst many of the clergy articulated a strong communal model of ministry their work was, in the main, orientated towards specifically church activities of a sacerdotal and pastoral nature, although, of course, pastoral work, such as visiting, may dovetail well with more formal community care provision.

Job Satisfaction

Notwithstanding the many problems experienced by ministers of religion, their life is, on the whole, deeply rewarding. Thus when we asked the clergy in the postal survey to indicate the areas of their work which gave them the most satisfaction we received an overwhelming response. Nearly all the clergy (92%) specified some aspect of their work which they found rewarding, with only two per cent commenting that no part of their ministry was particularly rewarding. Of course, this is not an unexpected finding. Most studies in the sociology of work uncover a high degree of job satisfaction, whatever the occupation. The interesting question to ask, though, is what constitutes the source of satisfaction. A distinction is commonly drawn between expressive and instrumental satisfaction (See Newby 1977; Newby et al 1978). Instrumental satisfaction refers to financial rewards or satisfaction derived from being in control of the work process. Thus a factory worker may express instrumental rewards when he highlights the wage packet as the main cause of satisfaction, or a farmer who cites his business independence. Expressive rewards concern non-pecuniary benefits resulting from the intrinsic nature and worth of the work. It is common for workers to combine, in differing degrees, both aspects. However, the clergy fall almost entirely within the expressive category. None identified financial reward, nor even freehold, and only three mentioned their own personal spiritual development. Instead the rewards cited were largely intrinsic aspects of their sacerdotal and pastoral roles. Interestingly, none identified administrative or organisational tasks as specific sources of satisfaction.

The rewards may be divided into four main groups - pastoral, ecclesiastical, sacerdotal, and community, as shown in Table 21. These are not necessarily strictly mutually exclusive. Indeed many clergy cited aspects in more than one group. Moreover there are grey areas, especially regarding the first three, but they do seem to reflect broad areas of reward and interest. Pastoral refers to ministry to individuals; ecclesiastical to ministry to the church; sacerdotal to the worship of God; and community to a sense of belonging and community.

Pastoral rewards were the most commonly cited. These refer to all aspects of the care of people. Some of this is a very general care and

TABLE 21. Rewarding Aspects of Ministry - Basic Frequencies

	No of Clergy	% of Responses
Pastoral	522	43
Ecclesiastical	296	24
Sacerdotal	265	22
Community	41	3
Personal	3	-
Other	90	8

concern for any in need. In the words of one respondent,

> The steady care of all within the parishes, be they linked with the church or not.

Visiting figured highly on the list:

> Visiting - being allowed the privilege of access to people's homes, lives, problems.
> Visiting the elderly and housebound and those in hospital.

Others referred to the care of individuals within the church, the pleasures derived from providing spiritual direction and nurture, for example:

> Helping people struggle on in the Christian way of life - and seeing their pilgrimage progress despite church structures.
> Seeing "ordinary" people of all ages becoming "aware and alive" and finding in the church a sense of hope and joy and a sense of being *valued* as a person.

The category also includes quite specific aspects of the work such as counselling the bereaved, and the conducting of funerals.

The ecclesiastical category has much in common with the pastoral, but the focus is on the church itself. Thus whereas a pastoral response might have been to emphasise the reward of nurturing an individual within the church, the ecclesiastical response was to emphasise church growth as such or the warmth of the congregation:

> Generous congregation in terms of prayer and praise and giving financially. A loved and loving people who I care about

deeply. There is a real sense of fellowship in our worship.

The measure of success seen in a doubling of church-going, high numbers of baptisms, confirmations etc. Remarkable increase in income.

Signs of spiritual growth, and a new awakening, a return of hope, the grasping of vision.

The ecclesiastical category also includes the encouragement received through wider church developments such as lay ministry and ecumenism:

There is a nucleus of many committed Christians who offer tremendous support and encouragement for plans to develop lay ministry and lay participation in all aspects of church life.

Development of lay ministry to the point where the parish continues to function well during a personal crisis (over many weeks).

Ecumenical friendship in an area where all churches minister to the same problems of social and economic deprivation.

Sacerdotal refers to the conduct of worship and the eucharist and the special role of the priest. It perhaps captures the catholic dimension more than the ecclesiastical or pastoral:

Preaching and the other *distinctive* aspects of being a priest and pastor. I don't enjoy merely drinking nice cups of tea out of nice cups with nice people.

The joy of the worship and the response of the folk as we offer the Eucharist together.

The improvement in liturgy, particularly in the attendance at Mass, and a growing sense of that being at the heart of the Christian life.

Also included in this group were those who cited the rewards stemming from the more personal role of simply being the parish priest:

Being seen as "the parish priest" by many who are not church goers.

The acceptance of the "vicar" within the total community – without any overt willingness to come to church, except of course for weddings and funerals!

No matter how crazy it all is the people are quite inexplicably well disposed towards church and rector, and one feels very loved.

Community rewards are those associated with rural life or the benefits pertaining to life in a rural community:

> Participating in a close knit community.
> Working and moving in such a beautiful valley.
> The tranquility of rural areas and the satisfaction of having a garden to grow flowers etc.

Others commented on the nature of the people in rural communities:

> People seem more open in rural areas than they were when I worked in town or built-up areas. I think this is because of pressures of living in large towns. People seem to keep themselves to themselves, unlike rural.
> The love and loyalty of the people of rural Lincolnshire.
> In rural ministry everyone belongs to the church unless they tell you otherwise. This sense of the church at the centre of the community is so very rewarding and is seen at times of joy (like the carnival) and times of sorrow (when all the village come to the funeral) and of course at major festivals which are 'village events'.
> I feel that people born and bred in a rural environment have a natural kind of theology, they see God at work in nature and get great joy out of being part of that natural process. I tend to share that joy, and am really privileged to be part of it.

Within these categories there were some variations of detail according to the churchmanship of the incumbent. Thus within the pastoral responses, work with young people/families was noted as particularly rewarding by nearly a quarter of traditional catholics (24%) but only ten per cent of conservative evangelicals. By contrast evangelicals were three times as likely as their catholic colleagues to mention the reward of witnessing individual spiritual growth. In the ecclesiastical category 15% of evangelicals saw church growth as rewarding, compared to only seven per cent of catholics. In the sacerdotal group, the occasional offices were found to be the most rewarding by modern catholics (13%), and the least rewarding by conservative evangelicals (five per cent).

As far as rurality is concerned there were somewhat fewer variations than with churchmanship. Within the pastoral group the clergy with totally rural benefices were the least likely to mention the growth of individuals and work with young people but most likely to refer to the rewards associated with visiting and more general aspects of pastoral work. This contrast between a general and a specific source of satisfaction was also evident with sacerdotal and community rewards. In rural areas the clergy felt themselves to be more implicitly part of the rural scene and articulated rewards in terms of a general sense of wellbeing associated with being the priest in the community. In urban areas, by contrast, involvement in the community was more explicitly defined in terms of church work and social action.

The generally high levels of satisfaction should not detract from the existence of many problems too. The postal questionnaire respondents were asked to indicate, in their own words, the main problems they faced in their ministry. As with the rewards, the question was an open one, and respondents were able to list as many problems as they wished. Of the 572 respondents, the vast majority (534 or 93%) specified problems. Predictably some mentioned problems of administration and finance, but these accounted for just 14% of the total number of responses. Problems often associated with specifically rural circumstances, the difficulties of multi-parish work and small congregations, accounted for just five per cent of responses. Far and away the most common answers concerned the negative side of one of the aspects of the work which gave rise to satisfaction – ecclesiastical concerns. Thus clergy lamented lack of commitment from their congregations, tensions within their congregations, inward-looking churches, and conservatism. The single most important category in this large group of ecclesiastical concerns was the lack of lay leadership mentioned by 18% of respondents and accounting for 8% of all responses. By contrast the negative side of pastoral and sacerdotal work received relatively few specific mentions. For many the main problem was just inadequate time to undertake the work.

The Clergy at Leisure

Ministry is a vocation and as such its demands are great, if not all embracing. There are those whose understanding of that vocation is such that they express an ontological view of the priesthood. Thus, by definition, they can never be separated on this earth from their priestly state of 'being'. Even those who reject the ontological argument find, in practice, that it is difficult to be off duty, not least because of the time demands mentioned in the last section. Only a quarter of the clergy interviewed (23) said without any qualifications that they were able to feel genuinely off-duty. By far the most common response was that it was only possible to feel off-duty when away from the parish, or even from the area. More than a quarter of the clergy simply said that they did not ever manage to feel genuinely off-duty. Several priests commented on the fact that time off in the parish did not work because the clergy were still "available" and contactable by telephone. As a result even so-called "leisure activities" were no respite from duty.

While the work produces high levels of satisfaction and reward, these derive from a giving to others and to the church, and a high investment of the self in the cares and concerns of others. If the giving is too constant and not accompanied by times for refreshment the rewards of ministry can easily degenerate into feelings of being drained and inadequate. Friendships, leisure, and family life will define the possibilities for such refreshment. However, the clergyman faces peculiar difficulties of etiquette with regard to friendships and even leisure activities and family life. Thus Charles Forder's instructions to incumbents on the question of friendships were stark indeed:

> Undoubtedly personal friendships with particular church families lead to the suspicion among the rest of the congregation that the priest is under the domination of these friends, and indeed, the suspicion is often justified. These difficulties are intensified when there is a change of incumbent. ... the priest must practically cut himself off from former friends, and even the link of correspondence is hardly wise, and is certainly unfair to the next incumbent. (Forder 1947: 352)

These strictures continue to play an important part in the lives of many clergy, as we discovered in the interview survey. The clergy were asked whether they found it possible to make close friendships with people within their parishes. Well over half the clergy interviewed (59%) felt either that it was impossible or inadvisable to make close friendships inside the parish, or that it was only possible with certain problems or limitations. Several of these respondents commented on the fact that although they were able to be "friendly" with large numbers of people, their position precluded more intimate relationships:

> Not close friends, but friendly – shouldn't have marked friends of a close nature in the parish.
>
> Not a good thing for the parish priest to make really close friendships as such. On fairly close terms with a number of people, but not intimate.

In some cases it was obvious that clergy had been taught to avoid close friendships in their training. One said "Not really, you're not supposed to" and another that "We were taught that you shouldn't make friendships - instead you should make acquaintances". The main reason given for this was the problem of being seen to show favouritism, something upon which several respondents remarked.

Another hindrance to the development of close friendships within the parish was the issue of confidentiality, and the fact that keeping a certain professional distance meant that it was hard really to talk to parishioners:

> You have to be very discreet because of confidentiality.
> Have tried not to - you can't really talk over problems with parishioners.

Because of this one clergyman referred to the "invisible barrier" which he felt inevitably existed in his relationships with parishioners. Another respondent said that it was the parishioners who wanted this distance between them and him in order for him to fulfil their ideal of a priest. As he commented:

> More indefinable is the spiritual necessity for distance, on their part, not mine. They want me to be the Priest on Sunday, the Holy Man.

A further group of clergy spoke of the fact that that they had no real *desire* to form close friendships, either because they felt there were no parishioners with whom they could form freindships, or because of the wearying effects of dealing with people in their working life. For some, though, friendships were clearly very important:

> In each parish I have at least one good friend who encourages me to rattle on. We sit in the farmhouse kitchen and have a good chat.
> I have three to four very good friends in the parishes - built up over the years.
> It's important to have friends because they're people, not just because they're involved in the church.

Some clergy felt that they were going against the conventional wisdom in making close friendships, and as a result questioned those who said or taught that such friendships should not be cultivated:

We were told not to - but I'm not like that. I prefer to be thought of as "just somebody else", not the vicar.

Only two clergy mentioned the effect of the rurality of their benefices, or of the types of community in which they worked, upon the desirability or practicability of making close friendships. One Durham respondent working in an ex-pit village commented:

The dynamics of a community like this are so difficult, so I haven't gone out of my way to make close friendships. There would be a problem if I had very close friendships here - it could be very divisive.

Few of the clergy had developed strong friendships with clergy in the surrounding area. Only a fifth of the respondents actually said that they had been able to form close friendships with nearby clergy, and a further 11% said that this was limited to only one or two key individuals who they often named.

If friendships pose a serious difficulty for many clergy, so too do relationships within the family and, in particular, the conflicting demands upon time. Those interviewed were asked whether they had ever experienced any conflict of loyalty between the family and the parish. The majority of clergy (67%) had at some time experienced conflict of loyalties between family and parish, and it is worth noting that in most of these cases this conflict was something which they were currently experiencing, not something which had only happened in the past. By far the most common conflict of loyalties was between the demands upon time of the parish and family which occurred in day to day life. Nearly half of all those who said that they experienced some conflicts mentioned the problem of time, either generally or more specifically in terms of trying to give enough time to the family. Several spoke of this as something which was an inevitable part of life:

You learn to live with it - it's never resolved.
Yes, very much so, it's been there from the start.

This conflict was obviously a particular problem for married clergy. As one respondent commented "Yes, any married priest would find this". Another, single priest answered the question concerning conflicts of loyalty with the family by saying "No, but I think a married clergyman would". Similarly, another unmarried clergyman extolled the benefits of the single life in terms of being free from any such conflicts:

> No. There must always be a temptation [for married clergy] to neglect family. It's very good to be free of family responsibilities, to be able to go wherever God calls. Even clergy with families should put God first before their own preferences.

Those clergy who had families, and experienced something of these conflicts, talked about them in various ways. Some commented generally on the pull between work and family:

> Yes, pressure of time, forcing out the family.
>
> Yes, always. Family gets a rough deal ..... it's hard to keep a balance between work and family.

Others explicitly stated that in their ordering of priorities there were times when the parish had to come first:

> Family would say the parish wins.
>
> Yes. Responsibilities to the parish come first and it leads to family and friends being squeezed out.

As a result many were aware that their families as a whole, and in particular their children, had suffered through lack of time being spent with them. Some clergy commented more specifically on ways in which parish demands conflicted with family demands, especially over leisure time. In this context weekends, days off, and evenings could be particular sources of tension:

> Family have felt they don't have enough claims on my time as they should – never free at weekends, restricts weekend activity.
>
> Yes, parish unaware of it. Time – always on call. Evening calls etc. – people mostly call during *their* [family's] leisure time.

Three clergymen referred to rural urban differences in the extent to which conflicts of loyalty were likely to arise. One respondent found that being in a rural area was easier:

> There is always tension, but less here, because demands are less than in a busy urban parish.

By contrast, two incumbents found that moving to the country created more conflicts of loyalty, although of a different kind. In these two cases, the problem was of the distance to facilities and activities for their children:

> Yes, especially in the country where things always happen in the town for kids.
>
> I'm very conscious that I've brought the family here. The older children feel the loss of the former place and facilities - the bus costs 95p into D....

The remaining one third of clergy said that they had not experienced conflicts of loyalty between family and parish. Only a few of these made any comment or gave any reasons for the fact that they avoided such tension. The one way in which potential conflicts did seem to be avoided by some respondents was simply by ensuring that the family always came first in any conflict of interests, in contrast to those quoted earlier who said that often it was the parish that "won".

Those interviewed were asked whether they felt they had sufficient time off and whether they took a particular day off. Forty one per cent said they did have sufficient time off, 31% that they did not. However, other clergy gave answers which suggested that their time off was insufficient, even if not stated in so many words. Eight per cent said that their wives felt they did not have enough time off (whatever they themselves thought), and eight percent said that it was up to them how much they took and some of these said that through their own fault this was not enough. Six per cent identified specific problems in taking either holidays or Sundays off (without answering the question more generally). Sixty one per cent had a specified day off compared to 38% who did not. However, in practice 21 of the 61 rarely achieved this and a further 15 only sometimes. Some even commented that they could end up more busy on that day, as people knew they were likely to be available at home! The question of holidays was one on which many clergy focused. A major problem was finding adequate cover from retired clergy, who were often said to be in short supply:

> There's a problem getting stand-ins for when I'm on holiday I need two retired priests to take over because of the schedule of services.
>
> Holidays are hard - I need a priest to cover, but they're hard to find, and it gets harder. Some areas don't have many retired clergy, and the few there are have many demands.

The other reason why clergy found it difficult to take holidays was the lack of time and sheer pressure of work. At least two clergymen said it simply wasn't worth going away because of the extra work it created in organisation, and because of the work which had accumulated on their return.

Conclusions

Our basic conclusion is that the content and meaning of clergy work remains firmly within traditional understandings of the parochial ministry and of the parson as the focus for that ministry. The clergy are hard working, they perceive their tasks in fairly traditional terms, and exhibit relatively high levels of job satisfaction. It is at this point that we run up against the thrust of much recent theology of ministry, which not only questions the efficacy of a clerically based ministry, but does so, in some cases, on the assumption that the traditional role of the clergyman has largely broken down. Our findings demonstrate that such post mortems for the parochial ministry are premature. Moreover whether it is entirely appropriate to develop a theology of ministry with only passing reference to the content of the office must now be open to question.

(1) Churchmanship has long been important within the Church of England as a major means of expressing both its Catholic descent and the influence of the Protestant Reformation. From the later nineteenth century it was strongly reinforced by the styles of training offered through the emergent theological colleges, and their special role in recruiting and influencing Anglican clergy (Towler and Coxon 1979). In the postal questionnaire survey we decided to explore the distinction between catholic, central, and evangelical forms of churchmanship by offering respondents the five categories of conservative evangelical, open evangelical, central, modern catholic and traditional catholic. Respondents were asked to tick only one of these responses. These subdivisions proved to be important in many aspects of this project and churchmanship has come to serve as one of our key variables in analysing many other factors.

Because the question of churchmanship may not be entirely easy to ascertain, not least because of twentieth century developments in religiosity (although in fact our respondents seemed to encounter few difficulties in selecting a designation), we also offered a further, and separate, opportunity for the respondents to identify themselves as charismatic, liberal, or radical.

5

Communities and Congregations

This chapter considers the question of whether the Church of England is becoming sectarian. It is a chapter about attitudes and the nature of relationships within rural parishes and especially about the idea of parish 'community'. But to use the term community is immediately to be reminded that some words live many lives, and community is one of them. There are good reasons why community cannot be simply defined for on the one hand it is used in an everyday sense by people wanting to describe their social world or that of a particular group. On the other hand it has also been used by specialists as a technical term, with sociologists, anthropologists, geographers, historians and theologians all stressing different aspects which interest them.

Christian theologians, for example, have use the word community to express beliefs about the Kingdom of God, the People of God, the Family of God, or simply to describe groups of believers. So in this chapter, as in much of this book, we are very much aware that 'community' is a word which expresses ideals more than it reflects actual life situations. Some scholars have already established this point very clearly. One such study of rural communities which clarifies the discussion is that of Howard Newby (1979; see also Bell and Newby 1971). Newby underlines what he called the 'rhetoric of community' which can be found in many post-war studies of change in British rural areas. These studies were often grounded in a nostalgic sanctifying of agricultural villages, often obscuring real changes that have taken place in village life or lamenting them.

Newby pinpoints three main uses of community. First, community can refer to an actual settlement, a geographical description. Second there is the pattern of social relationships between residents which is a more sociological definition. Third is the sense of belonging involving a shared emotional experience. It is this third sort of community, a community of feeling, which Newby characterises as underlying many people's use of the word in connection with villages. Such feelings of community might better be called 'communion', though as this is so hard to evaluate there is probably little to be gained by discussing whether such a communion or sense of community has changed over the years.

Another step forward in understanding community came with the work of Marilyn Strathern and others who studied one English village, Elmdon in Essex, throughout the nineteen sixties from an anthropological perspective (1981). Strathern focusses on the question of kinship and family relationships among longstanding members of the village and relates these to largely middle class newcomers to the village. This is obviously important because of the way commuter villages are referred to by many in the church and elsewhere who talk about recent developments in country life in England. Two models of village society, based on the opinions of Elmdon residents, emerge from her work and they are useful when considering church opinions on 'community'. One is the *community model* and the other the *interest group* model.

The 'community model' sees the village as a microcosm, a small world of its own where people have obligations and duties towards each other all serving the ultimate good of 'the village' itself. There are two versions of this model depending on whether relationships are thought of as democratic or hierarchical. The democratic version seemed to be held by some middle class newcomers to the village for whom village life was a picture of fellow villagers acting together for the mutual good of all. The hierarchical version was held by more upper middle class people who saw themselves as having duties and responsibilities to other villagers who might not be able to help themselves in the best possible way.

Strathern suggests that longstanding villagers themselves held to a form of hierarchical model, one which she calls an 'interest group model'. This view does not stress the importance of total village unity, but works instead on the assumption that groups of people do what is best for them as a group irrespective of the welfare of other groups. Here there is no ideal picture of 'the village' whose good is sought, rather the village is a set of different groups such that, 'as a whole the village (= all its residents) cannot be a community' (1981:48).

Time changes things in most areas of life and certainly this has been the case in Elmdon. Frances Oxford wrote an update on the village as it was in the later nineteen seventies. She underlines what she calls the 'cosy community' model of village life which many newcomers seem to entertain. It is an even stronger version of Strathern's community model. Some come to live in the village because of its romantic image of friendly residents living interdependently in a tightly knit set of relationships. Many of these people are commuters and her analysis suggests that the village they come home to at night is 'one they have largely created for themselves' (1981:222).

This view of village life produces a desire to conserve the way things are for posterity, indeed keeping things as they are comes to be part of village activity. In this we see an aspect of community life in which an ideal and romantic sense of the rural village takes shape through political and other action to preserve the character of the village where people have come to live. Thus ideas of community and village vary from group to group. Long resident working class people differ from middle class incomers, while upper class incomers and some similarly upper class long term villagers may have yet another view.

This is consistent with the conclusion reached by Anthony Cohen in his anthropological studies of communities. He suggests that 'the symbols of community are mental constructs' (1985:19). Going further he claims that 'the symbolic expression of community ... increases as the actual geo-social boundaries of the community are undermined, blurred, or weakened' (1985:50). So we might expect newcomers to a village where traditional kinship ties have been weakened through emigration of locally born people in search of jobs or houses to mark out with explicit concern the boundaries of 'their' village and community. The birth of committees or groups aimed at village conservation or preservation is one good example of that process. All this is important not only because the church can be politically involved in conservation but also because it can be seen as part of an ideal village history.

The vicar too is, potentially, a central figure both in conservation and as an ideal personification or image of an integrated community. This poses several important theological and pastoral questions. If the priest believes the Christian message calls people and groups to change or widen their outlooks he may soon be at odds with a tradition minded congregation. If he calls parishioners to a sense of practical, social, economic or moral responsibility for less privileged people elsewhere he may be seen as disturbing the calm of a chosen place of residence. In other words if the vicar is believed to be a bastion of tradition he will be blamed if he questions an idealised view of tradition.

But it is not only newcomers to villages who have ideal images of what a community should be. Christian theology itself has views on how people should live together. Here too it is easy for a cosy community model to be dominant. Some Christians read the account of early believers in the Acts of the Apostles and see there a model of intimate sharing and mutual concern which becomes their own religious model of community. Indeed the twentieth century has witnessed the birth of numerous movements involving communal life with shared economies and obligations. The Church of England has not been without its own ideals of society arguing, for example, that prosperous parishes should share wealth with the disadvantaged. We should therefore expect to find that rural clergy have some fundamental presuppositions about community life in relation to their ministry. A major issue surrounds priests' views of their people and indeed concerns the very identity of their 'people'. Do priests take all residents in their parish to be their real object of ministry or do they select certain people from the mass? If so, who is selected? We shall explore other specifically theological aspects of priests' thinking in Chapter 9 but now we focus on their views, theology, and opinion of community in relation to the church.

Clergy, Congregation and Parishioners

Chapter 2 outlined the historical basis of parish ministry including the traditional outlook still reflected in today's ordination services where priests are called to serve God in a church that serves the nation. This becomes dramatically clear when a priest becomes an incumbent and is formally given charge to pastor those in his geographical parish area. But what are the actual attitudes of priests as they face their parish work? Do they accept this traditional perspective or see it as radically unrealistic in modern situations?

The single theme of parochial identity emerged from the opinions collected in our project as of central importance. It has two aspects: one concerns the parish focused ministry, and the other the congregation focused ministry. In parish ministries all those in the geographical parish are viewed as people to be cared for. This follows the ideal historical or traditional pattern of the Church of England's cure of souls by the vicar. No distinction is drawn between regular church members and others.

In congregation focused ministries those who attend and support the ongoing life of the Church are viewed as the major object of the priest's endeavours.

While this pen portrait presents too sharp a distinction as far as most clergy are concerned it nevertheless provides a basis for approaching and interpreting our information. This distinction between a parish or congregation focus for ministry can be related to the sociologist's distinction between churches and sects. For our purposes we can see the parish focused ministry as an example of a church style of religious outlook while the congregation focused ministry has some similarity with the sectarian outlook. But we must emphasize very strongly that the resemblance is only partial and is made for theoretical reasons to stress the sense of intense group membership of a voluntary kind.

General comments have been made in recent years to the effect that the Church of England is becoming sectarian. This is a strong criticism and deserves serious consideration. Often the word has been used very loosely to indicate that the church is becoming increasingly inward looking and tends to shut out those who are not whole-heartedly behind its services and outlook. The key issue of spirituality here is intensity of commitment. Sometimes this refers to a narrow focus on the eucharist, on Charismatic forms of worship, or healing. In this chapter we will assess this criticism in the light of actual information gathered from parishes. As a criticism it is interesting because it is often raised by those who prefer a broad and open church-like outlook on life.

At the beginning of this century Ernst Troeltsch (1912) identified a trend in Christian history distinguishing those who accommodated to the broad life of the world and acted as those who had forgotten the incisive ethical teachings of Jesus, from those who sharply protested at this slack form of discipleship. Such protest typified the sectarian outlook. The idea of sectarian religion had a very positive overtone to it in Troeltsch's work. Sects were moments and movements of protest within an overall Christian society. For him Christian history swung, pendulum like, between institutionalised faith and zealous reformation. This basically theological model of church and sect was later developed by sociologists of religion, who stripped it of theological overtones and gave it the added purpose of analysing non-Christian cultures (Wilson, 1973).

Sociologists have often used such descriptions, or ideal types as they are called, when seeking to consider social change. So it is that the distinction between a 'church' and a 'sect', or between church-like tendencies in a movement and sect-like tendencies in a movement is of great help when looking at the history of religion and shifts from one stance to another. David Martin used this distinction between church and sect along with the additional idea of denomination in his overview of the sociology of English religion in 1967, and Bryan Wilson for many years has been involved in classifying religious movements and still sees the church-sect distinction as a useful tool in analysing religion (1982:89). In a similar way, Michael Hornsby-Smith has commented on it in his work on Roman Catholic parishes in England (1989:203).

Church of England: Church or Sect?

So what of the Church of England today? Does it have parish-churchly and congregational-sectarian tendencies, and if so how extensive are they? It is obvious that the church-sect analysis runs close alongside the issue of 'community'. Is community best expressed in a parish-churchly style of religion or in a congregational-sectarian outlook? This important question raises the issue of context, and in particular the rural context. Today more than ever studies of religion need to emphasise the importance of particular contexts because of the power of context to influence the shape taken by religious life (Lewis, 1986). In terms of the Church of England this is particularly so in relation to various rural, suburban, or urban settings.

We are now in a position to discuss the long standing issue in the sociology of religion concerning the nature of relationships between people in religious groups. This theme is often discussed by distinguishing between 'community' and 'association'. Anthony Russell in his book on country parishes concluded that, 'the rural church in many areas has come to assume the character of a eucharistic sect as opposed to that of a community church' (1986:248). Involved in his assertion are the two sets of sociological problems just outlined. On the one hand is the church-sect distinctions and now, before we consider the data from the parishes, we outline the traditional community-association distinction.

Communal and Associational Models

When Richard Hooker gave us one of the very first full discussions of the nature of the Church of England in its Reformed state as 'the Church of God established amongst us' he clearly pointed to the distinction, "the order", which he believed to exist between the clergy and the people. The clergy were a 'state whereunto the rest of God's people must be subject', (Bk III. cap.xi. 20). There is no question about the responsibility and duty of ministers. They serve entire communities which are local parishes of a national church. A narrow sectarian focus of ministering to a gathered congregation is quite out of the question. Hooker was sure that private groups, narrow conventicles, tended to heresy, and to a perversion of healthy religion (V. xii. 2). As time has gone on ministry has come to be conceived in broader terms and not only as invested in the threefold order of bishop, priest and deacon.

Guy Mayfield in his introduction to *The Church of England* published in 1958 stressed the long established point that historically the Church of England was made up, practically speaking, of four ranks: bishops, priests and deacons, and after them the laity. He observed that the later nineteenth century witnessed a widening gap between the people as the laity, and a narrower and more self-selecting laity relatively closely involved in church life. Here opportunity arose for a narrow congregation-focused religion which might lead to an alienation of the broader population. The separation of civil and ecclesiastical parishes led to the parishioner becoming a ratepayer in a civil parish (2nd ed. 1963:57). The addition of lay readers in 1866 began a great variety of additional forms of semi-clerical and clerical groups. Patterns of leadership were becoming more complex and in a sense more congregation focused.

The sociologist Ferdinand Toennies drew particular attention to some of these dynamics of social relationships in human groups through his distinction between Community (or *Gemeinschaft* in his original German) and Association (or *Gesellschaft*). These terms reflect both the mentality and behaviour of groups and have become widely used in discussing the quality of relationships in religious groups, and in rural areas. They were two different modes of thinking and acting. Since people sometimes refer to community churches and associational churches it is important to grasp what Toennies meant.

Toennies saw himself as organising and systematising ideas that others had had and which were known to all of us through our practical experience of life. Through and within our families we learn community (gemeinschaft), and this differs from the more public life of society (gesellschaft) where we associate together for particular rational or economic ends. Marriage too involves a community (gemeinschaft) of persons while the business or company in which we work is an association (gesellschaft). For Toennies community is a very old form of human interaction whereas association is a newer phenomenon which he associated with the rise of urban life. Community has positive connotations of a living and organic wholeness, whereas association turns our thoughts more to mechnical, rational, and purposeful ends (1955:39).

Toennies was, of course, well aware that simple distinctions do not tell all the truth. They help to set frameworks for discussion but they are not the conclusion of the debate. So it is when we talk, for example, of rural village life. Simplistically we might speak of village life as a community of interacting persons known to each other and committed through kinship to various duties served by the established parish church and its vicar. By contrast we might speak of the town with its rational modes of control and the contractual basis of voluntary association with churches available for use when necessary by those with need of them, much as any social service, with its professional priest.

What we find in real life is something far less simple. As far as the priest is concerned the social context is important because it does seem to influence the style of ministry adopted and corresponding types of church. We will see that the community-association model is of limited importance but does seem to be related to rural contexts to some degree. It is a useful theoretical idea in general discussion but loses its power when applied too directly to actual churches.

Our evidence shows that the distinction between rural and urban contexts plays an important part in the thinking of rural priests and cannot be abandoned in arguing that modern Britain has a relatively simple professional priesthood, or a relatively uniform cultural life. The practical experience of rural ministry, and indeed of ministry itself, seems to provide as substantial an influence on ministerial attitudes as the professional training received at theological colleges. Practical experience is gained in immediate contexts and contexts are influenced by change and by time. Two historical sketches will illustrate aspects of historical change in Anglican Ministry, theological ideas of ministry, and some of the sociological descriptions of human groups already discussed.

The Changing Rural Ideal of Priest and Parish

The ideal of George Herbert with its omnicompetent priest dedicatedly and piously serving his people presumes a community based scheme. Indeed as Toennies saw in religion itself, the parish is a sort of extension of the family. This ideal type which depicts the church as administerer of sacraments of salvation through the priest called 'father', makes the point clearly.

With the nineteenth century division of ecclesiastical and civil parish, and with the expansion of towns another possible model emerges where the priest serves at least two categories of people; the inner faithful on the one hand and the wider population on the other. There is a faithful group at the heart of Christian worship, prayer, and sacraments existing to worship God and to serve the wider group beyond. The priest is central to such a 'remnant' as its pastoral director. As the twentieth century proceeds ministry becomes increasingly complex with the growth of specialist ministries and various groupings of clergy to serve large or dispersed populations.

How then do these various ideal types and patterns of ministry, church, and community, reflect the actual experience of the priests we studied? Returning to the data of the Rural Church Project and the hundred clergy interviewed in depth we asked how they saw themselves in relation to those they served. This issue was approached through two major questions. The first dealt with the priest's view of whether he served all in his geographical parish or only a gathered congregation; the second explored the area of folk religion and whether the priest felt that people took advantage of the church for their own ends.

Ministry to Parish or Select Congregation

Table 22 shows a clear threefold split between those claiming to serve all the parish, those serving their congregations, and those attempting to serve both.

TABLE 22. *Do You See Your Ministry Primarily in Terms of Serving All Who Live in the Parish or Serving the Members of Your Congregation?*

Serve all parishioners	43%
Serve gathered congregation	23%
Serve both	27%
No response	7%
Total	100%

The largest single category is represented by those with a parish wide ministry, reflecting very much the traditional picture of Anglican practice. These respondents are, on the whole, fully in accord with the idea of a state church and of subjects who are properly related to the church and who can legitimately expect to be served by it. The outlook is one which we might call 'pastoral gemeinschaft', with the parish as the arena of pastoral activity. This represents a continuation of the Anglican ideal. Some of the clergy put it like this:

All need to know the church cares for them.
The church is *not* just for the faithful few.
My ministry is to *all* the people.
I visit the non-churchgoers most.

One of the more unusual examples of this was the clergyman whose parish included a tourist caravan site. He said that he regarded the visiting caravaners as his parishioners while they were in residence.

Twenty seven percent felt they served both the parish and the congregation. In some ways this is an interesting and telling group. Many of these clergy spoke in a very realistic way about their legal responsibilities as incumbents whose job it was to baptise, marry, bury, and to be generally interested in the welfare of the people in their parishes. But they also stressed the importance of the regular congregation as a different group whose existence was important for their own ministry. If the traditional Church of England ideal has been that of the whole-parish ministry the contemporary practical reality seems to involve the faithful congregation alongside the ministry to the occasional attender. The emergence of the congregation as an explicit focus for the pastoral task is a telling feature of more recent church life. This model encompasses ministry to the broader community, for the regular worshipping group may be seen as the corporate basis for the vicar's largely personal ministry to individuals 'outside' regular church participation. The gathered community in church must be trained to enable its members to serve non-attenders in the world. If anything the clergy in this category stressed this function of the church body more than their own personal ministry. The contemporary gathered Church of England is, in the eyes of these clergy, a church preparing for wider service. Some clergy put it like this:

There are two groups. The Family of God as the leaven in the lump of the Community.
The church is gathered to serve, not to be a ghetto.

The gathered need training to encompass all.
The function of the gathered congregation is to be
concerned with the rest of the community.
The gathered people of God are sent out to save the
world: they can't be inward looking.

Other clergy see intricate theoretical sides to the situation too. One argued that his church was a church in its vision of serving all but was a sect in terms of the personal commitment of individual members. Another spoke of the problem of level of attendance. Since many people attended on some one-off occasion it was better to view church-going not in terms of a strict division between attenders and non-attenders but more as concentric circles with ripples moving outward. Another shifted the focus from the moment of united worship to the focus of the congregation's everyday life arguing that people live as a wider community but with the potential to become a Christian community.

However, although the notion of the congregation as gathered to serve the community was common, a more sectarian model was rare. Thus the language used by the clergy did not reflect the idea of the congregation as a group clearly distinguished from non-members and with a zeal to expand its number. Only one clergyman spoke in this way and also spoke of attempting to restore his church to a pattern of biblical authority. In that particular community the Anglican Church has practically have given up its traditional role which has fallen to the local Methodist Church. Even when great stress is placed on the gathered congregation as the focus of priestly activity there remains a concern that the congregation should also be of service to others. In this sense the ideal of the priest serving the whole parish has become transformed into the congregation serving the parish. This is, perhaps, a realistic theoretical response to the growth in number of parishioners and parishes served by one person. It gives some hope to priests that their work may have realisable goals and they themselves find some encouragement from their more committed members.

Still if we add together those who saw themselves as serving all resident parishioners and those who linked residents and their regular congregation we have a 70% response, a large group of clergy asserting the importance of the resident public as their proper pastoral concern whether or not they went on to talk about regular congregation members.

This leaves a most interesting group of clergy who saw serving the regular congregation as their prime occupation. It is important to emphasise that the majority of these did not talk the language of exclusivism. Even though nearly a quarter of these clergy could be said to be narrowly focused on a select congregation and in that sense were potentially sectarian with a sharp distinction between those inside their group and those on the outside, the way they talked did not necessarily give this impression. Quite often they used very practical explanations of their view in terms of the stark number of residents who simply could not be adequately dealt with pastorally. But very frequently the emphasis went on the nature of the commitment of the faithful attenders:

> The church is the faithful.
> The church is the called out community of God.
> Coming to church is an act of witness.
> The church is the meeting place of Christians.

Those who stressed the gathered congregation were very clear that this was the object of their ministry, but so too did those who were deeply concerned about resident parishioners of infrequent attendance. Both the more inclusive and more exclusive attitudes towards ministry have consequences for the idea of church and community. One strand of the complex relationship between clergy and community involves the idea of the clergy being 'used' by infrequently attending parishioners for occasional services. Some might view this call on the clergy's time as an intrusion while others might not. To see just what the clergy thought we took up the theme with them, by asking whether they ever 'felt that people take advantage of the church for their own convenience in marriage, baptism, or funerals?' The question was directed quite intentionally at these three particular rites which are often singled out as of concern to the clergy.

Of those interviewed who thought that people did take advantage of the church (74%) approximately ten per cent added phrases such as 'of course they do', or 'most definitely yes'. These comments along with the high level of clergy thinking that advantage was taken of them must be interpreted carefully lest their response be read as negative or carping. On fuller analysis it quickly becomes clear that most are not at all distressed by this situation. In very many cases what emerged was a sense of pastoral opportunity occasioned by the demands made upon them as clergy.

Two basic attitudes seem to emerge from an analysis of clergy comments and they are typically expresssed as, 'We exist for this', and 'It gives us an opportunity'. Those who speak of 'existing for this' often made reference to being part of the established church, a status which many clergy clearly viewed as pastorally advantageous. Not all clergy elaborated on their response but more than two-thirds did so. Of the responses that were given approximately 60% focused on the state church and 40% on pastoral opportunity. By and large the clergy saw creative potential in being used by others. Relatively few spoke of annoyance and resentment felt towards those imposing on them and even when they did speak in that way they tended to add that it was only on 'bad days' that they felt like that.

'We say that we are the servants of Christ and when we are treated like servants we complain.'
'I bend over backwards to help.'

Such attitudes demonstrate a practical and open attitude to irregular attenders quite devoid of any exclusive air generated by a gathered community. Clergy often spoke as individuals free to be used by others and whose identity was not at risk by so doing. Seldom did the clergy give the impression of being high status individuals whose position as central church figures placed them beyond the reach of others. This brings us to the critical point where, looking at the church and people, we ask whose church it is.

Whose Church?

The discussion in this chapter so far has concentrated on views of the clergy. To obtain a more balanced view of the church we also sought the opinions of lay people including those on the Civil Electoral Roll and thus representing the general public (General Sample), and also those on Church Electoral Rolls (Church Roll Sample) who more directly speak for the church constituency.

There is one striking feature in these responses. Those in the church roll sample saw the church as more open than those drawn from the civil register. Seventy four per cent of church members thought the church was for everyone while 61% of the general public saw things that way. This suggests that as far as this sample, at least, is concerned the more immediately active church members see their own church in a wider light than those who were less involved. The accusation of a sectarian

TABLE 23. *For Which of These Groups Does the Church in Your Parish Exist in Practice?*

The church exists for:	General sample %	Church sample %
Everybody	61	74
Churchgoers only	22	18
Anglicans only	3	3
Other	1	2
Don't know	10	3
Refused	2	1
Total	100	100

spirit which always draws a firm boundary and demarcation line around itself would not seem to be justified as far as the majority of more active church people are concerned. Still there was a group of some 18% of members of the church sample who did think in the narrower way and who more or less matched 22% of the general public with a similar attitude.

What is perhaps interesting is that those most likely to think that the church was for members only were of male members of the general public. Twenty six per cent of men in the general sample thought in such terms of 'members only', a response that dropped to 16% of men on the church roll. In fact church–roll men were least likely of all respondents to see the church as for 'members only'. Church membership as such, then seems to foster an inclusive view rather than an exclusive view which suggests that the Church of England as a state church is at least not making its more active members possessive as far as church facilities are concerned.

Regional differences on this topic may, perhaps, be easier to interpret. Once more those the two samples differ but church members themselves differed across the country. Truro was an exception in terms of church and civil rolls. They closely resembled each other with approximately 56% believing the church was for all and 26% for churchgoers only. It is likely that the high church tradition of Truro, which had some 58% of clergy acknowledging a Catholic commitment, might increase a church focus while the strong Methodist history might also feed into a sense of groups belonging to their own church rather than to the Church of England. The fact that church and general population responses were similar might support this view.

Durham, Gloucester and Lincoln represented areas where similar numbers of people saw the Church as open to all, (67%, 66% and 64%). Church roll people in those dioceses were also very much committed to the open view, (90%, 73% and 83%). Durham stands out with 90% of church folk supporting the open view. In this Durham presents something of a problem for its pattern of churchmanship, and the historical strength of Methodism, is close to that of Truro. Perhaps a key to the problem lies in what some Truro clergy referred to as the strong regional tradition of Cornwall.

Whether or not these attitudes speak of the Church of England as being well established in the hearts and minds of the people will depend on the reader's perspective, but it is clear that for more than half of the public interviewed there was an acceptance of the church in quite a positive way. Certainly the views of church members reflect more the spirit of a church of the people than a church for a select few. In our study we have looked at formal membership of civil and church rolls. Needless to say there were people amongst the random selection of the civil rolls who were themselves Anglican, in fact 62%. Of the entire sample of four hundred and eighty nine people only 11% reckoned to have no religious allegiance at all. Along with the church roll sample they offer us a total of three hundred and fifty four individuals, 72% of the total sample, who claimed Anglican status. We used the criterion of attending church at least three times a year, in addition to any weddings, funerals, or baptisms, to distinguish between Anglican attenders and Anglican non-attenders. The fact that we have found differences between civil roll and church roll members on numerous issues suggests that the infrequent attenders amongst the general public tend to have perspectives which differ from more regular churchgoers. Such variations we now take up by looking at the theme of belonging or attachment to church which we see as part of the nature of community.

Sense of Belonging

All the Anglicans were asked, in relation to the Church of England, what exactly is it that you feel you belong to? There were many kinds of answer but certain distinctive features did emerge and they show some important trends, as shown in Table 24.

TABLE 24. *All Anglicans: What Exactly is it That You Feel You Belong To?*

	Anglican attender		Anglican non-attender		All Anglicans	
	No	%	No	%	No	%
The C of E	23	14	23	12	46	13
Tradition/upbringing	30	18	58	31	88	25
A body of people/ voluntary society	35	22	13	7	48	14
Spiritual body	28	18	14	8	42	12
A denomination	16	10	12	6	28	8
Anglicanism not important	5	3	12	6	17	5
Nothing	4	3	29	15	33	9
Other/don't know	19	12	28	15	47	14
Totals	160	100	189	100	349	100

Roughly 13% of both attenders and non-attenders said in a simple way that they belonged to the Church of England. Nearly a quarter of attenders spoke of belonging to a community or to a group of people (22%), compared with only seven per cent of non-attenders. Conversely we found that nearly a third of non-attenders (31%) said they belonged to a tradition or were brought up in the tradition of the Church of England, while only 18% of attenders spoke in that way. Reference to a spiritual dimension of faith as the sense of belonging marked another 18% of attenders and eight per cent of non-attenders. If we combine a sense of not belonging and feeling that such an issue was unimportant we have six per cent of attenders and 21% of non-attenders. There would seem to be some justification for saying that being a member of the Church of England means more to many people than simply having been brought up in it or being C of E for the purpose of form filling.

In terms of formal church membership we found that of all the three hundred and forty nine who identified themselves as Anglicans nearly all had been baptised, (95%). When it came to Confirmation a definite distinction was apparent between the regular and infrequent attenders. Practically all attenders had been confirmed (92%) compared with less than half (47%) of the infrequent attenders. It is interesting to note that four per cent of the infrequent attenders did not know whether they had been confirmed or not. Overall over two-thirds of the Anglicans had been confirmed. This quite high level of confirmation may be due to the rural social context of the people interviewed. There are many reasons why people who have been baptised as infants do not attend church when adult. One of these concerns Confirmation and Holy Communion, an issue raised in the next chapter, but worth mentioning now as a potential barrier to attendance. Regular church attendance is likely to involve reception of holy communion. This will apply to the two or three major festivals frequented by the more irregular attenders as well as to weekly congregational activity. Those who, for whatever reason, have failed to come to Confirmation during their teenage years may well feel disqualified from participation later in their life.

Since there is no fundamentally strong theological reason for using Confirmation as the initiation rite for the eucharist, church leaders ought perhaps to revise this traditional English pattern of infant baptism and teenage confirmation as a mode of initiation. In terms of pastoral theology this might be critically important for some people. If it is true to say that participation in the eucharist is itself a means of knowing God through Christ then such a spiritual education might work better with an open access system rather than a closed system of qualification. In terms of practical religion confirmation may well operate as a necessary 'work' required before access to 'grace' is possible. Theologically speaking, that would be an unfortunate message to convey through a pattern of Christian ritual whose goal is a knowledge of the grace of God through the love of Christ. The Decade of Evangelism which the Church of England is following in the nineteen nineties might well involve a major ritual change in which a 'confirmation amnesty' is declared and the Holy Communion is opened to all baptised members of the Church. A call to the feast of love, forgiveness and acceptance might lead some of the long baptised to 'come home'. If the eucharist does indeed foster the knowledge and sense of God it might well be that further instruction in the faith would follow and that a service of Confirmation in the faith might ensue, not as a qualification for accessing the holy table but as a witness of faith. If the medium is the message and the message is grace in loving acceptance then Confirmation has failed for many in the Church of England. All this would involve attitudinal change, change in custom, and a serious theological rethink which might make sense to many people who at present find explanations less than plausible.

Since the Church of England already seems to play an important part in the overall sense of belonging not only for those who are its more regular attenders but also its more infrequent attenders who live in the countryside such a pattern of change might increase that identity and further a sense of more active church related spirituality. For the period covered by our study we can say that the church constitutes an element in the community identity of individuals whether they be regular or less frequent attenders. Full details of this are given in Chapter 8, but here let us simply observe that practically 80% of respondents, and it made little difference whether they were Anglican or non-Anglican, regular or non-attenders, saw the parish church as an important aspect of local life. The degree of importance varied as one would expect but relatively few members of the public saw the church building as unimportant; in fact only 16% of non-Anglican non-attenders had that view. Once more we stress that this is the picture in the rural areas we studied. We cannot say that the same response would be found in suburban, urban, or inner city areas, and in terms of everyday judgement we would not expect that to be the case.

The Vicar in Community and Association

In Chapter 4 we have already seen how priests distinguish between rural and urban church life in terms of rewards of their work. Here we need to pinpoint some of those attitudes as they touch upon a sense of community in rural parishes. It is all the more important to do so given the place of the church in local awareness as we have just discussed.

In terms of our evidence it seems that the degree of rurality itself makes a difference to the way the clergy see themselves interacting with their people. When asked about the rewards of their work we found that the sense of being a priest amongst his people was greatest not, as might have been expected, in very rural but in urban contexts.

In terms of our earlier analysis of community and association social contexts it may be that urban churches function as a church-community within a wider association as far as the priest is concerned. Society at large is associational in that people relate to others in more impersonal and formal ways as part of a market economy. The church and its congregation comes to form a network of more personal and intimate links. Friends may be made with other church members and leisure time activity may also be church related through informal friendship as well as in organized church groups. Some of these groups are likely to meet in the homes of congregation members. The vicar plays a large part in these church oriented events, he has a high social profile within what can be seen as a network of community. The eucharist is often important as a single focal point of this network of relationships where the priest is symbolically and actually central. In the wider society of city or suburb the vicar will be much less well known and will be much less likely to have a natural place in other social networks. He is vicar of the community of church-network but not of the associational network of society at large.

The rural situation differs from this. The rather romantic view of rural religion might take the vicar as a central figure within a community of close knit and mutually responsible people. When we consider what rural priests say a different yet far more interesting picture emerges. While they did give slight emphasis to 'people and pastoral work' we should not immediately assume that this makes the church a community of closely related people after the suburban model. Interest in people and pastoral work with them does not mean one single thing. The growth of theories and schools of counselling over the last thirty years along with general ideas of community and group interaction has tended to produce an outlook on pastoral work which stresses the psychological, personal, and more intimate aspects of individual life. The term 'pastoral' need not, however, immediately evoke psychological or sociological ideas. There are levels of involvement of priest and people moving from the intimate one to one relationship of spiritual guidance or psychological counselling to involvement with families, groups, and organization to a very public person on formal occasions. There is involvement with people at all these levels but its nature and depth varies. We might characterize some of these differences by contrasting pastoral relationships aimed at the personal growth of individuals from organizational endeavour which seeks an efficient operation of groups of people.

Working with this kind of distinction in mind we found that rural priests liked working with people in general but did not seem to be extensively involved with the personal growth aspect of individual parishioners. Urban priests, by contrast, found the personal growth of church members a more central aspect of their work: in fact the urban stress on personal growth was twice as high as the rural. The urban situation implies a church of a community nature within a wider society of an associational type. The rural context has a less intimate sense of community at the congregational level. In rural areas we would expect people not to depend upon church based links for friends to the same degree as in the urban framework.

It is interesting that our survey of the laity showed that of those who expressed preferences on aspects of the content of church services 23% liked the exchange of the peace during the eucharist while 22% did not like it. This was the only feature of church services marked out for relatively large scale dislike. How we interpret this response is, as ever, problematic and we have no urban measures to place against it. Informal observation and comment suggests that this rite of 'sharing the peace' where the clergy and members of the congregation move about the church shaking hands or being more demonstrative with a hug and possibly a kiss has become widespread. It betokens a group of people whose interaction is symbolically expressed in church because the church is the pivot of their friendship and community. But there have been objections to this moment of informality in what is often a formal pattern of service. Those who object sometimes dislike any display of emotion during religious services. This could suggest a more associational than community sense of relationship. Indeed it is possible that village life in rural contexts does have a distinctive associational dimension to it. There is a high level of independence of person from person or family from family. Relations may be formal precisely because living involves relatively close proximity. Personal and family interests may conflict with those of others and involve a degree of distance from other people. Those other people may well be fellow members of the congregation, this is unlike the situation in towns where fellow members of the congregation will only impinge upon each others' lives in the weekday world if they want this to happen.

The paradox of rural and urban church life may well be that the rural parish church offers a more associational focus within a village life which also has associational dimensions to it within a wider sense of community. The urban parish church affords the possibility of a community base within a distinct associational social world. This would make sense of the clergy's work emphasis, with urban priests fostering individual growth of people who are in groups of more intimate relationships while rural priests encourage general social life at a more public level. Each type would be 'working with people' but not in the same way. There is some evidence to support this idea from the pattern of ministry in the five dioceses we have analysed. The pattern varies in relation to the nature of residence. The dioceses with the greater number of country town and mixed urban patterns also have the higher proportion of clergy seeing their work as directed to all those resident in their parishes.

People's View of Clergy

If the vicar has a view of parishioners it is equally true that they have views on their vicar. This is especially the case in rural areas where clergy have found a place in village life for the entirety of medieval and modern history. Today in our five dioceses we found that 29% of the general public said they knew their vicar reasonably or very well, with just about a third (34%) not knowing him very well. Thirteen per cent said they did not know him at all, while a final 23% said they had never met their vicar. All this suggests that two thirds of those interviewed had some link with their vicar while one third were not connected in any realistic way. Given the changes that have occurred in rural church organization in recent decades this figure might not be too disappointing for church leaders. Needless to say, older people were more likely to have some knowledge of their vicar. Some 47% of those under thirty five years of age in the general population sample either had not met their vicar or did not know him at all well. This dropped to 34% of the over sixty five age group. The overall figures suggest that about a third of the general public were without contact with or knowledge of their vicar. If the vicar is essential to the social presence of the church in rural areas then this might imply a very low profile of the church through its official clerical representative for a large minority of the communities studied.

Vicar's Village of Residence and Community Profile

Where the vicar lives is also an obvious yet vital issue when it comes to being known. When several parishes are united and served by one vicar the vicarage is, inevitably, located in but one of them. This means that the vicar's presence in each place differs as does the degree to which people come to know their incumbent. The evidence on this is striking when the population response is divided between the church and civil rolls. Table 25 shows that of those on the church roll 44% knew their vicar very well if he lived in their parish but if he lived elsewhere this number dropped to 24%. The figures for the general sample are considerably lower. At the next lower level of knowledge, those reckoning to know their vicar reasonably well, an interesting feature emerges. More people from the general sample now register a relationship, some 29% of those living in the same village but only 17% of those living elsewhere. But for those on the church roll the response is 44% and a slightly higher figure of 47%. In terms of not knowing the incumbent at all or of not having met him, some ten per cent of those on the church roll reckoned to be in this situation if they lived outside the vicarage village as opposed to only one per cent in the vicar's place of residence. The big difference emerges with those on the civil roll, if they live in the vicar's village 28% do not know him at all or have never met him, a figure that rises to 44% for those living elsewhere.

TABLE 25. How Well Do You Know Your Vicar?

	General No	sample %	Church No	sample %
When incumbent is resident in the parish				
Very well	12	7	34	44
Reasonably well	49	29	34	44
Not very well	61	36	9	11
Not at all	18	10	1	1
Never met him	31	18	-	-
Total	171	100	78	100
When incumbent is not resident in the parish				
Very well	9	5	17	24
Reasonably well	28	17	33	47
Not very well	56	34	13	19
Not at all	27	16	3	4
Never met him	47	28	4	6
Total	167	100	70	100

But we can be more specific than this because when the number of villages served by a priest rises to more than three, not knowing the vicar at all or not having met him begins to decrease. The pattern for the general sample is shown in Table 26.

The message here is slightly complex yet intelligible. The vicar is best known where he lives, becomes less well known when he has two parishes and then somewhat better known as he gains three or more further parishes. Other figures show that the level of familiarity in the increased number of villages is less than when he has only one or two

TABLE 26. *Not Knowing or Meeting Vicar and Number of Parishes (%)*

Number of parishes the vicar is responsible for

	1	2	3	4/5	6+
Not known & not met	34	51	41	24	29

villages. In other words, when clergymen have a large number of parishes they are known a little by a high proportion of people across those parishes. It is likely to be true that the actual population level of those many villages is low whereas the population of two parishes can be rather high. The consequences for the idea of community life are significant since familiarity with people both superficially and at greater depth as one means of pastoral access and service is reduced when there is no longer a resident priest. This fact is obvious to most but not to all rural clergy. If we compare these views of laity with what the rural clergy said in their interviews one interesting feature emerges for a significant minority of clergy. Just over a third of those interviewed (35%) did not think there was any major variation in their ministry between their village of residence and their other parish villages, though only 20% of these made a definite statement of no difference, others thought that in general there was no difference but added a few qualifications to this. Nearly a half of all the clergy serving in multi parish benefices did think there was a difference in their ministry to their village of residence and other villages visited.

If the pastoral practice of the Church of England depends upon a high degree of informal contact between priest and people then the above information will be important in discussion of the place of non stipendiary ministers and locally ordained ministers in village contexts.

Social Class, Vicar, and Community

Against the often repeated opinion of the Church of England as essentially of the upper, and middle classes with but little influence upon the working classes it is interesting to have some basic information of a more factual kind. Our evidence is useful here because it deals with the way in which people from different social classes spoke about their relationship with their vicar. The difference between the general and church roll samples is particularly interesting.

In the general sample there is a clear connection between social status and degree of familiarity with the vicar. As many as 43% of those in higher grade professional and managerial positions said they knew their vicar reasonably well or better, this compared with approximately 25% of social groups five and six covering routine non-manual workers, skilled and unskilled manual workers. In terms of not having met the vicar, over a quarter of the professional and managerial groups said they had not done so, this figure matches that of the manual working class groups.

As far as those who had never met their vicar were concerned the figure for social class one was exactly the same as social class six and comprised practically a quarter of the population (26%). Social class five, of semi and unskilled manual workers, registered 15% as not having met their vicar compared with 19% of class two and 18% of class three.

The claim that many working class people have little to do with the church, at least through the person of the vicar, would seem to be true for the majority of those covered in our laity survey. But the same is also true for the other social classes. Approximately a third of all groups in the general sample said they had neither met nor did they know their vicar. When we move to the church roll sample we inevitably found that most people had some personal contact with the vicar and the social class difference of contact was not particularly great. Given the population levels in many large rural towns and villages, especially when several are together in a united benefice, it may be surprising that clergy are reckoned to be as well known as these responses indicate. Though Chapter 8 looks in detail at church attendance it is worth mentioning here that our study showed that for the general population three quarters (76%) of non-manual workers had not attended church over the past year compared with just over half of the upper-middle (54%) and professional classes,(55%). Once we move to the church roll sample the scene changes with non-manual working class members having the highest rate of weekly attendance (36%) in the people we surveyed.

Magazines for the People

One feature of church life which impinges upon the wider population to some degree is the parish magazine. As part of our project we collected over three hundred magazines of which two hundred and sixty were for the month of November 1988. These were sent in by clergy contacted in the postal questionnaire. In subsequent interviews opportunity was taken to ask clergy if their magazines were specifically intended for a church readership or for overall community consumption, and whether they themselves saw the magazine as a significant pastoral opportunity. From the interviews we found that practically all benefices had magazines. About three quarters of the magazines were produced by the church (76%), some six percent by church and civic parish jointly, three percent by the local community, and two percent by deaneries. Of the clergy themselves 61% had been involved in magazine production in the survey week.

Of the magazines produced by the church just over 50% were said to be intended for all homes and residents in the geographical parish. Only eight percent were aimed solely at members of the congregation. A further 25% went to purchasers or subscribers thought to be more peripheral as church attenders or with an interest in the church. From this it seems that parish magazines serve as an extensive link between church and general population in rural areas and keeps lines of communication open as far as church events and matters are concerned.

By and large the rural clergy saw their magazines as a significant part of their ministry, indeed more than three quarters were of that opinion. Only five percent thought that magazines offered no real opportunity for their work while about 20% were quite unsure whether their magazines achieved a positive end or not. More than a quarter of the clergy specifically thought that their vicar's letter was the focus for pastoral benefit in their magazine. One vicar saw his letter as a sermon preached in people's homes and numerous views echoed that in some way or other, especially as a way of introducing some Christian theme to people who might not normally attend church.

A content analysis of vicars' letters for November 1988 was carried out by listing up to three topics or major themes in each letter and then relating the incidence of each topic to the total number of topics. In percentage terms we found that church centred activities and organizations took pride of position, (41%), followed by material directed to individual faith and life, (16%). Due to the fact that All Saints and All Souls Days fell into the month there was a high rate of reference to these events at about 12%, as also to Remembrance Day Services (6%). Aspects of personal faith and life occupied a relatively high profile of 16% which suggests that the idea of the letter serving as a sermon in people's homes is not inappropriate. Doctrinal questions and particular discussions of the Bible stood at about ten percent.

Specifically rural or even community focused issues of a particular kind were relatively rare at approximately two percent with a further two percent reference to Harvest Festival Services. The Archbishops' Commission On Rural Areas was specifically discussed by one magazine in the Southwell Diocese. Not too much weight can be given to this particular material for this single month since Remembrance Day, All Saints and All Souls occupied nearly 20% of comment which in other months might be 'free space' for other discussion. What is true is that the clergy saw Church magazines as a significant expression of an established and given pastoral relationship with people in the church though not necessarily of its regular congregation.

Conclusion

'Is the Church of England sectarian?' That was the question posed at the beginning of this chapter at least as far as more rural areas were concerned. Having now explored a variety of avenues and popular opinions the answer would *not* appear to be a resounding 'Yes'. In terms of the predominant clergy outlook the answer is a clear 'No'.

6

Ministry: Ordained and Lay

This chapter is essentially to do with the deployment of staff. The general trends in deployment and the implications for a theology of ministry are relatively well understood. The church's awareness of the complex problems of deployment surfaced in the inter-war period and the issues were aired in two reports, *Men, Money and the Ministry* (1937) and *Putting our House in Order* (1941). However it was Leslie Paul's report to the Church's Central Advisory Council for the Ministry published in 1964 which set the contemporary debates and developments in motion, not only in his recognition of the need for a radical proportionate (but not absolute) redeployment of clergy from country to town, but also in his plea, albeit a relatively muted one, for a greater role for the laity in ministry.

Both themes were taken up in subsequent years. That of clergy redeployment was considered by The Clergy Deployment Working Group under the chairmanship of the Bishop of Sheffield. Its report in 1974 provided a watershed in the church's methods for dealing with parochial deployment. Hitherto decisions had been based on a combination of diocesan policy and the system of patronage. Under the Sheffield 'formula' each diocesan bishop was asked to bring his clergy numbers in line with those agreed at a national level so as to allow the kind of changes envisaged by Paul. In practice this has meant that the more rural dioceses have lost clergy at a faster rate than some urban dioceses. The second major response to the Paul Report came in 1983 with John Tiller's report to the Advisory Council for the Church's Ministry (ACCM) on a strategy for ministry. Essentially the Tiller report took the debate forward in two key ways, his emphasis on new ways of structuring the church's parochial ministry and the full sharing of ministry with the laity.

This chapter considers two main issues which arise from these developments. First we look at the deployment of parochial clergy, including changes over time, in our five dioceses. Included in this consideration is the role of other stipendiary and volunteer staff who may complement stipendiary incumbents. This leads on to our second issue, namely the broader role of the laity and the extent to which lay ministry is developing in the manner envisaged by Paul and Tiller. A third aspect arising from the reports, that of parochial organisation and alternatives, is dealt with in the next chapter.

Measuring Change in Deployment

Many people look back to the inter-war days as a golden age for the rural church. The evils of pluralism had long disappeared and most parishes had their own clergyman who lived in a rectory or vicarage within the parish. He was likely to be prominent in local affairs and to have plenty of time to deal with a wide range of local issues and problems. Orwin (1944) in his book *Country planning: a study of rural problems* which was written during the war notes that,

> 'A country parson should interest himself in everything in which parishioners are concerned - though not necessarily to participate or even approve - whether it be allotments, pigs, the dramatic society, the local rates, the collection of salvage, pubs or football pools'. (p191-2)

This level of interest and activity implies, of course, a relatively small number of people per clergyman. But how well in practice were parishioners served between the wars? It is interesting that of the 11 benefices in Orwin's Oxfordshire case-study area, seven consisted of two or three parishes, and only four were single parishes. In fact, Orwin was in favour of a radical reorganisation of the rural church based on the rural deanery, this being a relatively early version of John Tiller's ideas. Orwin's idea was to provide a staff of clergy for each deanery, proportionate to its population and ease of communications, with the incumbent of the most important town or village being the rural dean who would coordinate all spiritual and pastoral work within the deanery.

In the Rural Church Project we decided to explore in depth the deployment of the clergy in our five chosen dioceses in both 1931 and

1988. This involved a considerable amount of work collating information from records held by the Church Commissioners and diocesan record offices. The earlier date was chosen so as to link the pattern of incumbencies with the results of the 1931 population census. The first step was to produce maps of the ecclesiastical parishes, for both dates, and then to determine their populations. For 1931 this latter task was relatively simple as the census data were provided for ecclesiastical as well as civil units. For 1988 it was more difficult as ecclesiastical parish data were not available, and the most recent census was for 1981. To overcome this problem, the most recent population estimates made by the relevant county councils were used and figures were derived for the ecclesiastical parishes. In Durham civil parish population estimates were not available so diocesan handbook estimates were used instead. As a result of this detailed work we are able to present pairs of maps of the five dioceses (Figures 3 to 12). From these we can see both the extent of changes in parochial structure and how the population per incumbent changed between 1931 and 1988.

Changes in Parochial Organisation 1931-1988

The maps confirm that parochial organization in 1931 was dominated by the single parish benefice. Overall in the five dioceses, over three-quarters of incumbents (77%) held single parishes. The multi-parish benefice was relatively uncommon and usually contained only two parishes. A fifth of incumbents were in fact responsible for two parish benefices, but a mere three per cent held three or four parishes and none more than this.

The variation between the dioceses was considerable. In Durham, for example, 92% of the clergy held single parish benefices, while in Lincoln even at this date over a third (34%) were responsible for between two and four parishes. Nonetheless, even in Lincoln, no clergy held more than four parishes and only six per cent held three or four. Very few benefices consisting of three or more parishes were found outside Lincoln.

By 1988 enormous changes had taken place. Overall, in the five dioceses the proportion of priests holding single parish benefices fell from just over three-quarters (77%) in 1931 to just over half (55%) in 1988. In the same period the advent of two new forms of parochial organization occurred: the large multi-parish benefice (five or more

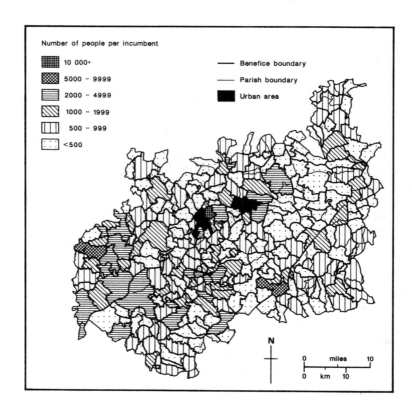

Figure 3: Population per Incumbent: Gloucester 1931.

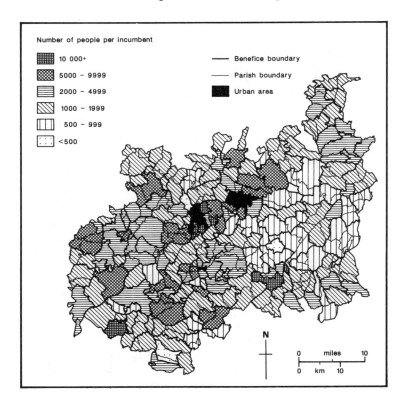

Figure 4: Population per Incumbent: Gloucester 1988.

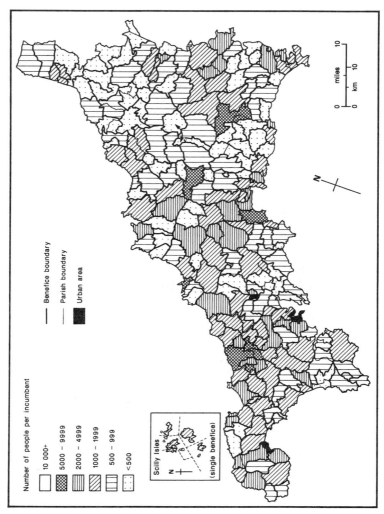

Figure 5: Population per Incumbent: Truro 1931.

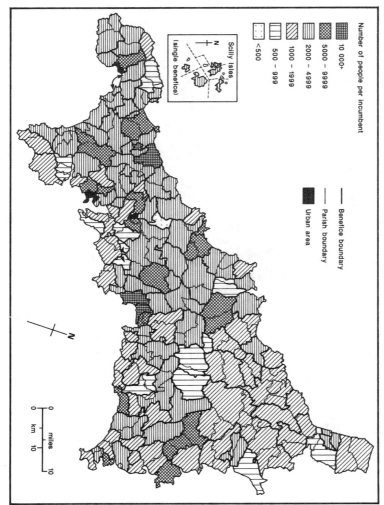

Figure 6: Population per Incumbent: Truro 1988.

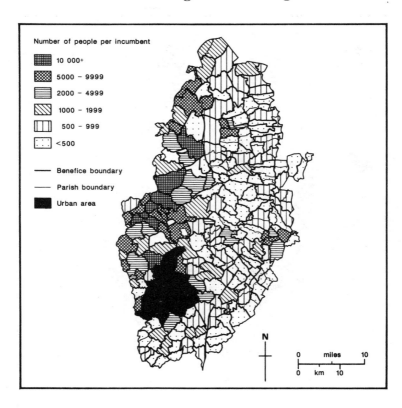

Figure 7: Population per Incumbent: Southwell 1931.

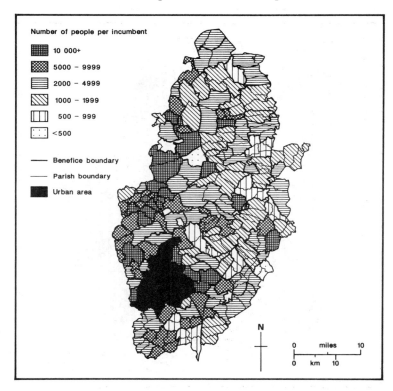

Figure 8: Population per Incumbent: Southwell 1988.

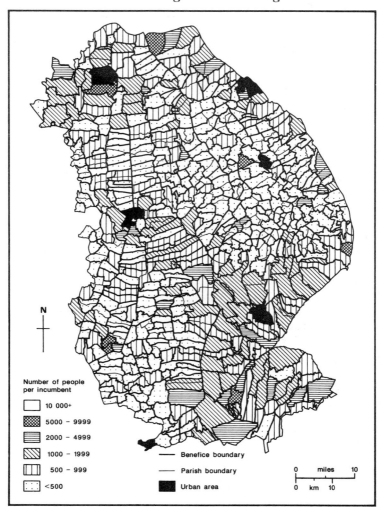

Figure 9: Population per Incumbent: Lincoln 1931.

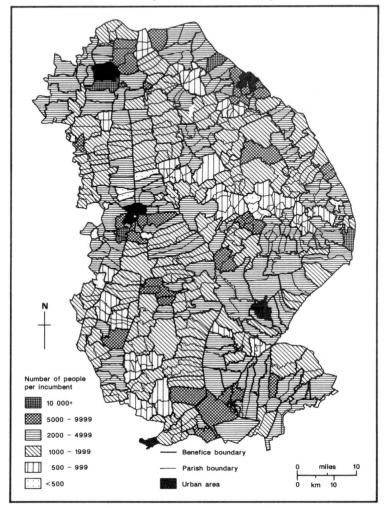

Figure 10: Population per Incumbent: Lincoln 1988.

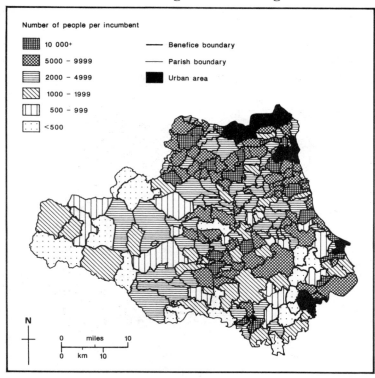

Figure 11: Population per Incumbent: Durham 1931.

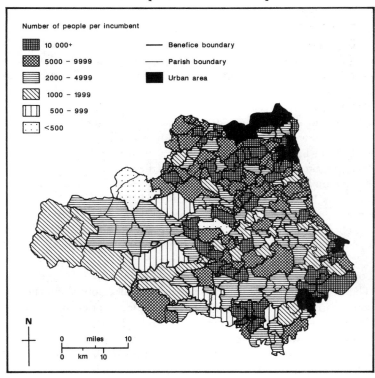

Figure 12: Population per Incumbent: Durham 1988.

parishes) and the team. Changes were even more dramatic at the diocesan level. Truro, for example, experienced a massive reduction in single parish benefices from a high level (88%) in 1931 to less than half (49%) in 1988. A doubling of the proportion of priests holding two-parish benefices also took place in Truro, alongside a substantial development of team ministry. In Lincoln, Gloucester and Truro less than half the clergy held single-parish benefices in 1988. Furthermore, in both Lincoln and Gloucester over half of the incumbents (54% and 52% respectively) now held multi-parish benefices.

Lincoln had the smallest proportion of single parish benefices in 1988, despite a policy of creating multi-settlement united parishes from former multi-parish units, of which there are at least four notable examples. In conjunction with this, Lincoln has witnessed the rise of the large multi-parish unit. It is the only one of the five dioceses to have benefices of more than six parishes: benefices of seven to 11 parishes make up five per cent of the Lincoln total.

In addition to variations between the dioceses, the maps show considerable variations *within* each of them in both 1931 and 1988. These consist of broad differences between urban regions, dominated by single parishes and a greater number of people per priest, and country areas where multi-parish benefices containing fewer people are more common. However, there are also significant variations between *different rural regions* in both clergy deployment and the parochial structure. The full effects of these massive changes in parochial organisation on the rural church are explored in detail in Chapter 7.

Changes in Population per Incumbent 1931-1988
The maps show clearly that in 1931 the great majority of incumbents were responsible for parishes with less than 1,500 souls. Indeed, over a third of incumbents (36%) held benefices containing less than 500 people, and over a half (55%) had less than 1,000 people in their care. The variation between dioceses was, nevertheless, considerable even at this date. Lincoln and Durham provide the extremes. Over half of Lincoln clergy (53%) were responsible for less than 500 people, and nearly three-quarters (74%) for less than 1,000 people. In Durham, at the other extreme, only seven per cent of incumbents were responsible for less than 500 people, but over half (51%) for 5,000 or more people.

By 1988 massive changes had taken place with only a fifth (225) of clergy holding benefices of less than 1,500 people. The change in the proportion of priests responsible for fewer than 500 people is particularly dramatic. These small benefices, so numerous in 1931 had virtually disappeared by 1988, and even the two per cent of clergy in charge of them often had another job within the diocese or were NSMs. The corollary of this decline in small benefices is of course the increase in large ones. Between 1931 and 1988 the proportion of priests with 5,000–9,999 parishioners doubled, and there was a tripling of the proportion with 10,000 or more. Accompanying this rise in the number of people cared for by one priest was a *decline* by *one third* in the actual number of incumbents in the five dioceses, from 1,499 in 1931 to 949 in 1988.

The decline of the smaller benefices has been most dramatic in those dioceses in which they were most common in 1931. As a result, by 1988, there was an almost uniform distribution between the dioceses of benefices containing fewer than 500 people. In fact, only one or two per cent of incumbents in *any* of the five dioceses held such benefices. Lincoln has undergone the most dramatic changes of all of the five survey dioceses between 1931 and 1988. It has also experienced the most radical reduction in the number of incumbents serving in the diocese. Over this period, the incumbent total fell by over half from 504 to 241 priests. The scale of these changes has had an effect on the social visibility of clergy in rural areas, and on the clergy as a group in terms of its own network of friends and colleagues.

Current Population of Benefices

For those benefices held by incumbents who responded to our postal survey we are able to present data showing the variation in the average number of people living in benefices by both diocese, and the rurality of the benefice. This information is shown in Table 27.

The average figure of just under 5,000 people in each benefice masked considerable diocesan variations with Durham having a mean benefice population two and a half times higher than that of Truro. As might be expected, the diocesan figures indicate that the more urban the diocese, the higher the average benefice population. The urban benefices had *five times* the average population of the totally rural ones. These figures go a long way towards explaining some of the fundamental differences between church life in town and country. It could be argued, of course, that it is not the number of people per benefice that is important, but the number of people per member of church staff. We will return to this point once we have dealt in detail with staffing issues.

TABLE 27. *Population per Benefice*

(i) Diocese	Population	Average benefice population	Number of benefices
All benefices	2,618,727	4,969	527
Gloucester	342,608	3,392	101
Truro	240,450	3,083	78
Southwell	612,345	6,378	96
Lincoln	463,114	3,646	127
Durham	960,210	7,682	125
(ii) Rurality			
All benefices	2,585,023	4,971	520
Totally rural	330,238	1,795	184
Partly rural	325,419	4,172	78
Small country town	451,080	5,245	86
Part urban/non rural	483,689	7,801	62
Urban	994,597	9,042	110

Staffing

Figures 13 to 17 show the status of incumbent for all rural benefices in the five dioceses in 1988. The maps also show the broad regions used for sampling purposes in our surveys of clergy and parishioners. Respondents in the postal survey were asked to describe their ecclesiastical status. The great majority (78%) were either vicars or rectors. Priests-in-charge (10%) formed the second largest category and were most likely to be found in rural benefices. This is clearly, in some instances, a consequence of the perceived need to keep parish structure relatively fluid prior to reorganisation. Team rectors and vicars were most common in the urban and partly urban benefices, although the maps indicate the large geographical area covered by some rural team ministries, especially in Truro.

Having considered the status of the incumbent, we turn to look at the full range of types of staff working in the parishes. There are various ways in which such staff can be classified. We asked the incumbents to

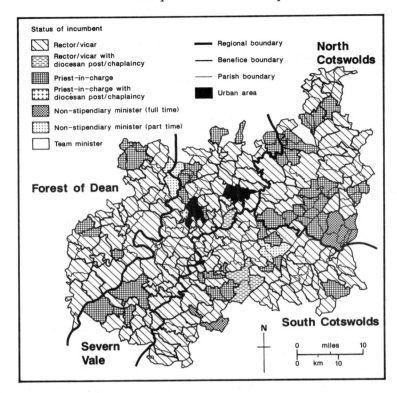

Figure 13: Status of Incumbent: Gloucester 1988.

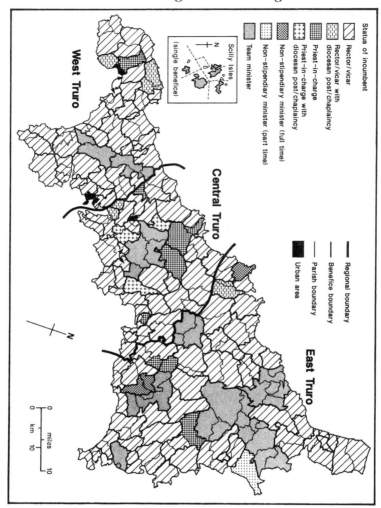

Figure 14: Status of Incumbent: Truro 1988.

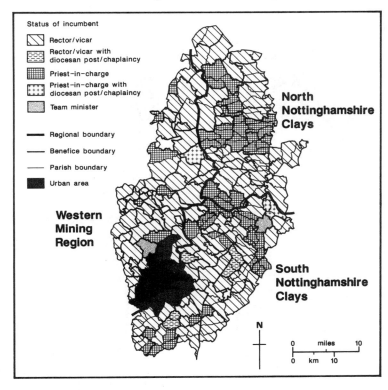

Figure 15: Status of Incumbent: Southwell 1988.

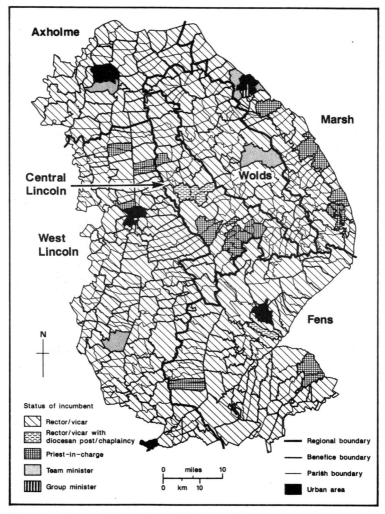

Figure 16: Status of Incumbent: Lincoln 1988.

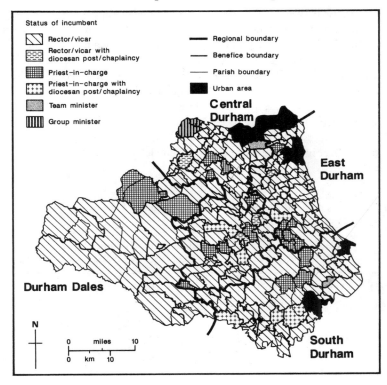

Figure 17: Status of Incumbent: Durham 1988.

distinguish between male and female staff, between stipendiary and non-stipendiary staff and also between full-time and part-time staff. Total staffing figures from the postal questionnaire are shown in Table 28. Of the total of 1,470 staff working in the 527 benefices just under half (47%) were full-time, and just over half (53%) were part-time. As might be expected, the largest group by far was that of rector or vicar, of which 97% were male and full-time. The occurrence of other types of stipendiary staff varied considerably: there were 112 curates and only one deaconess. The great majority of curates were male and full-time (83%). In contrast, all 18 deacons were female, 55% of whom were part-time.

TABLE 28. Total Number of Staff in Benefices

	Male				Female				
	full time		part time		full time		part time		
	No	%	No	%	No	%	No	%	Total
(a) Stipendiary staff									
Vicar/rector	506	97	15	3	-	-	-	-	521
Curate	93	83	4	3	13	12	2	2	112
Deacon	-	-	-	-	8	44	10	56	18
Deaconess	-	-	-	-	1	100	-	-	1
Licensed lay worker	7	78	-	-	1	11	1	11	9
Other stip	10	42	9	37	1	4	4	17	24
(b) Non-stipendiary staff									
NSM	15	14	70	63	8	7	19	16	112
Retired clergy	25	17	116	79	1	1	4	3	146
Readers	58	16	216	62	6	2	70	20	350
Trainee readers	1	4	18	75	1	4	4	17	24
Lay workers	1	2	19	44	1	2	23	52	44
Other non-stipenderies	9	8	39	36	4	4	57	52	109

Note: excludes team ministries

The frequency of different kinds of non-stipendiary staff was more evenly spread than that of stipendiary staff. The largest group was that of readers (350), with the next most important being retired clergy and non-stipendiary ministers. There were relatively few lay workers. The majority of readers, retired clergy and NSMs were male and part-time. Less than a quarter of NSMs (23%) and readers (22%), but over half (54%) the lay workers, were women. An important general conclusion to be drawn from this analysis of the pattern of staffing is that women are considerably less likely than men to hold stipendiary posts, and are also less likely to hold full-time posts. They are more likely, however, to carry out unpaid, relatively informal, work. Although there is a very wide range of staff working in the parishes, the actual proportion of parishes which make use of these staff is still very small. For example, 85% of benefices have no full-time male curate; 99% have no stipendiary lay workers; 71% have no part-time male readers; 89% have no part-time female readers and 88% have no male part-time NSMs.

How does staffing vary with the rurality of the benefice? One way to answer this is simply to consider the average number of staff in rural and urban benefices. Table 29 shows that half (49%) of the totally rural benefices had a single member of staff, and only eight per cent of this group had five or more staff. Partly rural benefices were also characterised by small numbers of staff. In contrast, only a fifth of the partly urban, and small country town benefices, had a single member of staff, and these two categories were much more likely to have five or more staff (34% and 28% respectively). Interestingly, the urban benefices were more likely to have only one member of staff than the small country towns, and less likely to have large numbers of staff. The possible reasons for this are discussed below when considering the average number of staff per benefice.

We can now move to explore in greater detail how the characteristics of staff vary between rural and urban benefices. Table 30 shows the average number of different kinds of staff per benefice. Overall each benefice has on average 2.8 members of staff. But this masks considerable differences between benefices, especially regarding part-time staff.

Church personnel resources are often seen in terms of full-time clergy alone, but our evidence shows that while the full-time component is clearly the single most important category, the presence of part-time assistance can be very important, especially if we consider rurality. Thus, there is a direct correlation between the average number of full-time staff and rurality, with totally rural benefices having an average of 1.1 and urban benefices an average of 1.9. If we consider part time staff a rather

TABLE 29. *Total Number of Staff per Benefice, by Rurality*

No of staff	Totally rural		Partly rural		Small country towns		Part urban /non rural		Urban		Total
	No	%	No	%	No	%	No	%	No	%	%
One	90	49	31	40	17	20	12	20	32	29	(35)
Two	35	19	15	19	17	20	14	23	28	26	(21)
Three	29	16	16	21	17	20	11	17	22	20	(18)
Four	10	5	5	6	4	5	2	3	10	9	(6)
Five +	13	8	10	13	25	28	21	34	18	16	(17)
No data	7	4	1	1	6	7	2	3	-	-	(3)
Total	184	100	78	100	86	100	62	100	110	100	

Note: excludes team ministries

TABLE 30. *Average Number of Different Types of Staff per Benefice, by Rurality*

Rurality	Full time	Part time	Stip.	Non stip.	Lay	Female	All
All benefices	1.5	1.3	1.3	1.5	0.8	0.5	2.8
Totally rural	1.1	0.9	1.0	1.1	0.6	0.3	2.1
Partly rural	1.3	1.3	1.3	1.3	0.8	0.4	2.6
Small country town	1.6	2.3	1.3	2.6	1.1	0.7	3.9
Part urban/non rural	1.7	2.0	1.6	2.1	1.3	0.8	3.7
Urban	1.9	0.9	1.6	1.2	0.8	0.4	2.8

Note: excludes team ministries

different picture emerges. Here, the urban and totally rural benefices both had an average of less than one person, whereas in small country towns the average was well over two people. Indeed this pattern is repeated, with subtle variations, for non-stipendiary, lay and female staff. An explanation for this state of affairs is that it is in the small country towns and the suburban areas that larger pools of suitable candidates for these voluntary posts are likely to live.

Other factors are also important, of course, and Table 31 shows that the churchmanship of the incumbent can have a strong influence on the likelihood of different types of staff working within a parish. The general rule is the more evangelical the clergyman, the greater the number of staff he is likely to have around him. This relationship is especially clear in the case of lay staff, where the average number of staff in conservative evangelical benefices is very nearly three times as high as that for traditional catholic benefices. This is likely to be linked to the evangelical belief in 'every member ministry'. Open evangelical clergymen are most likely to have female staff while the least likely group to have female staff is the traditional catholics.

TABLE 31. Average Number of Different Types of Staff per Benefice, by Churchmanship of Incumbent

Churchmanship	Full time	Part time	Stip.	Non stip.	Lay	Female	All
All benefices	1.5	1.4	1.3	1.5	0.8	0.5	2.8
Conserv. evangelical	1.9	1.4	1.3	2.0	1.5	0.5	3.3
Open evangelical	1.5	2.1	1.4	2.2	1.4	0.7	3.6
Central	1.4	1.4	1.3	1.5	0.7	0.4	2.8
Modern catholic	1.5	1.1	1.4	1.3	0.7	0.5	2.7
Trad. catholic	1.2	1.2	1.1	1.3	0.5	0.2	2.4

Note: excludes team ministries

So, when the staffing of benefices is considered in detail it can be seen that some of the most interesting variation was in what might be termed the 'unofficial' types of staff, as opposed to incumbent clergy, that is women, part-timers, those who were not paid, and lay staff. The numbers of such staff in a benefice were clearly affected by both its rurality and the churchmanship of the incumbent. There were also variations at the diocesan level. Gloucester, for example, stood out as the diocese with most part-time staff, while Durham and Truro had the fewest part-time and non-stipendiary staff and Lincoln had the fewest lay staff. To some extent it appears that these 'unofficial' staff were being used to supplement gaps in the provision of full-time permanent staff. Durham, for instance, had the largest mean number of stipendiary staff and the lowest mean number of non-stipendiaries.

Finally we need to consider the relationship between the number of staff in a benefice and its population. Table 27 showed considerable variations in the number of people per benefice. Table 32 shows similar information but takes account of the total number of full-time staff in the benefices. The number of full-time staff working in the benefices does little to redress the imbalances shown in Table 27. The more urban dioceses have the highest mean number of people per full-time member of staff. Rurality is still the key variable with urban benefices having nearly four times more people per full-time member of staff than totally rural benefices.

Our evidence shows that there is clearly a move towards the diversification of ministry along the lines envisaged by Leslie Paul and John Tiller. However the information presented tells us relatively little about either the nature of the work undertaken by these additional staff or the amount of time they are able to devote. Still less can the figures convey a sense of the theology of ministry which lies behind such a pattern of deployment. So we turn now to a consideration of lay ministry more generally and, in particular, the theology of ministry.

Lay Ministry

Just as the theology of the laity has become an important theoretical concern in recent years so too has the practical issue of the laity as a resource for leadership in rural churches. In the postal questionnaire we asked the clergy to give their views on the importance of the development of lay ministry for the running of their parishes. Their answers provide important comparative data on the perceived role of lay ministry in both rural and urban benefices. They demonstrate the great importance which clergy attach to the development of lay ministry in their parishes. As many as 59% felt that the development of lay ministry was vital or very important, whereas only four per cent of the total said that it was unimportant or unlikely to happen. However, nearly a quarter of the respondents, while stating that the development of lay ministry *was* important, qualified the statement in some way, either by pointing out the practical problems they faced in its development, or alluding to other limitations to the extent to which lay ministry should be allowed to grow.

Many respondents made quite detailed comments on the issue of lay ministry which threw considerable light on the continuing debate in the

Table 32. *Population per Full-Time Staff in Benefice*

(i) Diocese	Population	Average benefice population	Number of benefices
All benefices	1,876,829	3,709	506
Gloucester	232,497	2,447	95
Truro	184,568	2,528	73
Southwell	424,850	4,472	95
Lincoln	340,553	2,769	123
Durham	694,359	5,786	120
(ii) Rurality			
All benefices	1,859,509	3,719	500
Totally rural	283,281	1,657	171
Partly rural	247,387	3,343	74
Small country town	340,091	4,049	84
Part urban/non rural	304,075	4,985	61
Urban	684,674	6,224	110

church today. The clergy who saw the development of lay ministry in their parishes as vital or very important fell into two main groups. The first group gave *theological* reasons for the importance of developing lay ministry, in particular the desire for "every member ministry". The second stressed the *practical* necessity of lay ministry owing to the pressure on existing clergy, the lack of ordained ministry, and the sheer impossibility of providing adequate care without lay help. The practical need for lay help was voiced by both rural and urban clergy, although some rural priests commented on the need for special lay help in rural areas, especially in multi-parish benefices.

Those clergy who perceived, or who had experienced, problems in developing ministry in practice gave two main inter-linked reasons which were concerned with lay attitudes and lay availability. The main problems mentioned were the traditional expectations people have of the vicar, and their consequent reluctance to accept the ministry of the laity. It was felt that people did not wish to become involved either because of unwillingness (linked with lay attitudes), or because of a sheer lack of people with the time or ability. An additional practical problem which clergy mentioned was the fact that involving the laity in ministry could be more time consuming and difficult than doing the work themselves.

The main limitations to lay ministry noted by the clergy regarded either the manner or the extent to which it should develop. Some stressed that lay ministry should not develop at the expense of ordained ministry, or divert attention away from the needs for more ordained staff. Others pointed out the need to stop lay ministry from becoming too formalised. It was felt that there was a danger of the laity becoming "clericalised" and several clergy explicitly commented on the risk of "turning lay people into crypto-clergymen". A final aspect of this view was that a formalised lay ministry risked taking the laity away from their work and witness in the community.

It was found that evangelical clergymen were more likely to favour the development of lay ministry than catholic clergy. As many as 82% of open evangelicals considered the development of lay ministry in their parishes as vital or very important compared to well under half (41%) of traditional catholics. Clergy from the catholic wing of the church were also more likely, in general terms, to qualify their answers by stressing certain problems or limitations.

In general, the development of lay ministry was perceived as much more important in more populous benefices - nearly three quarters of incumbents (72%) in benefices of 10,000 or more people saw the development of lay ministry as vital, compared to only just over half (51%) those in benefices with populations of less than 1,000. Conversely, clergy in the smallest benefices were the most likely to say that growth of lay ministry was unimportant *or* to perceive or have experienced problems in developing lay ministry. Similarly, when our rurality classification is used, it was the clergy with totally rural benefices who were least likely to regard the development of lay ministry in their parishes as of vital importance. A quarter of totally rural clergy referred to the problems which could, or did, limit the growth of lay ministry, compared to only seven per cent of respondents in part urban/non rural areas.

Lay Ministry: Views of the Rural Clergy

The rural clergy we interviewed were asked how, ideally, they would define lay ministry. The wide range of responses clearly indicated that the term lay ministry meant very different things to different people. The principal divisions were between those who defined lay ministry in terms of *what* was involved, those who focused more on *who* was involved, and those who were concerned with the relationship between lay ministry and the role of the clergy.

We first of all consider the views of clergy who defined lay ministry in terms of the activities or functions involved. Some respondents focused on defining the *spheres* within which lay ministry should take place, others concentrated more on the *nature* of activities involved. Looking first at the spheres of involvement, several clergy, placed the emphasis on the church as the arena for lay ministry, as opposed to "the world". Others, however, explicitly stated that the term lay ministry should not be restricted to "church" activities but should include ministry at home, at work and in the community:

> Every Christian has a ministry which he or she is called to exercise in different ways in different spheres of life.... at the place of work or home, or to the community - *some* only within the church.

Several respondents said that they viewed lay ministry as simply "being" a Christian, in whatever sphere of life, and did not therefore see it as encompassing specific activities. Others emphasised that any involvement on the part of the laity could be classed as lay ministry. Several clergy however did give some idea of the sorts of activities or roles that they felt were appropriate for the laity, mainly in terms of church related functions. In general, the clergy perceived lay involvement in very broad terms. Some said all aspects of church life could be undertaken by the laity, including in a few cases the celebration of the Eucharist; others felt that everything except for the sacramental life of the church came under the remit of lay ministry. Two aspects of church life in particular were singled out for lay participation: involvement in worship and evangelism.

The most frequent response from clergy who defined lay ministry in terms of *dramatis personae* was that lay ministry was ministry of "the whole people of God", involving everybody in the congregation, rather than being restricted to a few with particular gifts or functions. Some respondents, rather than seeing lay ministry as something which de facto involved *all* the laity, said that they felt it should involve as many as possible. Others, although few in number, had a more restricted view of who they envisaged being involved in the ministry of the laity - seeing limitations either in terms of function or ability. Finally, a small number of clergy defined those to be involved in lay ministry in negative terms, namely, those who were *not* ordained.

The relationship between lay ministry and the ordained clergy was commented upon by several respondents. One view was that lay ministry was necessary mainly to assist the clergy, with delegation from the clergy to the laity when the need arose. In this sense the ministry of laity was implicitly seen as something additional and distinct, and sometimes even secondary, to the work of the clergy. By contrast the more widely expressed opinion, was that the ministry of clergy and laity was a shared one, in which both were as important as the other. In this context some clergymen stressed that they themselves were part of the "laos", and that there was no difference between lay and ordained ministry. In this context at least two incumbents questioned the idea that the clergy were indispensible, and that they alone were able to perform most of the duties of office.

The rural clergy interviewed were asked how important they felt lay ministry was for the future of the rural church. The majority felt that lay ministry was essential or very important for the future of the rural church. More than half (53%) said it was crucial or very important, and a further 13% described it as "important". Ten per cent defined it as very important but felt there were certain problems or limitations in its development. Seven per cent said the development of lay ministry was equally important in both rural and urban areas. Only twelve per cent of the respondents, did not give an overall view on the importance of lay ministry, but rather mentioned the problems, qualifications or limitations involved in its development. Even so, none of these actually said that the development of lay ministry was unimportant.

In general, the reasons which were given for the development of lay ministry in the countryside can be divided into the practical and the theological, although obviously there was some overlap. The practical reasons were generally clearly related specifically to rural areas and mainly revolved around a current or anticipated shortage of clergy, and the consequent increase in the number of parishes under the care of one priest. Lay ministry was viewed as a vital practical necessity by several clergy, if the church was properly to fulfil its role. The theologically based comments were generally relevant to both town and country and were associated with the view that all Christians should by definition be involved in lay ministry.

Clergy Perception of Lay-Priest Distinction

The clergy interviewed were asked what particular attributes they possessed as priests which non-ordained people lacked. This question encouraged the clergy to reflect upon themselves and their job in relation to the lives lived by their people. As an open-ended question it elicited a wide variety of response. A content analysis showed the following variety of concerns and topics (Table 33).

TABLE 33. Distinction Between Clerical-Lay Attributes

Response	% of Clergy
No essential difference	23
Training and theological college	19
Authority of church or bishop	16
Eucharistic role, ritual leader	9
Ordination, grace of orders	7
Vocation	5
Status as parson-vicar in parish	5
Focus of unity and wide perspective	4
Confidence of people,confidentiality	3
Availablity for parishioners	3
Outsider to parish	2
Prayer	2
Absolution	2
	100

These responses can be variously interpreted depending on the way in which the categories are aligned. But before considering a few possibilities attention must be drawn to the most surprising feature, namely that some 23% of clergy did not see any attribute pertaining to themselves which distinguished in any basic way between them and the laity of their parish:

> Forty years ago I would have said the Grace of Orders now I don't think there's any difference.

> There is no difference. I have a good education and my voice can be heard clearly, that's about it.

The training and theological college factor was strongly stressed by one in five clergy (19%) and seems to play a very important part in clergy's self-perception. This being the case it is appropriate to include at this point the response which the clergy made to a cognate issue of the priesthood viewed as a profession. When asked in the interview survey if they saw their employment in terms of being a job, profession, or vocation, or some other designation, we found that over half (58%) saw vocation as a prime designation, 17% saw vocation and profession as joint descriptors and only four per cent saw profession alone as a suitable designation. It would seem, therefore, that the emphasis on college has more to do with preparing for the fulfilment of a vocation or calling rather than with professional training as such. Nonetheless when asked about the actual attributes or qualities which separated them as priests from laity the issue of vocation was given a low priority, and the clergy actively dislike ideas of separation between them and their people.

Attitude to Readers, Non-Stipendiary and Locally Ordained Ministers

We explore here the rural clergy's views of the non-ordained work of the reader, the ordained pattern of work of non-stipendiary priests and of the more geographically restricted locally ordained priests. These groups are included together since it could be argued that there is a perceived gradation of priest-lay identity as one moves from ordained parish priest through NSM-LOM, to readers to lay member of congregation. Table 34 shows the general similarity of perspective on both readers and NSMs but the quite different view taken of LOMs.

TABLE 34. Rural Clergy Views on Readers, NSMs and LOMs (%)

Readers			NSMs			LOMs		
Good	Problems	Bad	Good	Problems	Bad	Good	Problems	Bad
44	46	4	46	36	9	44	16	32

Approximately the same percentage of clergy considered each of the offices to provide a very good form of service and ministry. They had no complaints and few qualms. Indeed they often praised the work of readers and NSMs on the basis of first-hand experience. One interpretation of this might be that clergy wanted both reader and NSM schemes to work and be developed in the church, especially within the rural situation. They could see numerous problems but thought those problems should be broached and resolved. The LOM scheme, by contrast, did not seem to fire the imagination so that when problems were anticipated the clergy were less inclined to perceive solutions. In addition, because so few clergy had direct experience of LOMs, they were possibly more inclined to see them as either good or bad.

The single most commonly mentioned problem area concerned the role conflict felt by both clergy and readers following the development of NSM and LOM patterns of ministry. The increase in eucharistic services alongside a decline in Matins and Evensong has meant that the traditional sphere of readers' operation has decreased. The subsequent use of readers for administering the chalice at Holy Communion or the question of whether they should use the Reserved Sacrament in a Holy Communion service conducted by themselves were frequently mentioned topics. A few clergy even questioned whether the office now had a purpose. One Gloucester clergyman regarded readers as belonging to a 'totally redundant Victorian order of things', a Truro incumbent saw readers as 'outmoded' while a Lincoln priest thought readers 'should be abolished'.

Non-stipendiary ministers received no such criticisms. On the contrary some went so far as to see them as 'the salvation of the rural church' and most saw them as useful as long as their work was well managed. NSMs were however very often viewed as 'additional curates' and not as 'worker priests'. Numerous clergy thought that a NSM who lived in an area for a very long time might be a problem to successive parish priests. Many Gloucester clergy argued that their diocese would be greatly hindered without NSMs. Several clergy suggested that with the rise in the number of NSMs the role of readers was bound to decline. A similar 'threat' to clergy was occasionally mentioned. Some thought that too much was asked of NSMs and that parish work and pastoral responsibility was a full time job. Several respondents expressed concern that the role of some NSMs was confined to the conducting of Sunday worship. They felt that the Anglican ideal of a ministry combining liturgical practice and pastoral concern was in danger of being lost. One person even suggested that NSM ministry was for those who lacked the courage to be a full-time priest. These concerns seem to show up a confusion about the role of the NSM other than that of celebrant. Because the formal designation of worker-priest does not tend to be used the fulfilling of a priestly role by NSMs in work or other spheres may not always be adequately recognised by stipendiary priests.

162   *Church and Religion in Rural England*

Turning now to LOMs, those ordained to serve in a particular locality, we encounter a major problem of 'orders'. Is it possible to be a priest in the Anglican Church and not be 'acceptable' throughout the Anglican Communion? We carefully monitored, therefore, the views of the clergy on whether the idea of local ministry was a bad one because of the notion of a restricted ministry. On average 10% of clergy commented negatively on LOMs to this effect. It varied from 14% of Durham clergy interviewed to none of Southwell clergy. Other comments on LOMs included the fact that they were "too close" to the people, that a "prophet was not without honour except in his own country" , that such a person might continue to serve for too long a period, and that they get "all the kudos and none of the responsibility". All in all the idea of the non-stipendiary seemed to take preference over that of local ordained priests. This might be expected since for centuries the Anglican church has operated an itinerant priesthood even though it presupposes long periods of residence.

Parishioners' Views on Lay Ministry

We sought the views of parishioners on a number of different aspects of lay ministry in an effort to discover how acceptable an increase in the role of lay ministers might be to rural people. Anglican respondents were told that in recent years it had been suggested that other people in the parish should conduct jobs traditionally done by the vicar and their views on this were requested. Just over half (55%) of the Anglican attenders thought that lay people should undertake tasks traditionally done by the vicar and only 17% disagreed. A fairly high proportion (28%) expressed neither a positive nor a negative view, either because they did not hold an opinion on the matter or because they felt that their response would depend on the task to be undertaken.

It should be noted that the question did not specify *which* tasks might be performed by lay people. Thus we have a general response to a general question. We now consider responses to a more specific question. All respondents were asked their opinion as to whether it was important for someone from the church to visit people in the parish. The response was overwhelmingly positive: 82% of respondents who were Anglicans felt that such visiting was important, along with almost three-quarters (73%) of non-Anglicans. However, when we asked who from the church would be a suitable visitor, the most frequent response supported the traditional role of the clergyman. Over three-quarters (76%) of the non-

Anglicans mentioned the vicar alone as a person suitable to visit from the church; this proportion fell slightly to 68% of the Anglicans.

In order to attempt to resolve the apparent contradictions surfacing from these different approaches to lay ministry, we turn now to a consideration of the acceptability of lay ministry on a range of specified tasks. All Anglicans were asked whether they would be happy for their vicar to allow other people to carry out various tasks. For the same tasks we asked whether the respondents would themselves be prepared to carry out various specified tasks, and if, in fact, they already did carry out such tasks. The results are provided in Table 35.

Table 35. Anglican Attenders: Acceptance and Experience of Lay Ministry (No = 160)

	Accept other people to...		Willing to perform		Already perform	
	No	%	No	%	No	%
Visiting people	123	77	91	57	26	16
Administrative assistance	152	95	76	48	25	16
Reading lessons	152	95	84	53	47	29
Leading prayers	123	77	47	29	17	11
Preaching sermons	100	63	17	11	3	2
Administering the chalice	71	44	23	14	5	3
Conducting the service	105	66	17	11	5	3

Note: totals do not add up to 100 as only the 'yes' response for each aspect is given

If we look first at visiting we find that again the position is reversed with 77% of Anglicans attenders prepared to accept a lay ministry of visiting. A clearer, although complex, picture is now beginning to emerge on the question of visiting as an example of lay ministry. On the one hand there is an acceptance of the principles of lay ministry in general and of visiting in particular. On the other hand, the expectation of ministry in practice remains fairly firmly within a traditional clerical-centred model. This raises as many questions as it answers. One reading might be that the results reflect a desire by lay people for greater lay participation in ministry which is frustrated by the clergy. Alternatively, the tension might merely reflect lay caution and, therefore, represents a salutary lesson to clergy who might obtain general approval from their congregations for an expansion of lay minstry, only for such a course of action to engender a very mixed response when it is put into practice.

The other tasks listed in Table 35 show a wide range of acceptability. The types of lay ministry the respondents were most likely to accept were the reading of lessons and the provision of administrative assistance. Lay people leading prayers, giving sermons and taking services were somewhat less acceptable. Least acceptable of all was lay help in administering the chalice.

There was considerable variation in the responses when people were asked what tasks they would actually be *prepared to perform*. Over half the Anglican attenders were willing to visit and read lessons and just under half were prepared to provide administrative assistance. However, no more than one in ten was prepared to take services or administer the chalice. The table also shows that although many Anglican attenders claimed they were prepared to perform various types of lay ministry, relatively few actually did so.

With regard to other church-related tasks which lay people may perform we asked a separate question of Anglican attenders, who were shown a card with a list of different ways of helping at services, and asked to state whether they helped in these ways. Apart from the tasks shown in Table 35, the most frequently undertaken tasks were serving coffee (20%), acting as a sidesman (11%) and being in a choir or music group (six per cent). Just under a third held some position of responsibility in the church. By far the most frequently mentioned position of responsibility was membership of the parochial church council. The only other frequently mentioned position was that of churchwarden (six per cent). There were very few lay readers, Sunday school teachers or youth club or study group leaders in the sample.

Conclusions

The evidence we have presented in this chapter confirms that there have been significant changes in the way the rural church is organised. The policy of reducing the imbalance in manpower between the rural and urban dioceses has clearly had an influence on the number of parishes likely to comprise a benefice and the number of parishioners that a rural clergyman will have in his care. But perhaps one of the most interesting findings, illustrated by the maps, is that these changes are in some ways less extensive than might be supposed. The large multi-parish benefice, for example, which features so strongly in media portrayals of the modern church, certainly exists, but it is hardly the norm which Russell (1986: 243) has claimed it to be. Moreover, compared to most urban parishes, rural parishes are still proportionately over-provided with clergy. This fact is of vital importance if we are to understand why parish life and religion in the countryside have their own distinctive characteristics.

It is enlightening to compare the provision of clergymen in rural areas with that of other professions. A recent study of legal services in rural Britain found that contrary to expectations, rural areas were not badly provided with solicitors in numerical terms. Indeed, it was found that the less urban a district was, the greater the chance that it would have a relatively low ratio of population to solicitors (Watkins, Blacksell and Economides 1988). There is also a parallel here with the provision of doctors in rural areas. Phillips and Williams (1984: 191-2) have noted that 'rural locations often appear to be quite adequately staffed purely in terms of the ratio of patients to health care professionals' and go on to point out that relatively rural areas such as East Anglia tend to have the smallest proportion of general practitioners with list sizes of more than 2,000 persons.

It is clear, therefore, that the relative over-provision of clergy in rural parishes is paralleled by over provision of members of the other principal professions. The reasons for this are complex. The location of professionals, like that of most services, is a compromise between the need to be located centrally, in order to provide an efficient service, and the need to be dispersed, in order to be close to those who require the services provided. In the case of solicitors, many factors encourage their concentration in the larger commercial, financial and administrative centres. Yet a group of factors has been identified which tend to encourage their dispersal in rural areas. Some solicitors, for example, may prefer to forgo the high status associated with the larger city practices, in order to gain high status within a small town community. Others may prefer to work in rural areas because of the attractiveness of the countryside and to avoid commuting. The situation is rather more complex in the case of clergymen. Although some may well be affected by these sorts of considerations our survey results indicate that clergymen are less able to make a free choice as to where they move as their choice is often circumscribed by the availability of benefices and the views of their bishops. It is clear, however, that one of the principal reasons for the apparent over-provision of clergymen in rural areas is the resilience and strength of the parochial system.

7

Organising Rural Churches

In this chapter we investigate the views of clergy and parishioners on the organisation of the Church of England in the countryside. The chapter is divided into three main sections. The first is concerned mainly with the structure of benefices. Considerable attention is paid to the current standard model of organisation, the multi-parish benefice. In addition we examine attitudes to team ministry, and people's views of the ideal form of church organisation in the countryside. The second is devoted to church buildings themselves. Is the Church of England too concerned with the upkeep of its buildings? Should certain churches be made redundant? What is the current condition of rural churches? We also examine parishioners' views of the importance of churches. The third section is concerned with the clergy's views on the organisation of the church at levels above that of the parish and benefice. Here we deal with the relevance of the deanery and the diocese, the importance of the different synods and attitudes to the established nature of the church.

Parochial Organisation

Multi-parish Benefices
   Chapter 6 showed the multi-parish benefice to be one of the main innovations in parish organisation over the last 60 years. Our interview survey of incumbents paid particular attention to this development. The 65 clergy who held multi-parish benefices or recently united parishes, were asked questions relating to the formation of their groups and the operation of ministry in them. The coherence of multi-parish groups was investigated by asking the clergy whether their groups made sense *geographically* and *socially*. Their answers indicated that nearly two thirds

of clergy felt that their groups generally did make sense in geographical terms, and over half thought their benefices generally made sense in social terms. In general terms the groupings were more acceptable geographically than socially with several clergy explicitly stating that they possesed a geographical but *not* social rationale.

Most of the reasons given in support of the geographical sense of parish groupings were related to proximity and 'natural' geographic areas. A number of clergy remarked that their groups made geographical sense because they were "compact". Some drew out the importance of respecting natural boundaries such as rivers, others stressed the importance of having good road connections. Common administrative boundaries or areas also informed the geographic sense of groupings. One two-parish priest felt that it helped that both his ecclesiastical parishes belonged to the same civil parish. Another found that his benefice grouping helped mend an 'artificial' break caused by the ecclesiastical parish boundaries.

The most important criticisms of the nature of multi-parish groups concerned the shape or area of the benefices. Several priests mentioned difficulties in their groups related to distances of five miles or more between the vicarage and outlying parishes (constituting at the least a ten mile round trip). Others noted problems connected with roads. One priest had problems because his villages were "not on the normal routes", and two reported their benefices as geographically illogical because they were split by major roads. Problems were also reported by clergy holding groups that crossed county and district boundaries and those whose groups lay outside the main county of the diocese.

Few clergy outlined very explicit reasons to justify the designation of their multi-parish groups as socially sensible. Some of them just said that the parishes which made up their groups were "similar types of parishes" or in the words of another six-parish priest a "coherent entity", or even an "obvious cluster of villages". Another gave as his explanation the fact that the people from his five parishes "mix quite well". The only other factor which was put forward as an explanation of the social sense of multi-parish groupings was the existence of a focus such as a common school.

Several related a lack of social sense in their groupings to major differences between their communities which frequently resulted in a lack of social mixing. In certain cases, social indifference was heightened into rivalry and animosity by specific historical factors. The importance of locality identity was echoed in the comments of the Durham priest who found some tensions between his two very small parishes and the larger one because of different occupation structures: "the farmer's life is quite different from the commercial salesman's life". Another reason for lack of social cohesion was when the different parishes in a group looked to differing areas outside the benefice for their social identity.

It was clear that several clergy felt that social and geographical aspects had been overridden by other concerns when the group was formed. In addition at least three priests mentioned that change in the structure of their groups was imminent to make them 'viable' for a full-time priest. In two cases it was reported that the deanery needed to lose one priest to be in line with the Sheffield quota, but one two-parish priest thought the "Sheffield report needs to be rewritten". The size of the benefice in terms of parishes was another issue commented upon. At one extreme was the two-parish priest who felt he had "suffered from having two parishes" with the result that he had to be like the "sorcerer's appentice". At the other was the four-parish priest who felt his group should be enlarged.

Parochialism as an Obstacle to Multi-Parish Ministry

One of the problems associated with multi-parish benefices is often thought to be that of the parochialism of the residents. Indeed this view is confirmed to some extent by the evidence we present in Chapter 8 on the organisation of church services. In order to explore this issue in greater depth we asked the clergy directly whether they thought that parochialism was an obstacle to the working of their multi-parish groups. Nearly half (46%) of the clergy thought that parochialism was an obstacle to the working of their groups. A further five recognised some parochialism but thought it did not have a severe negative effect on the working of their groups. By contrast, over a third of respondents (35%) stated that parochialism was *not* an obstacle to ministry in their groups.

Many clergy stated that they still encountered parochial attitudes which hindered the working of their groups, and sometimes their initial formation. The most frequently cited way in which parochialism hampered the ministry of multi-parish groups was people not attending services outside their parish; in particular this was linked to allegiance to the parish church. This issue is discussed further in Chapter 8. In some instances parochialism was explained by reference to the specific nature of the parishes concerned. One priest thought the parochial nature of one of his parishes could be related to it being an estate village, containing tenant farmers and estate workers. In Durham parochialism was noted amongst ex-mining settlements. One clergyman reported "hostility like in African tribal terms" whereby they joke and "poke fun" but still know they are "related".

In some cases, incomer/local terminology was brought into play to explain parochialism, with the incomers depicted as the worst offenders. One priest felt that although his two parishes were "fiercely independent" they would work together if it was left up to the "local" people to decide; he laid the blame upon the "incomers at P... [who] prevent it". Another clergyman who held three parishes in plurality felt that where people were the "most educated" (these were incomers) "they are the most insular". In other cases parochialism was associated with parishioners' resentment over not having their own vicar, or with recent members of a grouping.

A number of clergy found parochialism an obstacle to their plans or aspirations for parochial reorganization, and in particular their desire to form their multi-parish groups into united parishes:

> The boundaries between the parishes are lunatic, but the churchwardens were insistent that they remained the same when the group was formed.

Another parish priest who saw what he described as "old parochial ideas" as "ridiculous" thought that it would "make more sense" if his three parishes were made into one single parish, particularly since there would be "less duplication". However, he could not implement unification since he knew "the people like it as it is". It is not surprising, therefore, that parishioners were reported as opposing parish reorganization. Two clergy related their people's fear of parochial reorganisation being imposed upon them, with an accompanying loss of churches and PCCs and an obligation to travel elsewhere to worship. One two-parish priest reported that "both parishes feel threatened", and his attempts to increase group unity by the introduction of a joint standing committee were met by resistance in one parish who were suspicious that this might be the "thin end of the wedge" in a move to one PCC. While obviously sympathising with their fear of reorganization being imposed upon them, the priest thought that "one central body to discuss issues affecting all parishes" made sense, especially if more parishes were added to the group in the future. The priest's interpretation of parishioners' attitudes as a negative type of parochialism must, therefore, be seen in the light of his own vested interest.

One priest outlined his views on parochialism and how to deal with it. For him parochialism was an "obstacle to the Kingdom of God" but also "a fact of life". He advised against confrontation with parochialism as that would only lead to "antagonism". Instead he advocated "working with what is good in it - [a] sense of caring, community" and then to try to "look out" beyond the parish. In fact, a number of clergy who generally thought parochialism was an obstacle to their ministry also mentioned that it did have certain positive aspects. These were outlined more clearly by the four-parish priest who felt that the way in which parochialism was defined was crucial in any assessment of its role. He saw the parochial system as generally "good" because it provided a "small unit to identify with" but added the provisos that the identification should be "open-ended" and that the parish will "go with other parishes and be welcomed".

The most important reason put forward to explain why parochialism was not an obstacle to ministry was that the parishes within the benefice were operated separately and so there was no group mentality to be obstructed by parochialism. Indeed parochialism was often seen as an asset in such a context. In the opinion of one priest of two parishes which "work as separate parishes" and just "share an incumbent", their parochialism was "not a bad thing" as it was "better to share with Christians in own parish". Only a few clergy stated that they had faced and overcome parochialism in the working of their multi-parish groups. One priest felt that the smooth running of his united parish was especially attributable to the fact that one of the ex-parishes did not have its own PCC before it became part of the united parish. Another three-parish priest who did not think parochialism was an obstacle related this to his attempts "to do things as a group". Two others felt that the passage of time had helped to overcome parochialism, although the general feeling was that it was a "gradual but long process", requiring careful and sensitive attention.

It is apparent that clergy felt that parochialism was almost universally an issue and frequently an obstacle to ministry if multi-parish groups were to be operated as groups and not separately. However, with time and effort on the part of clergy the signs are that it can be combated. But several priests felt parochialism must be dealt with without threatening people and creating antagonism. The positive aspects of parochialism were recognised by many, but there were some who displayed vested interests and who shunned a consultative approach in these matters. Can parochialism be dealt with in a fair and sensitive manner if changes to parochial organization have to be pushed through because of financial restrictions at the diocesan level? As one single-parish priest stated "parish amalgamation can be badly prepared and done" and the clergyman usually is the one who is answerable.

Parochial Variations in Ministry

The incumbent of a multi-parish group has to live somewhere, and he often lives in the largest village within his benefice. We were interested to discover whether the clergy felt there was any variation in their ministry between the parish where they lived and the other parish(es) in their benefices and asked the clergy whether this was so. Half of them considered that their ministry definitely varied in favour of their parish of residence and a further five agreed generally with this but added some qualification usually related to their efforts to combat the variation. This bias of ministry in favour of the parish of residence has repercussions in terms of the treatment of small and large parishes since multi-parish clergy were much more likely to live in the largest parish in their benefice than elsewhere: of the 61 multi-parish clergy interviewed, two-thirds lived in the largest parish in their benefice. The implication of this is that smaller parishes are more on their own, receiving less attention from the priest, a factor which could be crucial if they are marginal in terms of support anyway.

Many clergy stressed that they became "better known" in their home parishes and that they knew more about the people in the parish where they lived. Some emphasised how the day-to-day activities of living in a community, such as doing the shopping or exercising the dog, facilitated walking around and meeting people. Walking around was seen as a particularly important part of ministry, and was found to be difficult to do where the priest did not live. One priest described the variation as inevitable because he went around on foot a great deal in the parish where he lived, whereas in his other parish there was a "temptation to use the car". Another admitted the difference was "because I don't walk around S... as much as I walk around here". Despite his holding a mid-week service at S... [his second parish], having coffee at the WI, going into the school and frequenting the pub, he still felt it was not the same because it was "difficult just to walk around". Even one priest who felt his ministry did not vary between his five parishes thought there was a need to encourage priests to do more walking about in their ministry and stated, "I don't do enough". Connected with this was the extra "effort" that many clergy indicated was necessary to motivate them to go elsewhere.

Living within one parish instilled a feeling of belonging in several clergy which they did not have for their other parishes. One stated that although he believed that where he lived should not affect his ministry it did, and he identified more readily with the people where he lived. Another priest drew an essential division between his 'home' parish where he felt he knew people and was known better, and his other parish where he felt "an outsider except with the regular congregation". A number of clergy felt that the variation in their ministry in favour of the parish of residence was heightened by people there expecting more from a resident priest. In contrast, parishes without a resident priest tended to be much more self-sufficient and independent.

What were the practical effects of this variation in ministry? In several cases the result was that they spent less time ministering in the parishes in which they did not live. One priest who tried to do the same for both felt he failed because of time limitation with the implication that although he tried to visit his other parish three times a week, his home parish had priority by default. Another had consciously to give time to visiting outside his home parish to overcome this problem. This need to make an effort to spend time in the other parishes was noted by a number of clergy. At the other extreme was the priest who ran only a "maintenance ministry" in one of his three parishes, visiting it "really only if needed".

Many of the minority of just over a third of clergy who thought there was no major variation in their ministry between the parishes noted that they had to make conscious attempts to prevent a variation in favour of the parish of residence. Indeed, some clergy reported quite complex plans to help equalise their time in different places. One priest outlined his detailed timetable which allowed him to spend one weekday in each of his five parishes, the same day being allocated to each parish every week. Another priest, who was adamant that his ministry did not vary, reported that he had his week carefully worked out so that people in the parish where he lived would see him no more than the rest of his parishioners. Others, although considering that their ministry did not vary felt that there were subtle differences such as those caused by their being seen about their home parish more than their outlying ones. The form of settlement could also have an effect: one incumbent found difficulty visiting in one parish because it consisted mainly of scattered farms.

The same group of clergy was asked whether there was any resentment in their benefices over one parish having to "share the vicar" with other parishes. Views were equallly divided on this question. Although resentment was often widespread, in some cases it was only "one or two people" who could upset the working of a whole benefice. In a number of cases clergy reported there was most resentment in a particular parish or with a particular group of people. Often it was the parish where the priest lived that most resented sharing him. One three-parish priest related how the parish where he lived "regard Rector as 'theirs'... - they can't take it in their stride" when he is elsewhere - whilst the other two parishes were "not so possessive". Another priest reported people in the largest of his four parishes resenting him "dashing off after morning service" as they would prefer him to stay for coffee. In another case, the clergyman reported resentment with which he agreed because the parish was "geographically marginal" to the rest of the six-parish benefice.

A major reason given in explanation of this resentment was having to accept fewer services, in some cases with the added resentment of paying the same money. One incumbent thought that there was almost a bitterness because the parishioners paid the same quota as another parish but got fewer services in return. The priest of one five-parish benefice expressed sympathy for his parishioners' resentment as each parish could only have one service per Sunday and it was hard if people differed over what it should be. Several clergy mentioned that there was some resentment but that most parishioners accepted the situation. Indeed, many of the incumbents who thought there was currently no resentment indicated that in the past there had been but that with the passage of time people had got used to the situation and that they felt there was nothing they could do about it anyway.

Parishioners' Views of Church Organisation

The views of the clergy on parochial organisation may of course be quite different from those of their parishioners. In order to explore the parishioners views on whether ministry varies between the parishes we asked them a series of questions concerning the grouping of parishes. All the Anglicans surveyed were asked whether they thought that the effectiveness of the church was altered by the grouping of parishes. Just under half felt that the grouping of parishes altered the effectiveness of the church; a third felt it had no effect and the remainder did not know. Very few people considered that this effect was positive – most thought that the grouping of parishes resulted in the vicar having less time for people and being less in touch, and hence in the church's effectiveness being diminished. The only ways in which grouping was seen to be beneficial was in bringing communities together, and making parishes more self supporting.

There was a clear relationship between the answers to this question and the type of benefice in which the respondent lived. Two thirds of the respondents in benefices with six or more parishes considered that the grouping of parishes did alter in some way the effectiveness of the church. The proportion of respondents holding this view falls consistently with the number of parishes in the benefice down to 39% in the case of single-parish benefices. Interestingly, the results showed that there was little connection between the age of the respondent and the answers given to this question. Over half of attenders from all age-groups considered that the grouping of parishes did alter church effectiveness. There was little evidence therefore to support the view of some clergy that it was the older parishioners who were most likely to be opposed to the grouping of parishes.

The Anglicans in the sample were asked whether they would rather have a part-time minister chosen from within their parish or congregation, or a full-time minister who would be responsible for a group of parishes. Those who attended church were far more likely to prefer the full-time minister option (80%) compared to the part-time parochially based minister (14%). Furthermore, a majority of non-attenders were still in favour of full-time ministers. For attenders, therefore, the persona of a full-time minister was clearly of importance, even if he did have to be responsible for other parishes as well.

We explored parishioners' views of parish organisation further by asking them how important they considered it to be for an individual parish to have a vicar of its own. Two-thirds of both the general and church roll samples considered it to be 'important' or 'very important' for each parish to have its own vicar. Those aged 65 or more were the most likely to hold this view, and those aged less than 35 were the least

likely. Another interesting point to emerge is that those parishioners
who had lived in the parish all their lives and who were on the church
electoral roll, showed a strong preference for the one priest per parish
model which, presumably, many of them will recall from their younger
days.

Clergy Attitudes to Team Ministries

One of the newer developments concerning parochial organisation
is that of team ministry (Russell 1975). In Chapter 6 it was shown that
several rural teams had been established, particularly in Truro. We
decided to assess the clergy's views of this novel form of ministry and
asked them their general opinion of team ministry, and whether they
saw it as the future pattern of ministry in the countryside. The six
respondents who were team ministers were asked some additional
questions about the working of their teams. The general views of clergy
on this subject were varied. A third were not generally in favour of team
ministries and a similar proportion were in favour. An important sub-
group although generally in favour considered this type of ministry to
be mainly suitable in towns. A large proportion (16%) had not formed
any definite opinion about team ministry, or held mixed views which
could not easily be categorised.

A number of clergy held strong views on the issue of team ministry.
One stated that he was "100% dead against it - the ultimate disaster.
People relate to people, not organisations". He thought that team
ministry commended itself to people in central offices who "think they
can organise people like pawns on a chessboard". Many of their
comments indicated that clergy considered team ministry to be definitely
second best to the parochial system, and unsuited to rural areas: "It's a
lot of poppycock. You are known as a shepherd...you cannot say there
are three shepherds." Another point of view was that lay ministry should
be developed in preference to team ministry. One respondent considered
that the country vicar 'one man band' had to change. The vicar should
become the "leader of a group of lay people". Another thought that
"every rural priest can have his own team if he wishes by training his own
people", while a third considered that a curate and a vicar are cheaper
than a team, and work well in coherent rural groups.

Those respondents who were generally in favour of team ministry
had varied reasons for being so, and many were rather tentative in their
support. Some saw the development of team ministry as the inevitable

consequence of the growth of specialisation in the ministry, while others would only be in favour of team ministry as long they were still able to be in charge of specific geographical areas. One respondent was in favour of team ministries because of the artificiality of parish boundaries. Another view was that in a team ministry there would be a gain from the support of fellow team members. One incumbent noted that he enjoyed being his own man, but that life might be "lighter" if he was part of a team.

The most frequently mentioned area of concern with team ministry was that of staffing arrangement and management. One clergyman at times felt lonely in his parish and said he would like to have colleagues, but knew that "team members can also feel more isolated if they don't get on with others in the team." This opinion was certainly backed up by one of the clergy who had personal experience of team ministry:

> At L... we had one big church and five small parishes. Most of us lived in the town - distances were not great. We felt like curates there, though we all had areas of pastoral care... Here everything is different...we are independent...when I started here I rang the team rector and he said "why are you ringing me?". The team rector does not come to church services [held by team vicars] but does sometimes attend PCC meetings. I take one or two problems to the team rector but it's like he's not listening. I've got somebody in the parish who bosses me about like a schoolboy... I tell the team rector, but he's not interested.

Several respondents considered that clergy find it difficult to work together because they are so "individualistic". One pointed out that the 'group dynamics' of a team are likely to change over time with changes of membership. In his experience, this could result in a complete change of team ethos. He went on to say that "certain people will not fit in".

There were clearly some management problems within teams. One clergyman considered the system set up "an artificial hierarchical position, with the diocese dealing with the team rector" and thought that there should be 'rotating chairmen'. Another considered that staffing needed very careful attention because team vicars tended to get looked upon as curates. One respondent who had previous experience of team ministry in a town felt they worked best if they met the following six conditions:

    i need to be at least five clergy
   ii each church needs to have a person to whom parishioners
       can relate specially, but not exclusively
  iii great care in selecting people
  iv good organisational structure
   v bring lay people into team
  vi need administrative back-up.

The seven respondents who were currently members of teams were asked several specific questions about the functioning of their teams. With such a small number of respondents it is difficult to make any worthwhile generalisations, but a few interesting points can be made. The first is that six of the seven respondents had responsibility for a particular parish or group of parishes within the team. In other words, it appears that within this small group of rural team ministries, the parochial system is still alive and well. The second main point is that the members of the teams do in most cases hold regular meetings. The third point, however, is that half the team members did not consider their team to work 'as a team' at all, while half did.

We also asked the clergy whether they saw team ministry as a future pattern of ministry in the countryside. The response to this question was fairly evenly balanced between those who did not see team ministry as a future pattern of ministry in the countryside (35%) and those who did (34%). The picture is not as clear cut as these figures might suggest, with several of those in favour of team ministries having reservations, and several of those against supporting greater collaboration of some sort. Moreover there was a large proportion (16%) of 'don't knows'. One respondent could see advantages in having some rural team ministries but hoped that "there will still be plenty of parishes with their own priests."

Despite the general air of uncertainty over this question, several clergy had very definite views on the subject. Those who did not see team ministry as a future pattern of ministry in the countryside generally preferred the current parochial system. Those who saw team ministry as a future pattern of ministry in the countryside tended to be split into two main camps. First there were those who saw it as a development forced upon the clergy by changing circumstances such as reductions in staff and second, there were those who saw various benefits. One noted that "if you are on your own, there is more stress", another considered team ministry to be a better way forward than lay ministry and a third felt that team ministries "will have to come in the country if you want to give the country parishes any sort of balanced ministry".

A relatively small group of respondents favoured the use of the deanery or similar sized grouping of parishes as the basis for team type ministries. One commented that the best way forward "may be to have most of the deanery under one big team, but this is a big step to take" and in one case the respondent considered the local deanery chapter "to be close, and we do use each others' gifts a bit...[the deanery] does work like a team in a sense". Another respondent saw the deanery as "the key" to the problem, and thought that the rural dean should be given more status and become the team leader. In a similar vein, a Gloucester respondent wondered whether "we should explore the old minster pattern – with the clergy living together in the town and going out to satellite villages." A Lincoln clergyman working in a team ministry based on a small country town noted, in this respect, that "there is some resentment by the villages of [the town]. They feel they lose out, but really they get a better deal than they would otherwise." We return to role of the deanery in a later section.

Parochial Ideals

Almost two thirds of the clergy considered that *ideally* each parish should have a priest of its own, whereas only a fifth disagreed. However, a large group of those who agreed with the proposition felt it to be unrealistic in the present circumstances. A commonly held view, exposed by the answers to other questions in the survey as well as this one, was that parishioners needed a clergyman they felt 'belonged to them'. One respondent noted that "they should have someone they feel is their own clergyman, as opposed to the idea of curates slipping out of towns to take a few services". Another thought that "there is a strong desire of people to have a visible person to whom they relate on matters of spirit – a sort of 'totem pole'". A third commented that "I'm very much in favour of a parochially based clergy as opposed to sector ministries. We must be deployed on a parochial system."

The minority of respondents who did not consider that in ideal terms there should be a priest in every parish was largely of the opinion that the clergy should be distributed according to the population. As can be seen from the answers to the other questions discussed in this section, however, there were very wide disparities between the clergy as to the number of people they would *like* to have in their benefice. One respondent did not consider the parish system ever worked properly "because it was unfair and anomalous. We have become obsessed by our parish system." Another simply stated that "people must cheerfully accept grouping", while one vicar with five parishes thought that "in country areas people can feel a benefit having to share their vicar".

When asked how many people they would like in their parish in an ideal world, the clergy interviewed gave a wide variety of responses. At one end of the spectrum was the team priest whose ideal consisted of only 200 people in a one church parish where "everybody went and the church was full". At the opposite end was the priest of an ex-mining village whose ideal was between 15,000 and 18,000 people, a figure obviously influenced by his feeling that his 5,000 people were "in some sense harder to get to grips with" than people were when he shared 22,000 as a curate. However, most of the 62 priests who specified an ideal population, indicated preferences of between 1,000 and 5,000 people. Only four priests thought fewer than 1,000 people in their charge ideal and only ten favoured more than 5,000.

A few clergy outlined general practical reasons in forming population limits and ideals but the ranges still varied greatly. For one priest 2,000 people were "as much as I can really manage", for another 10,000 were "as many as I can manage". Finance was also an influence, particularly in Durham. One priest of a single parish stated that his ideal was around 7,500 "thinking in terms of manpower and money required for payment", but "if there were no constraints I would make the population smaller". At least 12 priests referred to the facility of knowing people in answering this question. Many stated population limits beyond which they believed it was impossible to know most people, but these limits varied from the incumbent who considered that "no priest can know more than 200 people" to the one who thought it was "very difficult to maintain personal links with excess of 5,000."

Some clergy differentiated ideal population sizes according to location or locality. In particular, there was reference to distinct 'rural' circumstances. One priest of two parishes saw a population of 2,000–2,500 "in the country an absolute maximum". Another gave a similar estimate: "for one church, one parson – in a rural area – 2–3,000 is quite enough." In a number of cases geographical *area* was seen as a crucial factor determining optimum size and some denied the relevance of numbers altogether because of the overwhelming importance of area.

The clergy interviewed were also asked how many churches they would like in their charge in an ideal world. Around two thirds favoured only *one* church, a "one church ideal", and many agreed with the sentiment expressed by one priest that it was "a privilege to have one". In several cases it was clear that having only one church was seen as generally "much easier", leaving more time for dealing with people and yielding less administration. Some indicated that the ideal way for the church to serve the parish was for there to be one church "central to the community". In fact for one priest the ideal was "one church, one community". For others, the single church was important as a means of bringing together the church community. One priest who had previously looked after one church for 20 years felt the single church to be "ideal because the whole church family comes together in one place" rather than being "fragmented" as in his current three parish benefice.

Another priest with a similar one church ideal made a different criticism of church policy. He saw the single church as a potential "spiritual centre" to which people should come rather than attending churches "dotted around all over the place", the legacy of different communications and church attendance patterns. He advised a rethinking of the policy which keeps such churches open. However, many other clergy did not agree. Although one priest of five rural parishes felt that one church was "much easier", he doubted the value of the question and his answer because a greenfield site would be needed if ideals were to be put into practice. Another priest of four rural parishes stated that although one church may be ideal in terms of administration and expense, he "wouldn't want one church if it meant four had to close".

A fifth of the respondents were critical of the single church ideal and some actually disagreed that one church was in any way ideal: "In a rural situation, four is the optimum or three, [I] wouldn't want to go back to one man - one parish." A four-parish priest found "joy and variety in different congregations". A number of other priests referred to the development and involvement of lay resources as relevant to the ideal number of churches. A small number of clergy denied the importance of the number of people and churches in the care of one priest. In the case of one priest, Christian commitment overrode all consideration of ideal parish size or ideal number of churches. Others queried the importance of churches and parishes in the composition of their ideal situations. One saw it rather as "largely a question of geographical area" a stress that some priests made in relation to the ideal number of people they would like in their care.

Church Buildings

Building Upkeep

The upkeep of church buildings is undoubtedly one of the principal reasons for holding charitable events in the parishes of England. Sometimes parish life seems to be an endless round of church fetes, garden parties, whist drives, luncheons, and coffee mornings. Almost all these things have as their *raison d'etre* fund raising for the church, and in most cases the funds raised will be used to help repair the fabric of the church. We asked the clergy and the parishioners a number of questions to ascertain their views on the question of the maintenance of church buildings.

The great majority of incumbents (88%) considered their churches to be in reasonable shape, but 11% had at least one church in poor condition. This does not mean, of course, that considerable efforts are not needed to keep the buildings in reasonable condition. One Gloucester clergyman pointed out, for example, that although the church at F.... was in reasonable physical shape, there was "a programme of non-urgent work which will cost £30,000". The parish had £15,000 in hand because of legacies. At another of his churches, "three-quarters of the roof was redone six or seven years ago. This cost £6,000; we had £3,000 and the rest was found in six months".

Moreover, it is clear that although most churches could be classed as reasonable, there may be sudden requirements for very large sums of money, often following upon a visit and report from the diocesan architect. In some cases it is unlikely that the parish can bear the expense. In one instance, a church in very poor condition only had a congregation of from three to eight people, yet £100,000 was required to repair the roof. The vicar thought that redundancy was likely, but said "I won't let it close in my time... it's a gem". The question of redundancy is discussed fully below, but the overall impression gained from the survey was that parishes were able to raise surprisingly large sums of money if the continuing existence of their church was threatened. In one Gloucester parish, for example, the clergyman wanted to close down S.... Church and turn it over to the Redundant Churches Board, but the parishioners insisted on keeping it open, even though, as the clergyman put it, "double figures is a victory" there. They had to find £75,000 for the roof, and received a great deal of financial support, especially from Americans who lived in flats in the big house. To the respondent's surprise they "would write out cheques during the service at collection!"

In some instances, the church building was kept in good repair through the generosity of individual families. This was especially true where the church was situated close to the big house:

> At H.... the court family pay for everything. Apart from the family and the organist, there are only one or two others, yet we can carry on paying the quota.

Such dependence upon the goodwill of local landowners was sometimes viewed with trepidation by the clergy. In one case a vicar had 'weaned' his PCC away from relying upon the local estate to look after the church. In another, a church which needed 'thousands' spent on it was in effect the private chapel of a local landowner and the clergyman was put in a difficult position as he had to keep on reminding the landowner that repairs were necessary.

As building upkeep required such large sums of money, the respondents were asked whether they considered it to be a preoccupation for the clergy. The responses indicated that almost half of the respondents considered building upkeep to be a preoccupation, but over a third thought it was not. Some respondents were very concerned about the amount of time spent on fund raising for buildings, and felt that this state of affairs meant there was too little time to deal with more important issues:

> The PCC talks all the time about buildings, but only talks for a few minutes about religion;
>
> Buildings demand a disproportionate amount of time and divert us from moral issues of the day such as AIDS and women priests.

One clergyman went so far as to suggest that the government should "nationalise all ancient parish churches and rent them back to the parish". Another considered that "there should be a national scheme to look after church buildings, to take the strain of care and maintenance." These were extreme views. A more representative view was that building upkeep was a " *constant* burden, but not a problem". Other respondents pointed out that they, or their parishioners, thoroughly enjoyed this type of work: "Spare us these yuppie theology guys who don't clear [blocked up] water out of drains!"

Sometimes, however, the political skills of the clergy were tested when different groups within the parish wanted to concentrate on different types of upkeep. In one parish there was a "constant battle" between those who wished to beautify the churches and make them like their homes, and those who wanted to do hidden [structural] work. Another problem voiced by some clergy was the relatively small grants available from English Heritage and the fact that VAT was payable on church repairs. In addition, one respondent considered that English Heritage was "bureaucratic, unfeeling and incompetent and only interested in putting the building back to what it was like in yesteryear. They are a real pain and hassle to deal with." The same man also pointed out the problem of increasing insurance premiums which for his benefice had gone up 150% in the last four years.

Redundant Churches

One of the consequences of the development of the multi-parish system is that an incumbent has a number of churches in his charge. In an earlier section we discussed clergy ideals as to the number of parishes and churches for which they would like to be responsible and discovered that the majority had an ideal of a single church. We now turn to consider the views of the clergy on whether the norm of at least one church per parish should be maintained. The rural clergy interviewed were asked how important they considered it to be for each parish or community to have its own church building. It is clear from their answers, with 83% stating that they did think this was important, that their ideal and personal views were tempered by the practical necessity of keeping churches open. Only 10% thought that it was not important for each parish or community to have its own church, the remainder saying that it depended on the circumstances.

Many clergy considered that a building was crucial to the maintenance of a presence by the Church of England in the parish, especially in rural districts where parishioners were considered to be 'conservative' and to feel 'very strongly' that their parish church should remain in use. They made the point that if rural churches were closed, many members of the congregation would be lost as they would tend not to attend services in other churches:

> Church membership is non-transferable. If you close one they won't go to another. Maintenance here *is* ministry.
>
> In a town, the church is second to the created Christian

community. In rural areas there is a need for a monument representing an idea that will not be reached in human terms.

Churches are often the most visually impressive buildings in villages. In areas where there is a scattered form of settlement rather than nucleated villages, as in most of Cornwall, the Forest of Dean, fenland Lincolnshire and parts of Durham, they may be the principal binding factor in the formation of parish identity. Many clergy stressed that they felt the parish church was essential as a focus for the local community:

> In this Celtic spread it's the one thing, the only thing, it gives the community a centre; without it, the raison d'etre of a 'place' is lost. [The church] is essential for the community.... In some ways the only thing we've got is the church in some of the remoter areas.

Some respondents saw potential advantages in reducing the number of churches in terms of efficiency and economics, but felt that in practical terms these benefits were outweighed by the wishes of the congregations to retain their own churches. The following quotations show clearly the way that the wishes of the parishioners influence the views of the clergy:

> Personally I think it would be a good idea if there was one building for ten villages, and everyone goes to that instead of several small populations. To the people [however] it is very important.
> Being realistic we are overchurched. The group would work well with two rather than four buildings. If I tried to close them there would be trouble from the folks who don't use them except for hatch, match, despatch...symbol of continuity with the past.

Of those clergy who felt it was unimportant for every parish to have its own church building, a number were adamant in their views that there were simply far too many churches in rural areas and that this was having a deleterious effect on religious life in the countryside:

> This is a luxury we cannot afford - it's spiritually stultifying. Too much effort goes on keeping buildings open...people travel to pubs - why not for church? The church is seen as something other than a spiritual centre.... It's impossible to stimulate spiritual worship with a handful of people and a parson dashing around.

It is clear that although many clergy would like to have fewer churches in their charge they are heavily influenced by the views of their parishioners. But what are the views of the residents of rural parishes in this respect? In our sample of twenty rural parishes we asked how important it was for a parish to have its own church (Table 36). The great majority of all respondents (87%) thought it was important or very important for a parish to have a church building of its own. This view was expressed more by those in the church roll (95%) than the general sample (83%). These figures confirm dramatically the views expressed by the clergy: there does appear to be overwhelming support for the continuance of the norm of at least one church per parish.

TABLE 36. Rural Parishioners: Importance of Parish Church

Importance of church	General sample		Church roll sample		Total sample	
	No	%	No	%	No	%
Very important	112	33	87	59	199	41
Important	170	50	54	36	224	46
Unimportant	42	12	3	2	45	9
Don't know	16	5	4	3	20	4
Not answered	1	0	–	–	1	0
Total	341	100	148	100	489	100

Having gauged the views of the clergy and parishioners on the importance of parish churches we went on specifically to discuss with them the issue of redundancy. The clergy's views on this issue were varied and difficult to classify. In simple terms, a fifth were in general favour of redundancy and over a quarter were against it. Many clergy, however, were neither generally for or against redundancy, pointing out that its applicability depended on a wide range of local issues. One group of respondents were opposed to the idea of redundancy, even if the numbers attending fell to very low levels indeed. One Lincoln respondent pointed out that a nearby parish has a redundant church and "every time I pass it I am unhappy". Other clergy expressed similar sentiments:

> Some people felt we should pull down St J.... But, although it's only used for half the year, it's very popular. It's a standing witness even when services are not held. [It would be a] terrible witness

if redundant. You have to be sensible and ensure it's not too draining on finance; but you have to look very carefully before you do it.

I don't agree with redundancy on the whole.... nor with new uses....neglected decay I support....churches are hallowed places. If they had closed down all the redundant churches in Cornwall 200 years ago we would have no churches in 90% of the villages today.

Another group were not totally against redundancy in theory, but in practice did not wish to implement it. A Southwell clergyman, for example, stated that his "gut feeling" was to retain churches. When he first looked at his benefice, on the map, he thought he would be closing the church in his smallest parish, but he changed his mind when he actually saw the building concerned and noted that "I would be heartbroken to preside over the closure of a building". One Gloucester respondent who in general considered that there were too many churches had a small chapel where attendance, apart from at harvest, was never higher than six. This chapel was already closed for the winter months, but he thought that "it would be an awful shame to close it as it is a lovely church".

One of the most frequently given reasons for being against redundancy was that rural populations are rising, or may rise, and if the church is retained there is always the possibility that there may be an increase in attendance. When the general rise in population numbers in rural areas described in Chapter 3 is taken into account, there is no doubt that this point of view has some validity:

Only in 1968 the archdeacon wanted to make T.... redundant. Now it is thriving. Villages are growing [now] and I think we have to think very carefully about redundancy.

Came to M.... and there was a regular congregation of three and at first I thought it should be made redundant. Now I see little point in making country churches redundant. It finances itself and would only be converted to a house. It is a presence and now numbers are up.

Those respondents that supported redundancy tended to do so in rather general terms. A Southwell respondent noted that he had "no worries or qualms about redundancy - it's the common-sense thing", a

Durham clergyman considered that "there is no way that the Church of England can go on supporting every little village church" . One Gloucester respondent said that it was an obvious point that when the congregation moves away there is no need for a church and went on to say that "It does not cheer me to see a church close, but you have to be realistic".

Very few respondents had actually closed down a church themselves. One who had closed a church seven years ago noted that there had been a tremendous uproar, "especially from those who had never attended" the church. He considered that a strange side-effect was that the closure had encouraged the parishioners to take care of the churchyard which had previously been unkempt but was now impeccable. He considered that he would be known for ever "as the vicar that closed B...." Another noted "I shut two churches in my urban phase...you have to leave if you do it!" On a more positive note, one respondent noted that the threat of closure can help to encourage attendance.

A frequent view was that as long as there were enough people in the parish, and the parishioners could afford to keep the church open, churches should not be made redundant. This begs the question, is there a minimum number of people for a viable church? When asked this question, well over half the clergy felt that it was impossible to give precise numbers. One noted, for example:

> It varies enormously according to the circumstances. T... survived with two or three people for quite a long time. Some younger families moved in and the church revived. With a regular congregation of ten you are viable and can make ends meet.

Of those that tried to give an estimate, 14 thought that at least ten regular attenders were required to make a church viable, ten thought that from 10–20 attenders were required, and nine thought that more than 20 attenders were needed. Even those who attempted to estimate minimum numbers generally qualified the number by stating that it would depend on the circumstances of the parish. Some respondents thought that the minimum size for a viable congregation was affected by the physical nature of the church. A Truro respondent thought that "minimum numbers depends on the size of the church building. At L.... 12–15 feels a reasonable congregation". A more frequent observation was that it was not the numbers attending that was important so much as the quality:

It depends on quality of numbers, and percentage of population. At P.... we get 15-20% of the population, although small numbers. Not minimum number but minimum commitment...could have large congregation but not necessarily viable. Had congregation of six in Yorkshire, but was viable.

Others had more definite ideas as to how many attenders they required. One Lincoln respondent considered that "you need at least twelve regular, definite, worshippers" and pointed out that "I've closed three [churches]: there's action!" Other views varied from the minimilist, "the minimum number of people for the celebration of holy communion is two. I don't care how many people are there" to requirements for attendances which would toll the death knell for many rural churches: "You need a regular congregation of 60-70 (not necessarily every Sunday). The cut off point is 20 - struggle; 30-40 picks up; 60 plus works better - there are more people to do the work".

In our survey of rural parishioners we asked whether a parish church should be closed if the numbers attending it become very small. The answers given show that this option is not generally favoured. Less than a third of all respondents (31%) broadly agreed that churches should be closed if the numbers became too small, whereas over half (54%) said that they should not be closed. Many people qualified their answers, however, epecially those people from the church roll sample, probably because they were more aware of the complexities surrounding the issue of church closure. Further analysis showed that people in certain dioceses were more likely to favour closure than others. In Gloucester, for example, only 24% agreed with closure, but in Lincoln this proportion was as high as 40%. The readiness of people in Lincoln to accept the closure of churches could be a reflection of the existing situation, as the diocese already has significantly more redundant churches than the other four survey dioceses. Another interesting point is that when the age of the respondent is taken into account, it is the youngest age-group (34 or under) that was most opposed to the closure of churches (16%) and the oldest (65 and over) who were least opposed. One explanation for this could be that as fewer people in the youngest age actually attended church, their view was more idealistic, whereas the caution of the oldest age group could represent a pragmatism based on some experience of the church.

Historical Importance

Churches are by far the most important architectural and historic feature in most parishes. The church forms a tremendously important element of most people's image of the English village. This significance has long been nurtured by some of the most potent forms of expression and perhaps most importantly in prose, poetry and the visual arts. Countless guide books reinforce the cultural importance of the parish church. On a more personal level church buildings are closely associated with the most important rites of passage, and churches and church yards contain many memorials of great personal significance. In order to gauge the clergy's views of the cultural values ascribed to church buildings, they were asked how important it was for their parish(es) to have an *old* church building. Over half (52%) thought that it was important but a large minority considered this to be unimportant. Several made the point that *they* did not mind whether a building was old or not, but their parishioners did: "I would cheerfully put a bomb under it and start again, but the people love it and feel its beauty".

Several clergy considered the age of their churches to be of great importance. Some linked this importance to broad ideas of English culture and one considered that the media view is that "churches should be built of stone and pleasantly weathered". One thought that people liked old churches because "they associate them with parts of their lives". A similar point was made by a Gloucester clergyman who considered that it was not the age that was important: "What's relevant is it's the church that they remember as children – part of their roots and heritage". Others were less clear:

> Yes, [old churches] do have significance for parishioners, but I'm not sure what the significance is. Search for belonging... symptom of disease of society...lack of roots.... church is adopted by newcomers because of something missing – the sense of belonging – in them.

A small minority of clergy felt antipathy towards old church buildings. One noted that "there is a sentimental attraction to old buildings, but I hope this is not the important issue." Others stressed that the church consisted of people and that the building must serve the parishioners rather than becoming a burden to them:

> Building at worst is a symbol of rural mythology...of a dreamed feudal age of tranquility and a rural idyll that never existed. At best,

building serves a worshipping community. But there is all the difference in the world between a group of people using building as expression of belief, and a museum or mausoleum.

We did not ask parishioners directly what their views were of old churches. We did however ask them whether they had 'looked round' any churches or religious buildings over the past year. The answers to this question are quite remarkable: almost two-thirds (63%) of the general sample had visited such buildings, and the figure was even higher (78%) for the church roll sample. All those who had visited churches were asked for their reasons for visiting churches and religious buildings. They were given four categories of reason - architectural, historical, spiritual, and general interest, and were asked to say which for them were related to their visiting. Overall the most popular reasons for visiting churches were architectural (54%) and general interest (53%). Historical interest was mentioned more frequently by those in the general sample, while not surprisingly, spiritual interest was mentioned by more (38%) of the church roll sample than the general sample (29%). Other reasons given for visiting churches included events such as flower festivals and concerts. Obviously the simple questions we asked only provide answers which touch the surface in terms of the reasons why people visit churches, but the answers do give an indication of the enormous numbers of people who like to visit churches, and a general idea of their reasons for doing so.

Finance

When asked about the importance of having an old parish church, one Lincoln respondent made the pragmatic point that without their historic appeal, rural churches would not be able to pay their way. We now turn to consider the views of the clergy on church finance. First of all, we asked the rural clergy whether their benefice had financial problems. The majority (60%) of clergy thought not. This proportion rises to 83% if those who did not answer the question are excluded. We found this a surprising answer, especially as many clergy had in their answers to other questions described in dramatic terms the costs involved in repairing and maintaining their churches. What are the reasons for this confident, if not complacent, attitude?

Several incumbents pointed out that there were wealthy people living in their benefice: "all the parishes have rich people." Others noted that their PCC often thought they had financial problems, but were in practice always able to meet the demands. Some respondents, however, were rather concerned that the church was relying on a relatively small proportion of their parish for financial support: "when I came here the church was in debt. Now we've got £6,000 in hand through various activities. It's the same people all the time." One group of incumbents were keen to point out that it was possible to reorganise fund raising in parishes, and to improve the financial situation by careful management:

> If a church is alive it looks after itself. The congregation were happy to take over buildings and finance. They were ready and waiting and delighted to be given the chance. They weren't allowed to before: the lay talent was there to be exploited...Two parishes have a 'financial services management group' which includes all churchwardens and two others. They do all the accounts and finances have been revolutionised... We have just spent £100,000 on a new roof. The lay people raised this in nine months.

The most frequent financial concern raised by the rural clergy was the level of quota payments demanded by the dioceses. One respondent considered that "the day I find it difficult to raise the quota is the day I know I should be moving somewhere else....because it's a sign of reluctance to support the personal ministry of church". Several respondents, however, were critical at what they considered to be high levels of quota. One Gloucester clergyman noted that his benefice had no financial problems, but that "we are beginning to jib at the level of quota now... this is a sore point". The following comment indicates that a number of parishes were finding it a considerable struggle to keep up their quota payments, and some were finding that the level of quota meant that there was little money left over for other purposes:

> The quota system is one of the biggest binds. The more you raise, the more you give. Because quota is nearly 70% of income you cannot escape this spiralling upwards.

In a few cases it had been decided not to pay the quota. In one instance, the clergyman and the PCC decided independently of each other not to meet the quota. They decided to pay 10% more than the previous year, not the 16% asked for, feeling that "the diocese should budget within its income". In another case, a complicated arrangement had been made between two parishes in the same benefice. Parish A, which had an annual income from 6-9 people of £250 was assessed for £270. A neighbouring parish (B) who could afford to pay their quota decided to withold theirs in defence of Parish A. The clergyman considered that Parish B "will probably pay for [Parish A's] quota and withhold their own!" In another case, all fund raising efforts were used to fund a repair bill of £60,000 over and above insurance, and as a result the parish owed quota. The clergyman went on to note:

> Giving is not enough to pay quota, so we cannot give much away elsewhere. Non-churchgoers helped with the rebuilding of the church but won't support the daily running of it. This is seen as a problem for the churchgoers. [Non-churchgoers] see the church as a club - if you like that sort of thing you can pay for it.

The clergy had very variable views of the level of giving in their parishes. Most felt it was was moderate; about a quarter considered the level of giving to be poor and only 14% considered it to be good. Some respondents painted a bleak picture. One pointed out that there was "a widespread erroneous belief that the Church Commissioner are well off and so people are not willing to give" He considered the overall level of giving to be poor and that people became upset if he suggested a suitable figure. Another needed £20,000 in order to replace lead stolen from the church roof. He wrote round to everyone in the parish, and was only able to raise £1,500. Another considered the level of giving to be "absolutely appalling... only 60p a piece."

All was not gloom, however, in some cases astonishingly high amounts were raised and the clergy considered people to be very generous:

> We usually raise £1,000 for foreign mission. One year, we had not got this amount so I wrote to all people on the PCC list and got £1,000 easily.
>
> We are blessed financially. We give away 20% of income to missions and charities. We are not a wealthy church - we are a church of people who give generously. When there is a material need the money is there.

Several clergy held special campaigns to raise money for particular purposes. The success of these varied greatly. One clergyman "had a kind of mission four years ago and stirred them up, but now they've gone back to sleep". Other campaigns appeared to be rather more successful:

"we've had projects... a drought drive raised £1,500. Some money is given to the Samaritans etc...." Some clergy had a strict rota of campaigns: "I have a major campaign every five years contacting 350-400 families, and a minor campaign every two years contacting around 80 largely new families."

A problem mentioned many times was that parishioners were happier to give if the charity was local, and especially if it concerned the church building. As earlier sections have shown, most parishes appear able, at irregular and widely spaced intervals, to raise sufficient funds to keep their church property in good condition. A Gloucester respondent noted that in respect of giving, "it's very much a feeling of let's look after ourselves. They are happy to keep the shrine going". In one instance, the incumbent even appeared to be taking advantage of a mistaken belief among his parishioners that funds raised went towards the church building:

> At St G.... there are four to five well attended events - may be up to half the total population. They think they are supporting the fabric I suppose, but in fact it all goes to costs.

In some cases the introduction of 'envelope schemes' had increased the level of giving, but views on the effectiveness of covenanting, and of stewardship campaigns, as ways raising the level of giving were varied:

> Giving is improving, but in rural areas you have to be careful about stewardship campaigns because 1) you could drive church to sectarian model and 2) you have to be careful not to despise the goodwill of coffee mornings and jumble sales. They're well supported and part of fellowship.

This quotation is particularly interesting as it brings out the fact that some incumbents favour traditional fund raising events such as church fetes, garden parties and so forth, whereas others actively disapprove of them. One respondent was pleased with the overall level of giving, but not with the methods because "most is raised by events".

Higher Levels of Church Organisation

The Deanery
Opinion on the rural deanery as an organisation was evenly divided

between those rural incumbents who felt it was important (31%) and those who felt it to be unimportant (29%). A further 11% invested the deanery with some value or potential, because they said that it should or could be more important in the future than it was at present. In addition, nine per cent of the clergy, answering specifically for their local situation, said that their own deaneries were good or important. In total therefore, there were considerably more incumbents who felt that the deanery had or could have an important role than there were those who thought it insignificant.

By far the most significant way in which the deanery was seen to be of value was in enabling mutual support and fellowship among the constituent clergy. The deanery chapter was seen by several clergy as the main way in which this support, sharing and fellowship could take place. Some clergy explicitly stated that it was the primary function of the deanery to provide this support and fellowship, and that it should not over concern itself with other matters:

> It does provide a place for the clergy and laity to get together and to find support and share similar problems - it shouldn't consist of a formal business meeting.

A much smaller number of respondents commented on a linked issue, namely that the deanery was important in enabling clergy to see themselves as part of the wider church, and to prevent them becoming too isolated in the affairs of their own parishes:

> It's very important. It's bigger than the parish or the team, yet not so big as to be unrealisable by the general people. It's a good corrective to have the deanery, it forces people to look outward, and stops them falling into little boxes.

The deanery was therefore felt by some clergy to be a layer of government of a size and order that people could identify with. This point was echoed by those who said that the deanery was more relevant and important than either the diocese or General Synod. Another way in which the deanery was seen to be important was in the provision and sharing of resources, in particular in terms of holiday cover, and help in the payment of quota.

Many of those who did not feel that the deanery was an important organisation stated that it did not work or had no function, without attributing any reason. Comments such as "I wonder what it's there for at times – a bit of a bore" and "it's a waste of time and money by and large" were frequent. However, among those who did elaborate on their views of the deanery, the most common remark was that the deanery was simply an inappropriate and unnecessary level of synodical government, as the following quotations show:

> It's all about how big should the unit be? Too much is made of the deanery – it's a layer that we can do without, it has no useful function.
> No importance whatsoever. The diocese is the unit, and the parishes are limbs and cells.

The other major criticism of the deanery was that it made no sense geographically, being imposed on parishes which could be very different, and which otherwise had no sense of corporate identity. One incumbent commented "the problem is that they are such amorphous areas and they don't relate to anything." Another felt that:

> It may work where there is a feeling of regional identity, but the present deanery structure is not local enough. The problem is that because the deaneries are organised administratively, they could not all be rural parishes.

Another problem with the deanery was felt to be that too much time was spent dealing with matters passed down through the tiers of church government, which could be irrelevant but nevertheless had to be discussed. Implicit in this, for some respondents, was the fact that the deanery was seen as a powerless organisation, with no corresponding movement up the hierarchy. This problem was mainly cited in relation to deanery synod, and it was apparent that many clergy thought that deanery synod (as opposed to the chapter) had no importance, or were critical of this particular aspect of the deanery. In addition, several stressed the difficulty in finding lay people to act as deanery synod representatives.

Several clergy stressed the importance of the leadership of the rural dean and described how the success of the deanery as an organisation had fluctuated with different deans. The other factor which influenced whether or not the deanery was important was its size and geographical composition. Another issue was whether the administratively imposed deanery happened to coincide with a geographical area with its own coherence and identity. As one incumbent commented "it only relates if it's a geographical area", and as another remarked "it may work where there is a feeling of regional identity".

Finally, ten incumbents said that whatever the current importance of the deanery, they felt that it could or should become more important in the future. In particular, some clergy thought that the deanery should increase in importance through investing the rural deans with more authority, even to the extent of making them bishops:

> Very important to have a local group of parishes. I would like to see it strengthened. The Rural Dean is the "local father in God".

However, it is a matter of considerable interest that none of the clergy took the opportunity when answering this question to suggest that the rural deanery should become the principal unit of local church organisation as argued by Tiller (1983).

The Diocese

In general the diocese was a rather more popular entity amongst the rural incumbents than the deanery. Just over half of the clergy said that the diocese helped in their ministry, or mentioned mainly positive aspects of the diocese. Fourteen per cent of the clergy mentioned both positive and negative aspects of the Diocese, and only eight per cent said it hindered their work, or made only negative comments. In addition a fairly high proportion of the clergy had no strong views, or failed to invest the diocese in general with any particular significance or relevance.

Two main areas were singled out for praise, or as ways in which the dioceses were helpful. The first was the staff and senior clergy of the diocese - in particular Bishops, but also Archdeacons. Several clergy commented on the support and help they received from their Bishops (16), and also from their Archdeacons (7), and in particular the fact that they were readily available and approachable. One respondent suggested that it was only the bishop that gave the diocese any value. Other clergy commented on the general helpfulness of the staff at Diocesan offices. The second way in which the dioceses were seen to help the ministry of respondents was through the provision of resources, advice and training and for their general administration, including that of housing and financial matters.

> Splendid. We're very lucky here. I don't know how they do

what they do, because the administrative budget is small for what they achieve.

The most frequent criticism of dioceses concerned the appointment of central diocesan staff – seven respondents commented on this. Some clergy were concerned at the number of such appointments, and others questioned the value of them, especially when staff had parish jobs as well:

..... there are six people, three ordained, running education. They've never been here – and they give chronic advice. The ..... adviser is the only parson I've ever sworn at. There are too many advisers – they should have parishes.

The bureaucracy involved in diocesan administration was another negative factor, which six clergy criticised. One said "I have watched it grow more and more bureaucratic – like the civil service", and others commented on the volume of paperwork and form filling. Others questioned the value of some of the diocesan meetings and committees. Another area of criticism related to the diocesan bishops. Six clergy were critical of their bishops, either because of the level of pastoral care they gave, or more generally in the way they ran the diocese. It should be said, however, that these criticisms were not widespread, as four of these six clergy came from the same diocese.

Finally, we must consider the views of those clergy who had neutral views about the diocese or who found it irrelevant. There were various reasons for this. A number of clergy said that they themselves tended to ignore the diocese, and preferred to carry on with their own independent ministry: "I have my own ministry, and the diocese is irrelevant". Several clergy said not that they ignored the diocese, but rather that the diocese simply made no difference and had no impact on their ministry and parishes at all. Others felt that the diocese was largely irrelevant because of their geographical location. For some this was a result of living on the periphery of their diocese, and hence being less able, because of travel time, to join in diocesan events and meetings. Some clergy explicitly stated that they felt disadvantaged because they were working in rural areas, and their dioceses were more geared to urban ministry.

Establishment

Many commentators have questioned the established nature of the

Church of England and consider it would be beneficial, as in Wales and Ireland, for the church to be disestablished. In order to obtain the views of the rural incumbents on this issue, we asked them what they felt were the losses and gains of being priests in the established church. Nearly all those interviewed answered the question, and many gave very full answers. Considerably more priests mentioned gains than losses: Over 80% of respondents listed the gains involved in being a priest in the established church, whereas just over a half (56%) mentioned losses. The answers given were very full, and often complex to categorise. It was obvious that the same issue could represent a gain to one person and a loss to another, or even both a gain and a loss to the same respondent. Looking first at "gains", Table 37 shows the main categories of advantage which our sample felt stemmed from being priests in the established church.

TABLE 37. *Gains of being a Priest in the Established Church*

	No. of clergy	% of respondents (n = 94)
Church/priest/community	58	62
Paid centrally/freedom from congregation	10	11
Nature of Anglicanism	6	6
National voice/importance	6	6
Support/authority of C of E	5	5
Other	9	10

By far the most common benefit which was felt to stem from being a priest in the established church was the category labelled "church/priest/community". The category included all answers referring to the place of the Anglican vicar and church in the community under the parochial system. It therefore refers to having the cure of all souls in the parish, the place of the vicar in the community, the access to homes and the opportunities for evangelism, and the attitudes of people to the church. Although this is a very large category it would be inappropriate to separate out the different strands quantitatively, as they are all interlinked.

The most common aspect of the church–vicar–community category to be mentioned referred to having the cure of *all* souls in the parish, and hence a *right* to minister to everybody and also an *expectation* that this will be the case, as fully explored in Chapter 5. Some clergy referred more explicitly in this context to the differences between the gathered and associational church models, and the fact that the "cure of all souls" prevented a ministry solely to the gathered congregation:

> We try to meet the needs of ordinary people – not an exclusive church – I never think in terms of whether they belong or qualify – all parishioners are potential friends to whom the church is always open for private prayer, devotion and the sacraments.

Linked with the benefits of being able to minister to the whole community, was the more specific sense in which simply being "the vicar" meant occupying a prescribed, recognised and accepted place in the community. Because of the acceptance in the community of the role of the Anglican vicar, several respondents elaborated further about the benefits this had for their ministry, especially in terms of the "rights" they felt it gave them, and in particular the access to people and their homes.

> I do feel I can visit everybody .... I'm given a right to call and see people, and it's the same with youth clubs and schools etc.

Some respondents explicitly referred to the *evangelistic* benefits of this access to people and community. Two respondents described the Church of England as "a good boat to fish from". One clergyman summed up what he saw to be the ideal relationship between church and community, in order for the Anglican church to make best advantage of its historic position in the community:

> The relation of church to society is critical. It needs to be a church in form and vision which relates to the community, but it needs to be sect-like in terms of commitment and involvement – this is the Anglican vocation.

The next most frequently mentioned benefit was the group of replies referring to the advantages of having a guaranteed stipend, and in particular the fact that this was centrally paid, thus ensuring a measure of independence from the congregation. One respondent summed up the situation with the comment "My free church brother is a damn sight less free than I am". Another advantage of the established church related to aspects of Anglicanism itself, in particular its tradition, doctrine and liturgy. Others stressed the importance of the church having a voice at the national level; and having the support and back-up of church structures and law.

It is interesting that the most commonly mentioned *loss* of being a priest in the established church mirrors the most frequently mentioned gain (Table 38). More than a fifth of the respondents said that the expectations placed upon them by the people because of the "cure of all souls", and the obligations of conducting the occasional offices, were a disadvantage of the Anglican church.

TABLE 38. Losses of being a Priest in the Established Church

	No of clergy	% of those who answered (n = 94)
Expectations/obligations in the community	21	22
Church law, structures and personnel	18	19
Image of the C of E	11	12
Government influence on the church	7	7
General decline of C of E	6	6
Other	8	8

Most of those who found that their expectations and obligations in the community had a negative side focused on the occasional offices. Some just referred to their obligations here in a general sense. Others expressed more explicit concern over the issue of being obliged to perform the occasional offices for people with no or minimal religious commitment, and the sense in which the church could therefore become "used", and perhaps even secularised. For one respondent the converse of the widespread demands made by the parish in general was the worry that members of the congregation may receive less care than was their due. As he expressed it "if there is no concentrated effort on church people they may lose out". In a similar vein, another incumbent said that community involvement could "swamp the identity of the church".

The second disadvantage of being a priest in the established church was that category concerned with aspects of the church's law, hierarchy and personnel. Nearly a fifth of respondents mentioned a loss which came under this broad heading. The major way in which the church's structure was found to be frustrating was the loss of freedom, due mainly to canon law and to bureaucracy. Another concern in this general category was that those in the hierarchy were out of touch, and failed to give support and leadership.

Another perceived loss concerned the general image of the Church of England. Several respondents said that for various reasons people had an incorrect image of the established church, especially in terms of its wealth. The fact that the image of the church received by parishioners was to a large extent governed by what went on at national level, rather than locally, was also mentioned. Another important category of "loss" concerns the influence of parliament and the government upon the church, and the ways in which this was seen to be undesirable. There were two aspects to this: the first was the issue of parliament having a say in the making of church law; the other concerned the involvement of government in the choice of bishops.

General Synod

The vast majority of clergy thought that General Synod bore little relation to life at the parish level. Only eight said that there was some relation between parish life and General Synod. This is not perhaps surprising, but what did take us aback was the strength of the views held about General Synod. Several phrases occurred repeatedly in incumbents' answers to the question. A number said that Synod and parish life were "totally unrelated", that Synod was "remote" or "far removed", or that it was "irrelevant".

The cause of Synod seeming so irrelevant to parish life was attributed by some clergy to their parishioners, and by others to Synod itself. As far as the parish was concerned, a number of clergy commented on the fact that their parishioners were simply not interested in the wider church. Others said that their parishioners were only interested when major issues were being debated or issues of practical relevance to themselves. One considered that the whole concept of Synod was wrong as far as his parishioners were concerned:

> The parish still looks to the Bishop. They get and read Synod reports, but they don't see it as authority - they see the Bishop as authority.

One of the key explanations for the irrelevance of General Synod was that it was unrepresentative of parishioners in general:

> The ordinary man in the pew can't go because they won't have
> the time unless retired or whatever.

Another factor was that General Synod was felt to be concerned with
issues unrelated to parish life, and to be unaware of the real problems.
One problem was that many parishioners actively disagreed with Synod
pronouncements, and hence wanted little to do with it. An image of
General Synod as always being at odds with itself also contributed to
disinterest from parishioners. The few clergy who felt that General
Synod did have some relation to parish life thought this way because of
the far-reaching effects of the decisions taken by Synod in relation to
such issues as the ordination of women.

We also asked the clergy what they thought was the significance of
General Synod in the Church of England. This question produced a
wide range of answers. The most common sort of response was from
those who only made criticisms or negative remarks about General
Synod. More than half the respondents came into this category. A
further quarter of the respondents stated some problems with Synod,
although recognising it was necessary or of some significance. In total,
then, more than three quarters of the respondents (78%) had some
criticism of General Synod. In total only just over a third (37%) of clergy
invested Synod with any significance or beneficial role, and it should be
stressed that many of these saw it simply as necessary, rather than
positively beneficial.

Some of those who were dissatisfied with General Synod simply
made negative comments expressing their feelings, rather than giving
any particular reasons. Some of the comments received are reflected in
the following:

> Pathetic, ridiculous, rubbish. The whole thing is a nonsense.
> No benefits whatsoever to the church. Most priests I know feel
> exactly the same.

Most priests, however, gave some reason for their negative view of
Synod, or criticised a particular aspect of it. The comments were very
wide ranging, and several clergy criticised more than one aspect. Table
39 shows the numbers who mentioned each of the main topics which
emerged.

TABLE 39. *Criticisms of General Synod*

	No. of clergy	% of clergy who responded (n = 73)
Unrepresentative	12	16
Opposed to synodical govt.	10	14
Cumbersome/bureaucratic	10	14
Wrong/irrelevant issues	10	14
Should meet less	5	7
Argue/factions	5	7
Too expensive	4	5

The most common complaint to be levelled against General Synod was that it is unrepresentative – this echoes the views of clergy discussed above concerning the relevance of Synod to parish life. Several made comments relating either to the laity who acted as Synod representatives or to the clergy on Synod, and expressed their concern at General Synod becoming biased:

> The problem is getting the right people there. It reflects the running of the church – both General Synod and the PCC are run by the retired middle class. Parish representation would be good if people took part – for example here only the PCC turn up at the AGM and promptly re-elect themselves. The church is run very much by a self-appointed organisation.
>
> Great danger that Synod is infiltrated by those with a strong socialist outlook – a danger of political bias.

The next three criticisms of General Synod were each mentioned by ten of the respondents. The first came from those who, out of principle, were opposed to synodical government. Some felt that democracy was simply not appropriate for church government. Others stressed the need to vest authority primarily in the Bishops or pointed out the tensions and conflicts involved, both theoretical and practical, between synodical and episcopal models of government. The next criticism of General Synod was that it was too cumbersome, hierarchical, and bureaucratic. The final frequent criticism of General Synod was that it concerned itself with the wrong issues.

A quarter of the clergy felt that General Synod was necessary or beneficial but qualified their acceptance with the problems which have been covered above. In particular, some felt that in *theory* Synod was a good idea, but that in practice it failed. Others urged more tolerance of Synod because they felt problems were inherent in any system of church government, and because although it was easy to complain about it, it was harder to find a viable alternative. Those who felt that Synod was necessary or significant gave various reasons for this point of view. One of the most frequent comments made was that General Synod was necessary as a democratic governing body: "ordinary people do get a say in the rules". Linked with this was Synod's significance as a decision making body and as a forum for discussion of a wide range of issues.

Diocesan Synod

The clergy's views of Diocesan Synod were also very varied and hard to classify. In general, they thought diocesan synod was more significant than General Synod, but even so considerably more than half the clergy (58%) were critical in some respect of Diocesan Synod. Interestingly 15% of respondents said that they felt Diocesan Synod was better or more significant than General Synod. It was also clear that the general tenor of the responses was less condemning than those concerning General Synod.

Looking first at the negative aspects of Diocesan Synod which were identified, eight clergy simply said that their criticisms of Diocesan Synod were identical to those concerning General Synod. However, among those who did express their views about Diocesan Synod, the most frequently mentioned complaint was that it did not relate to the parish and to day to day ministry. In total 14 clergy commented along these lines. This echoes the comments concerning General Synod, and many of the remarks made were fairly similar. One respondent working in a remote Dales parish explained more specifically how his Diocesan Synod tended to be urban orientated, thus contributing further to its lack of relevance. Linked to this point, three clergy commented on the way in which Diocesan Synod was particularly irrelevant or inappropriate in rural areas, especially if their parishioners were parochial in their outlook.

The second most common criticism of Diocesan Synod, mentioned by seven respondents, was that it was unrepresentative. This again echoes remarks made by many of the clergy in connection with General Synod. Some respondents specifically said that Diocesan Synod should comprise representatives from every parish, as used to be the case with diocesan conferences. Another criticism of the Diocesan Synod was that it drew clergy away from parish responsibilities, and encouraged them to be too much concerned with "power politics" and promotion.

There was a wide variety of other criticisms. Some incumbents felt that the Diocesan Synod met too frequently, others that it did not have enough power in terms of decision making, and that the issues debated often seemed to have foregone conclusions. One described Diocesan Synod as a good forum, but said that it had "no teeth". Two respondents felt that it was too concerned with financial matters, one that Diocesan Synod was too big, and in a similar vein another priest commented that "Diocesan Synod is not able to be in touch with God's work in every parish". Another incumbent said that his parishioners "still regard Diocesan Synod and the diocese as a whole as a bit of an imposition".

The two main benefits of the synod recognised by the clergy were that it acted as a forum for discussion and as a way to establish and find out the diocesan "view" on matters. Linked to this was the view that it brought clergy and laity together and provided an opportunity for fellowship. As many as fourteen respondents said that they found Diocesan Synod to be more significant than General Synod. The main reason for this was that, despite the criticisms outlined above, it was seen to have more relevance to life at the parish level. This was partly because it was a smaller and more "local" organisation. In addition the Diocesan Synod was seen as more relevant to parish life because it was concerned with finance and other issues which had a direct impact on the parishes.

Conclusions

Our examination of the views of the clergy and the parishioners towards multi-parish benefices indicates that although there are many problems associated with them, this form of parochial organisation is rapidly becoming accepted as the norm. The majority of clergy considered their grouping made sense in geographical terms, although only just over half felt they made sense socially. Many considered that parochialism was an obstacle to the working of their group although several positive aspects of parochialism were also outlined. The ministry of clergy did tend to vary from parish to parish and in particular was often biased towards their home parish. Views on team ministries were varied and around a third of the clergy saw it as a future pattern of ministry in the countryside. The parishioners certainly felt that the grouping of parishes altered the effectiveness of the church, but found the idea of having a full time minister responsible for a group of parishes preferable to the idea of a part-time minister chosen from within their parish or congregation. Two-thirds of the parishioners felt that ideally an individual parish should have a vicar of its own and a similar proportion of the clergy also held this ideal and would prefer to have a single church. It is clear that although the multi-parish benefice is increasingly the norm, many clergy and parishioners still yearn for a more traditional parish structure.

The strength of traditional views associated with the rural church was further demonstrated in connection with attitudes towards the church buildings themselves. Most churches appeared to be in reasonable physical condition and some clergy appeared almost complacent when discussing the financial aspects of church maintenance. Although many clergy felt they were preoccupied with looking after church buildings there was little suppport, either from clergy or parishioners, for the closure of churches if congregations were small. Indeed, many clergy felt that the current pattern of church buildings was a crucial element in the maintenance by the Church of England of a strong presence in the countryside. The historical and architectural importance of parish churches was also thought to be of great importance by clergy and parishioners alike.

When questioned about the levels of church organisation above the benefice the clergy showed a tremendous variety of response. The importance of the deanery was seen, generally, to consist of support and fellowship from neighbouring clergy. Relatively few thought the deanery to be of great value although several thought it should become more important in the future. The diocese was rather more popular than the deanery, especially in terms of the help and support provided by bishops and archdeacons and in the administrative back-up it provided. The views of the clergy on church establishment provided further data on the relative strength of communal and associational models of ministry which we discuss in Chapters 4 and 5. One group of clergy stressed the benefits of ministering to the whole community while another found such obligations to be a disadvantage. The final aspect of church organisation we questioned the clergy about, synodical government, was also by far the least popular. Very few clergy felt the General Synod had any relation with parish life, and the majority felt it to be of little significance in the Church of England.

8

Forms of Worship and Ecumenism

In this chapter we consider one of the most important public expressions of religion, attendance at church services. We then go on to investigate the extent of ecumenism in rural areas. The chapter is divided into three main sections. First of all we investigate the *level* of church attendance using data from our postal survey of all incumbents in the five dioceses. We also assess the *rate* of attendance in different kinds of benefice by relating the numbers attending church to the benefice population. We then go on to consider the type of people who attend church. Making use of data from our survey of the residents of 20 rural parishes, we consider who attends church at both regular Sunday services and at special services such as those associated with Christmas and Harvest. This section concludes with a review of the rural incumbents' views of the make-up of their congregations. The second main section explores the range of services on offer in the dioceses, and this range is compared with the preferences of the rural parishioners. Some of the issues involved in holding services in rural churches are investigated. In particular we focus on the clergy's views on united benefice services and small congregations. The third main section considers the extent and nature of ecumenical cooperation. Evidence is drawn from the three surveys to explore the effects of rural circumstances on ecumenism.

Church Attendance

Levels and Rates of Attendance
The level of church attendance is often considered to be a key issue affecting the Church of England today. It is thought to be one of few ways that the religiosity of the nation, and the popularity of the church

208

can be measured in any meaningful way. Low attendance is frequently identified with lack of success. Suburban churches with regularly large congregations are seen as healthy; small country churches with regular attendances in single figures may be castigated as inefficient failures. It is clearly important, therefore, that any measure of church attendance should be accurate. Yet such figures that are generally available, and frequently quoted, are rather limited in scope or of a very general nature.

In our survey we decided to assess church attendance over four consecutive Sundays in the autumn of 1988: October 16; October 23; October 30 and November 6. These dates were chosen as they avoided the period when most harvest festivals are held, but fall well before the onset of the Christmas season. It is, however, difficult, if not impossible, to class any four Sundays as normal. Usable statistics were provided by 527 of the clergymen who answered our postal questionnaire. Statistics were collected for attendance over the benefice as a whole and collected separately for people aged under 16.

The figures we collected show that the level of attendance varies from diocese to diocese, between town and country, and is associated to a considerable degree with the churchmanship of the incumbent. Overall, the average weekly attendance per benefice, was 129 people. Lincoln was the diocese with the lowest attendance (107) whereas the remaining four dioceses all had weekly attendances of more than 130. When attendance was considered in relation to the rurality of the benefice we found that it was much the lowest in the totally rural benefices (80 people a week). Indeed weekly attendance rates in small country town and part urban benefices were both more than twice that found in the totally rural benefices. There is hardly surprising, of course, because the totally rural benefices tend to have much smaller populations than the other kinds. To investigate this phenomenon more closely we can consider the relationship between church attendance and population at the benefice level (Table 40).

The table shows that there is a very close relationship between benefice population and attendance. As might be expected, the more people there are in a benefice, the greater the attendance is likely to be. Average weekly attendance in the largest benefices is almost four times as great as that found in small benefices with less than a 1,000 inhabitants. Size is not, however, the only factor affecting the level of attendance. When we looked at attendance in relation to the churchmanship of the incumbent, for example, we found that evangelical incumbents were

TABLE 40. *Average Weekly Benefice Attendance, by Benefice Population*

	Mean Population Attendance
All Benefices	128.8
less than 1,000	55.8
1,000-1,999	81.9
2,000-4,999	122.7
5,000-9,999	160.1
10,000+	200.6

likely to attract considerably greater attendances than catholics. Overall, benefices with conservative and open evangelical incumbents had average weekly attendances of over 160 people; the equivalent figure for benefices with traditional catholic incumbents was 110.

So far, we have considered the numbers of people attending church without relating this directly to the populations of the benefices. Table 41 shows the *proportion* of the total population of a benefice attending church per Sunday. This figure was calculated by using the average weekly benefice attendance and the total benefice population. The figures here will tend to overestimate the proportion of people attending church as we have not been able to take account of the number of people attending church more than once on the same Sunday. However, we consider that this will have little overall effect on the percentages.

TABLE 41. *The Proportion of the Total Population of the Benefices Attending Church*

Percentage attending church	Number of benefices	Percentage of benefices
less than 1%	40	7.6
1 to 1.9%	109	20.6
2 to 2.9%	102	19.4
3 to 3.9%	68	12.9
4 to 4.9%	72	13.7
5 to 5.9%	46	8.7
6 to 6.9%	31	5.9
7% or more	59	11.2
(average = 3.9%)	527	100.0

This table shows that the average weekly church attendance overall is only 3.9% of the total population. This average disguises considerable variations from benefice to benefice. For example, in 7.6% of the benefices, less than 1% of the population attend church on a Sunday. Moreover for almost half the benefices, the attendance rate is less than 3% of the total population. In just over a quarter (25.8%) of the benefices, attendance is greater than 5% of the population. Put starkly, this low proportion might be interpreted as an astonishing indictment of the weakness of the Church of England today. In a later section, we will examine data from our survey of rural parishioners which will help to ameliorate this picture.

The more one examines the attendance statistics, the more fascinating they become. When the diocesan figures were considered, for example, it was found that the dioceses of Gloucester (5.2%) and Truro (4.9%) had relatively high overall attendance rates, whereas Durham's (2.9%) was particularly low. It was found that the highest attendance rates tended to be in benefices with an evangelical and especially a conservative evangelical incumbent while the lowest rates were in benefices with catholic, and especially modern catholic, incumbents. The most interesting results are seen, however, when we consider attendance rates and the rurality and size of the benefice (Table 42).

TABLE 42. Average Benefice Attendance per Sunday, by Rurality and Benefice Population

Rurality	Mean Attendance	Population	Mean Attendance
Totally rural	5.3	< 1,000	8.1
Partly rural	4.0	1,000–1,999	5.5
Small country town	3.8	2,000–4,999	3.9
Part urban/non rural	2.9	5,000–9,999	2.4
Urban	2.3	10,000+	1.4

There is a dramatic relationship between rurality and the percentage of the population attending church on a Sunday. The totally rural benefices had by far the highest proportion attending (5.3%), followed by the partly rural benefices and small country towns. The lowest attendance rates were in the urban benefices which overall had a rate of attendance less than half that found in the totally rural benefices. That the key factor operating here is the size of the benefice is indicated by the right hand column of Table 42 where a most striking relationship is shown. The general rule is that the smaller the size of the benefice, the larger the proportion of people living within the benefice will attend church. In the 46 smallest benefices of less than 1,000 people, for example, the average benefice attendance was as high as 8.1%. This was over double the average attendance rate for all benefices of 3.9%. At the other end of the scale, in the 72 largest benefices of over 10,000 people, the average benefice attendance per Sunday was as low as 1.4%. This was considerably less than half the mean attendance rate for all benefices.

The information on church attendance clearly shows that the large congregations tend to be found in small country towns and suburban areas of England. It was no surprise, to find that the smallest congregations were to be found in the most rural areas, nor that rural congregations tended to have a rather lower proportion of young people compared to suburban congregations. When the proportion of the total population attending church was considered it was found, almost paradoxically, that it was in the smaller benefices that the highest rates of church attendance were to be found. This result points to the importance of the basic strengths of the rural church which we frequently come back to in this study, namely the way in which its parochial structure has enabled the rural areas to maintain a relatively high number of clergy and churches.

One of the most frequently raised church issues is the extent to which young people are attracted to church services. We collected information on church attendance over the four Sundays by people aged 16 years or less. The results show that attendance by young people varies according to the rurality of the benefice. Overall, a fifth (20.6%) of attenders were aged 16 or under, but this proportion varied from 18.4% in the case of totally rural parishes, to 24.2% in the case of the part-urban parishes. Further research is needed to explore the reasons for the relatively low attendance by young people in the most rural areas. Various factors are likely to be operating here, ranging from the more traditional types of services which tend to be offered in rural benefices (see later) to the relatively sparse population of young people in rural areas, especially during term time when many of the children of more wealthy families are away at school.

There is still much work to be carried out in order to understand the reasons for the geographical variations in the levels and rates of church attendance. One huge area that demands detailed examination is the historical geography of church attendance. The myth of almost complete church attendance in rural parishes in the late Victorian and Edwardian periods is frequently punctured by tantalisingly small scale and local assessments of attendance. Bennett (c1914) writing on rural life in Oxfordshire in the period immediately preceding the First World War, for example, noted that church attendance varied greatly, but that in his view the normal number of Sunday attendances at both church and chapel, amount to around 25-35% of the adult population. It is to be hoped that Gill's (1989) work on the history of church attendance in north east England will encourage further work in this field in order that full assessments of church attendance over a long time scale can be made. It must not be forgotten, however that such rates and levels are only broadbrush statistics which are easy to misinterpret. In the next section we explore in greater detail the nature of church attendance in rural areas by making use of results from our survey of rural parishioners.

Who Attends Church?

Information provided by the clergy has enabled us to present various statistics on the level and rates of church attendance. In this section we go into this subject in greater depth by making use of information gathered during our survey of 486 parishioners in twenty rural benefices (See Appendix). All those interviewed were asked how often, on average, they attended a regular Sunday service at church.

TABLE 43. Attendance of Sunday Services by Rural Parishioners

Attend Sunday service	General sample		Church sample		Total sample	
	No	%	No	%	No	%
1/week or more	25	7	39	26	64	13
<1/week-1/month	29	9	52	35	81	17
<1/month-3/yr	24	7	18	12	42	9
< 3/year	38	11	10	7	48	10
Not attend	222	66	29	20	251	51
Total	338	100	148	100	486	100

If we consider the general sample first, it is immediately apparent that two-thirds of the adult inhabitants in these rural parishes do not attend Sunday services. Seven per cent attend at least once a week, and nine per cent attend between less than once a week and once a month. The church electoral roll sample shows a very different picture with 61% of those interviewed attending church at least once a month or more. However, even here, only just over a quarter (26%) attend at least once a week, and perhaps more surprisingly, as many as a fifth of those on the church electoral roll do not attend Sunday services.

We can now go on to see what type of people tend to attend church, by looking at the characteristics of the attenders drawn from the random general sample. Our survey confirms that a considerably higher proportion of women attend church than men. A fifth of all women parishioners attended church once a month or more compared to only just over a tenth (11%) of men. Furthermore, three-quarters of the men interviewed did not attend Sunday services, compared to 58% of women. When the age of the parishioners is considered we find that there is, perhaps surprisingly, little connection bewteen age and attendance. For example, the proportion not attending church only varies from 61% for the 35-44 age group, to 70% for those aged 55 years or older. If we consider the frequency of attendance, however, the age groups with the highest proportion attending at least once a week are those aged 45-54 and the over 65s.

A more interesting pattern emerges when the length of time that a person has lived in the parish is considered. The most striking result is that the group who have always lived in the parish has the highest proportion (76%) of non-attenders. A high proportion of those who had lived in the parish for 10 years or less also did not attend church. In other words, it is those who have moved into the parish, and been resident for eleven years or more which are most likely to be church attenders. One explanation for this might be that a relatively high proportion of the middle-class incomers who have had time to settle down and become involved in parish life are church attenders. This is to some extent confirmed by our findings on the relationship between social class and attendance. We found that just over three-quarters (76%) of the non-manual workers had not attended church over the past year, compared to only just over half of the upper-middle (54%) and professional (55%) classes. Moreover, there was a direct and clear relationship between social class and frequency of attendance. Thus over a quarter (27%) of upper-middle category respondents attended church at least once a month, compared to 23% of class 1; 20% of class 3; 16% of class 5 and only eight per cent of class 6.

When we considered the relationship between employment status, as opposed to social class, and attendance it was found to be complicated. The groups with the lowest levels of attendance are the retired (29%) and those in full time employment (30%). The perhaps surprisingly low proportion of retired people attending church is explained by the high proportion of elderly people who are likely to find it difficult to get to church. Those with the highest rates of attendance are housewives (49%). Housewives attend church far more frequently than the other groups: 30% attend once a month or more often, this is more than double the equivalent figure (13%) for those in full time employment and much higher than the figure (17%) for the retired.

Attendance at Special Services

So far, we have been considering attendance of normal Sunday services. Account must now be taken of the number of respondents who did not necessarily go to church on a regular basis, but who did attend church services on special occasions. The interviewees were asked whether they had attended any specific church services in the last year. The specific services mentioned were (i) weddings, baptisms and funerals; (ii) services over the Christmas period; (iii) services over the Easter period; (iv) Harvest Festival and (v) Remembrance Sunday. Table 44 shows that 70% of the general sample attended church at the time of a wedding, baptism or funeral. Of the specific services, Christmas was the most popular with well over a third (39%) of the general sample attending at this time. The second most important special service was Harvest (31%). Easter was attended by just under a quarter (24%) of the respondents and Remembrance, only slightly lower, by a fifth. Attendance of these church services by respondents from the church electoral roll sample was consistently higher. The great majority (86%) had attended at least one wedding, baptism or funeral in the past year, and 80% attended a Christmas service. Easter and Harvest Festival were equally popular (72% and 71%), and over half (53%) attended a Remembrance service. Nonetheless, considering this is a sample drawn from the church electoral roll, it is surprising to find as many as 28% not attending at Easter or 20% at Christmas.

As might be expected from the earlier section dealing with attendance at Sunday services, we found that for all these special services women are more likely to attend than men. Interestingly, the types of service which were most evenly balanced in this respect were those associated with

TABLE 44. *Attendance at Special Services*

Type of service	Whether attend	General sample		Church sample		Total sample	
		No	%	No	%	No	%
Wedding,	yes	238	70	127	86	365	75
Baptism, Funeral	no	98	29	21	14	119	24
Christmas	yes	133	39	118	80	251	51
	no	204	60	30	20	234	48
Easter	yes	83	24	106	72	189	39
	no	254	75	41	28	295	60
Harvest	yes	105	31	105	71	210	43
	no	232	68	43	29	275	56
Remembrance	yes	67	20	79	53	146	30
	no	269	79	66	45	335	68
Total		341		148		489	

Note: the totals do not add up to 100% as a small number of people, never more than 2%, did not answer

rites of passage, but even here attendance by women was nine per cent higher than that by men. The service where the gender difference is least was Harvest Festival, where the male attendance rate was 67% of the female rate. At Christmas and Remembrance the attendance rate was 57% that of the women, and for Easter, the attendance rate (51%) was half that of women.

We also found that the age of respondents influences whether they are likely to attend particular types of service. As might be expected, attendance at the 'rites of passage' services was high for all age groups. However, the figures varied substantially. Thus as many as 90% of those aged between 45 and 54 had attended a wedding, baptism or funeral in the last year, compared to only 65% of those aged 35-44. Christmas attendance was highest (60%) for those aged between 35 and 54, possibly as they are the age group most likely to be taking children. It was lowest for the young adults (39%), and also low for those aged 65 or more (48%). Less than a fifth of the those aged 18-34 attended a service at Easter, whereas for the other age groups the proportion attending was consistently between 42% and 47%. A similar pattern occurred with Harvest Festival, although attendance was generally rather higher than Easter. The greatest link between age and attendance was shown by Remembrance services. Attendance by the young adults was low (17%), but it rose with each age group to 40% of those aged 65 or more.

The relationship between social class and attendance at special services was of particular interest. The one group of services for which this is not true is that associated with the rites of passage. Here, over 70% of all social classes had attended at least one such service in the past year. A rather different pattern emerges with Christmas services. Over two-thirds (67%) of the professional and managerial respondents had attended church at Christmas, compared to only just over a third (38%) of the manual workers. The relationship, here, is not simple, however, as 63% of the working non-manual group attended at Christmas, compared to 59% of the lower middle class. Over the Easter period, just over half (51%) the professional and managerial respondents had attended, compared to less than a quarter (24%) of the manual workers. Similarly half the number of manual workers (20%) compared to professional and managerial respondents (40%) attended at a Remembrance service. At Harvest, there is rather more of a balance between the different social classes, with 43% of the professionals and 38% of the manual workers attending.

Clergy Views on the Make-up of Their Congregations

The rural clergy interviewed were asked whether there were any groups in the parish which were not represented, or were under-represented, in their congregations. Their answers are quite difficult to interpret as many named more than one group of people, but it is clear that most of those interviewed felt that there were gaps of various sorts in their congregations, with only 13% stating that a good cross section of the local community attended church. Most of the groups which clergy mentioned as being under-represented were defined in terms of age. In total 60% of clergy cited some category of young people, ranging from young families through to children. The most frequently mentioned specific category was teenagers, cited by over a fifth of respondents. In some cases the problem of attracting teenagers was seen as essentially no different to that in urban churches. As one priest remarked "teenagers – but then where does one get them?"

However, other respondents felt that there were particular difficulties in trying to conduct youth work with this age group in rural areas. In general these related to the small numbers involved and scattered populations, with consequent transport difficulties, and also the problems that arose when schooling was based in a nearby town, which therefore became the focus of activities rather than the village. One respondent thought that the types of service on offer were offputting:

> Even the few [children] there are in the parishes don't come. It's easy to see why – Book of Common Prayer Holy Communion and Matins will turn young people off.

It is interesting to note that relatively few clergy specifically mentioned children as a missing group – only eight per cent – compared to those who mentioned teenagers. The increase in the number of Family Services held in the sample of parishes may be one factor in this, although some clergy felt that Family Services only generated a following for that particular service. Young couples – often specifically without children – and young families, were the other two groups which were mentioned as being under represented within the general "young people" grouping. Some felt that only if the couple had children would they attend church, and even then only perhaps for the rites of passage, and in particular baptism. Another view was that young children were a highly inhibiting factor on their parents' attendance at church.

The other categories to be mentioned were not defined in age terms, but rather in terms of occupation, length of time in the parish, gender, and social class. The most frequently mentioned of these groups was the category which included residents of council housing, and those variously referred to as "the lower social classes" or "working class" people. As one priest said, he was failing to attract the "real working class people, the old labouring people, the unchurched". One incumbent expressed the view that this was because of the middle class image of the church:

> There are fewer from the housing estate, though this is changing since I've been here. It's now not thought that the church is only for owner occupiers.

At the opposite extreme of the social spectrum, three incumbents mentioned that they had problems attracting the upper classes, or as one put it "the county set".

In different benefices both locals and incomers were cited as under represented groups in the congregation. Six clergy felt that the group variously described as incomers, commuters, or upwardly mobile people, were hard to attract, mainly because of other commitments, and in some cases lack of full time residence in the community. One described the missing group as "the upwardly mobile, because they're busy sailing, or washing the car, or something". By contrast, three incumbents explicitly stated that they had problems attracting local people. In one parish in Cornwall, this was because of traditional loyalties among local people to the Methodist church, although the clergyman concerned pointed out that "the locals come for the rites of passage". Farmers, a specific element of the 'locals' category, were described as a missing group by five clergymen. One noted that:

> The farming population is not very well represented. Of 30 farms, only two families are closely involved, and another three only marginally. The others don't come for Harvest Festival - the farmers don't relate to the village.

The final important category considered by clergy to be under represented in their congregation was that of men. They were mentioned by six clergy, four of them in Durham diocese. One incumbent described the social tradition which had built up in the villages in his parishes and which contributed to the problem:

> In all the villages here it's not the done thing for men to be mixed up with the church - they leave at the age of 11. But men will turn out in great numbers for funerals. Men are not against the church - there's no anti-church or anti-clerical feeling, it just isn't the done thing.

The general conclusion to be drawn from the answers to this question is that the vast majority of respondents were able to cite some group in the parish who were under represented in terms of church attendance. By far the most common group to be under represented was young people in general, and in particular teenagers. This partly reflects the national situation, but also the more specific problems of conducting youth work in rural areas. In general, the missing age groups were in the middle of the age range, rather than at either extreme - young children and elderly people being mentioned relatively rarely. By contrast, it was the middle range of the *social* spectrum who were most likely to attend.

One point that needs to be stressed is that it was apparent from some of the responses that the incumbent himself could be largely responsible for determining the make up of the congregation. This was especially the case with youth work, which could be very dependent on the skills and interests of the priest in question. As one respondent commented "Sadly, my predecessor killed the work with children. He inherited a youth club of 60-70 children. In two years nothing was left."

As a subsidiary question, clergy were asked whether there had been any changes in either the size or nature of their congregations since they had been in the parishes. Sixty five clergy responded to this question. It is hard to classify the answers by respondent as many clergy gave separate answers for each of the different parishes in their charge. In many cases the situation was not uniform across the benefice – more often numbers in one parish would be changing, and in the others static.

The most common response was that numbers had increased – this was mentioned by two fifths of clergy as being the situation in at least one of their parishes. However, it was obvious that in many cases this was a slow and undramatic increase, although some clergy did point to situations where the congregation had grown more markedly. By contrast, only six clergy – less than one in ten of those responding – noted a decline in numbers in any of their parishes. Where this was recorded, it was sometimes in part due to demographic changes such as an ageing population. As one priest explained "there is a decrease at H.... because as people die off they're not replaced".

Despite the problems in reaching young people generally, some respondents did seem to be making headway in this area. Nine said that the number of young people in the congregation had increased, and eight specifically mentioned an increase in the number of young families and children. However, as was noted above, this increase sometimes represented attendance at Family Services alone, rather than a more complete involvement in the church. The only other group to be cited as increasingly important in the congregation by a significant number of clergy was those who were newcomers to the parish. This may simply reflect the fact that such people represent an increasing proportion of the rural population, although this needs to be held in tension with the finding that some clergy found incomers to be an under-represented group in their congregations.

Church Services

The Range of Services Offered

In order to set our discussions of the views of parishioners and clergy on different types of services into context, we had first to obtain data about the range of services available in our five dioceses. We obtained this information by means of our postal questionnaire. The incumbents were asked to state the total number of services held in the four week period Sunday October 16th to Sunday 6th November inclusive. They were asked to specify the different types of service held. The three main categories provided were Communion, Morning prayer or Matins and Evensong or Evening Prayer. Within these three categories, provision was made for the incumbent to note whether services were BCP, ASB, 'Family' or other. In addition, incumbents were able to note whether they held any services that did not fit into any of the three main categories. In other words, we can present here a unique overview of the range and type of services held in the five dioceses.

Table 45 shows the average number of services per benefice for the three main types of service held over the four Sundays. This information is shown taking account of both the rurality of the benefice and the churchmanship of the incumbent. The bottom row of figures shows the average number of services for all five dioceses. They reveal that there were 14.2 services per benefice and 3.6 services per Sunday. In terms of number, communion services formed well over half (59%) of the total services, and evening services (24%) were more frequent than morning ones (13%). The dominance of communion services indicates the success of the liturgical movement as already discussed in Chapter 2.

In general there is little connection between the rurality of a benefice and the number of services that are likely to be held in it. The main exception to this rule is the situation in benefices classed as small country towns. The table shows that these benefices had consistently more communion, morning and evening services than any other type of benefice. Those with relatively low numbers of services were the totally rural or urban. The greater frequency of services in small country towns is clearly connected with the availability of a wide range of staff in these benefices as shown in Chapter 6.

The table shows that there is a very strong relationship between the churchmanship of the incumbent and the number of communion services. Benefices with traditional catholic clergy had a mean of 9.1

TABLE 45. *The Average Number of Different Types of Service per Benefice, by Rurality and Churchmanship*

	Communion	Morning	Evening	All
Rurality				
Totally rural	8.2	1.8	3.0	13.4
Partly rural	8.6	1.5	3.6	14.7
Small country town	9.4	2.3	4.0	16.5
Part urban/non rural	8.8	1.7	3.2	14.8
Urban	7.6	1.4	3.3	13.0
Churchmanship				
Conserv. evangelical	6.2	3.2	3.6	13.4
Open evangelical	7.7	2.8	3.5	14.8
Central	8.4	1.4	3.2	13.8
Modern catholic	9.0	1.4	3.3	14.4
Trad. catholic	9.1	1.8	3.5	15.1
All Benefices	8.4	1.7	3.4	14.2

Note: averages for family services and 'other' services are excluded from this table

communion services over the four sundays; central clergy had 8.4 and conservative evangelicals had 6.2. Although conservative evangelicals have the lowest mean number of communion services, the fact that they hold on average more than one per Sunday shows the effectiveness of the Parish Communion movement. The relationship between churchmanship and the number of morning services (non-communion) is the mirror image of that with communion services. Evangelical incumbents have considerably more morning services than catholic and central incumbents. Indeed conservative evangelicals have over double the number of such services compared to central and modern catholic clergy. Evening services are much more consistently held than either communion or morning services.

Although our survey results show that there are important variations in the frequency with which different types of service are held, the situation becomes even more interesting when the forms of the different types of service are considered. We asked the clergy to specify the number of services following both the *Book of Common Prayer* and the

Alternative Service Book. The average numbers of these different forms of service are given in Table 46. If we consider the figures for all benefices first, it can be seen that ASB communion is by far the most frequent form of service, with on average six services per benefice over the four Sundays, followed by BCP evensong and BCP communion. The reverse is true for both morning and evening prayer where the Prayer Book was more frequently used. Information was also gathered for family services, which had a low mean of 0.4 services per benefice over the four Sundays.

TABLE 46. *Average Number of Different Types of Service per Benefice Over the Four Sundays by Rurality and Churchmanship*

Rurality	Holy communion		Morning prayer		Evening prayer	
	BCP	ASB	BCP	ASB	BCP	ASB
Totally rural	2.3	5.5	1.0	.2	2.6	.3
Partly rural	1.8	6.0	.9	.3	2.6	.7
Small country town	2.4	6.0	1.2	.5	3.2	.5
Part urban/non rural	1.5	6.5	.3	.6	1.6	1.3
Urban	.8	6.4	.3	.6	2.0	1.0
Churchmanship						
Conserv. evangelical	2.5	3.2	1.1	.9	2.1	1.0
Open evangelical	2.4	4.8	.9	.5	2.1	1.0
Central	2.0	5.8	.8	.2	2.5	.5
Modern catholic	1.2	7.2	.5	.5	2.5	.6
Trad. catholic	1.5	6.9	.9	.5	2.7	.7
All benefices	1.8	6.0	.8	.4	2.4	.7

For some forms of service, the relationship between rurality and the forms of service held was very strong indeed. Morning prayer and evening prayer are held much more frequently in rural and small country town benefices than urban ones. BCP communion, on the other hand, seems to be especially dominant in small country towns and rare in both the extreme rural and urban benefices. Both ASB evensong and matins are inversely correlated with rurality. The type of service most often used, ASB communion, is popular across all types of benefice, with a tendency to be more frequent in the urban benefices.

The churchmanship of the incumbent is also a key factor in determining the frequency of different communion rites in the benefices. Evangelical clergy, for example, were more likely to take BCP communion services than catholic incumbents, while the latter were more likely to hold ASB communion services. Perhaps surprisingly, the group with the greatest use of family communion services were the traditional catholics. The conservative and open evangelical incumbents were much more likely to hold morning family services than were other types of respondent.

We may therefore conclude that both the rurality of the benefice and the churchmanship of the incumbent strongly influence the likelihood of different types and forms of services taking place within a benefice. Overall, it is clear that ASB communion was by far the most frequent service, followed by BCP evensong and BCP communion. One fascinating result is the considerably different profiles of service types for the five dioceses. For example, twice as many BCP communion services were held on average over the four Sundays in Gloucester diocese compared to Durham while Truro had almost four times the number of BCP morning prayer services than Durham. There is no room to discuss these diocesan variations in any great detail, but over the country as a whole there are quite considerable geographical variations in the types and forms of services taking place.

Preferred Type of Service

It is now possible to compare the range of services held with the preferences expressed by the residents of our twenty rural parishes. Those who attended Sunday services were asked to specify which type of service they most liked attending. Their answers are summarised in Table 47.

The most popular service by far was parish communion. This was followed by evensong and matins or morning prayer. Family services and early said communion were both rather less popular, and five per cent of the sample said they had no preference at all. If we compare these preferences with the frequency of services as shown in Table 45 it is interesting to see that the rank order is the same. In other words, the current range of services offered by incumbents is roughly in line with the preferences expressed by their parishioners.

We then went on to enquire which form of service the church attenders preferred, giving prompts for BCP and ASB. The results given

TABLE 47. *The Preferred Type of Service*

Type of Service	No	%
Parish communion	68	42
Evensong	39	24
Matins/morning prayer	33	20
Early said communion	20	12
Family service	22	13
Other	10	6
No preference	8	5
Refused/don't know	3	2

Note: although there were 163 attending Anglicans, some specified more than one service

clearly demonstrate the continued strength of support for the BCP. Forty five per cent said they preferred the Prayer Book, 26% expressed no preference and only 22% supported the ASB. This is interesting as it confirms that, in rural areas at least, the incumbents are increasing the proportion of ASB services rather faster than the parishioners might prefer. In general, it was the older respondents, aged 45 years or more, who tended to be in favour of BCP services, while the younger age-groups were more likely to express no preference.

Changes to the Pattern of Services

The rural clergy were asked for the reasons for the present pattern of Sunday services and whether the current pattern and type of services, their frequency and their timings had been inherited, reorganised, or resulted from a union of benefices. The answers we received showed that though a fifth of all respondents said that they had simply inherited the pattern of services from their predecessor, the great majority had made some changes. In many cases these were modifications of the inherited pattern, but a quarter of the respondents had made changes which they considered to be fundamental.

The most common changes concerned the types of service held, and in particular the introduction of family services which were in many cases non-eucharistic. Evensong was also frequently mentioned as a candidate for change. Seven clergy had reduced the number of evensongs, one commenting rather plaintively that "we used to have evensong but it didn't work - we kept trying, and gave it up". In contrast, five incumbents said that they had increased the number of evensongs, or had reintroduced the service after it had lapsed.

Another set of responses was concerned with changes to the frequency with which the eucharist was held. Slightly more incumbents were explicitly concerned to increase the importance of the eucharist than to lessen it. In practice however, it is likely that some of the non-eucharistic family services which were introduced may have been at the expense of communion services. It is not possible to tell from this question whether the overall trend is for the eucharist to become more or less important, although the more general increase in the prevalence of holy communion across the various traditions over the last 40 years must be borne in mind. Changes to the frequency with which the eucharist was held tended to depend a lot on the churchmanship of the individual incumbent, and the extent to which inherited patterns of worship fitted in with this. Some priests who took over incumbencies where there had been a weak tradition of communion services felt it necessary to increase the number of celebrations. Others reduced the number of holy communions and increased the number of non-eucharistic services, in order to broaden the appeal of the church. One priest commented that "we started a family service so that there would be some non-eucharistic services for non-confirmed people".

A second type of response referred to changes in the *timing* of services. In general, these comments were made by clergy in multi-parish benefices who were striving to arrive at a service pattern which was both workable and which suited their congregations. Some of these clergy were concerned about the consistency in service time and type from week to week in each parish. One view was that "the service in church ought to be the same time each Sunday". Others felt that this was not possible, especially in large multi-parish benefices. One incumbent therefore ended up with "different services held at different times each Sunday". Another described the pattern of services in his four parish benefice as "a bit of a railway timetable" but said "it's the only way to work it - you can't have set services every week". Another problem in multi-parish benefices occurred when each church wanted the "prime time" service preferably, of course, with the incumbent officiating.

In some cases the pattern of services was dictated by the number of staff available. One respondent had had to reduce the number of services because he became incumbent of the parish in which previously he had been assisting as NSM to the last incumbent, thus effectively reducing the number of staff by one. Some incumbents, who currently had curates or readers, guarded against the possibility of total disruption to the service pattern if such help should be lost by designing service patterns which could be worked by the incumbent alone, and therefore could be carried on without alteration. One incumbent who expected that his curate would not be replaced commented:

> It was set up to run as a one priest parish even though we've got two. It's sensible because when the curate leaves the pattern will stay the same.

There was obviously a sense, therefore, in which some clergy felt that a stable pattern of services was very important, even to the extent of preferring not to maximise the use of current staff resources rather than risking change.

A few clergy commented on the manner in which changes to the service pattern had taken place and who had instigated them. In some cases the clergy had obviously listened to the views of parishioners and were seeking to involve them in decisions. In one case, for example, the vicar stated that "I revived the 8.00am at one parish - I try to give them what they like." Indeed, two respondents had gone as far as carrying out questionnaire surveys in order to find out the views of their congregations concerning the types and times of services, and had made alterations as a result. In other parishes decisions were made with the PCC or church wardens:

> When the other two parishes were added on I got all the churchwardens around a table with a blank timetable and told them to put it together.

At the other end of the spectrum were the incumbents who worked out changes without consultation. One priest went so far as to say "I am the pope in my parish. I tell them which services are held". Finally, some clergy expressed a more generally cautious attitude towards changing services. Several referred to the fact that whatever changes were to be made, it needed to be done slowly, and not on immediate arrival in the parish. Thus one described the process of change as "evolution not revolution", and another remarked that "I waited a long time before I changed anything".

One popular caricature of the rural clergyman is that he dashes around his churches on a Sunday morning so quickly that he barely has time to chat with his parishioners. In order to check whether there was any truth in this theory, the clergy were asked whether their pattern of services was constrained by pressures of time. Many of those who answered this question said that they did feel pressured on a Sunday this being especially true of those with three or more churches. One priest with three churches simply said "Sundays are gruelling", and another, also with three parishes, commented that he was "completely 100%" constrained by time, and had to drop one of his services. He added that fortunately his parishioners "are sensible, and know that I am stretched to the limit". One set a limit on the number of services he took in his four-parish benefice on the basis that he could not effectively take more than three services on a Sunday.

Most of the comments, however, related more specifically to the way in which having to rush between services affected both the services, and in particular, the time for socialising afterwards, which many incumbents obviously viewed as vital. Other clergy remarked upon the problems of not being able to make it from one church to another on time. One commented:

> You feel like a performer when you arrive at church and all the cars are outside, and people are waiting for you to begin.

The situation was exacerbated in very rural areas by the sheer physical difficulty of getting from one church to another in a short time along narrow country lanes. In some areas of Truro diocese tourist traffic increased this difficulty in summer. However, the problems of arriving late could be alleviated by the help of others; one incumbent of three churches praised his churchwardens at being so good at getting everything ready for him as he dashed between 8.30, 9.30, and 11am services. Another said "it's better now I have a lay reader – he can start the service if I am late".

Perhaps the main conclusion to be drawn from this assessment of the clergy's views on the current pattern of services is the remarkable lack of innovation. Although more than three quarters of the clergy interviewed had made some changes to the patterns of services they inherited, in most cases these were minor alterations. It is clear that in multi-parish benefices it could be very hard to arrive at a workable pattern of services which was also acceptable to the separate parishes. Moreover many clergy felt constrained by time on Sundays, especially in terms of not being able to take full advantage of the time after services to socialise with their parishioners. The general consensus seemed to be that a stable service pattern was desirable. Indeed, some clergy felt it so important to guard against change that they arranged a service pattern that could withstand a decline in staffing levels.

Services in Multi-parish Groups

In this section we touch on the issue of the organisation of rural churches which is dealt with in detail in Chapter 7. Here we are concerned with whether people attend church services in churches other than their parish church. The 65 rural clergy with multi-parish benefices, or recently united parishes, were asked about the extent to which people living in multi-parish benefices attended services at churches in other parishes in the group. This is obviously a crucial factor for clergy attempting to establish workable service patterns in such benefices, where it may not be physically possible for each church to have a service every week.

The vast majority of clergy did say that there was some movement between parishes for services, but nearly all answered in very guarded terms, saying that the amount of movement was very small and infrequent, and often restricted to certain services. Very few were able to respond in such a wholehearted manner as one clergyman who said "yes, people do - it's just part of life". Many described the extent of attendance at other churches as taking place only by "a handful" or "one or two". Others said that it was "exceptional" and was only undertaken "reluctantly". At least six incumbents said that very few travelled between parishes, but there was evidence of a certain committed core who did support services, wherever they were held.

Several clergy were more specific concerning the occasions upon which people would move between churches. Six said that people would attend the regular services in other churches in the benefice, if the particular time or type of service suited them. By contrast, five clergy said that people only attended services at other churches when they were formal united benefice services, and another four that this mixing only took place on festivals and other special occasions. A further five clergy referred to variations between parishes in the extent to which mixing took place. It was evident that in some multi-parish benefices one parish was less inclined to mix than the others. The following quotations suggest that the relationships within certain benefices were extraordinarily byzantine:

> It's one sided if it happens. There used to be some people who
> went to H... Evensong, but it was never reciprocated. One
> Evensong at H..., all the congregation were from S...
>   In O... and W... if there's no service in their own church, they
> won't go to the other. But G... people [without their own church]
> will go to either W... or O...

Some clergy gave an indication of the extent to which any movement
between parishes was increasing. Of those who answered the question,
responses were almost equally divided between those who said there was
no change, and those who felt that attendance at other churches was on
the increase. However, two incumbents expressed the view that
encouraging attendance at other churches was not necessarily a good
thing. One simply said that "I do not favour eclecticism", which he
presumably felt might result from pursuing such a policy unreservedly.
Another commented on the need for parish loyalty.

In the majority of multi-parish benefices, some sort of united service
for the whole group was held on at least one occasion. Considerably
more than half the clergy said that they held united services apart from
at festival times, and in total over two thirds said that they held them at
some time in the year. Just over a fifth of respondents said that they did
not hold united benefice services at any time. The most common time
to hold a united benefice service was on the fifth Sunday of the month.
In this way group services could be held without disrupting the usual
monthly service pattern, a consideration which at least one incumbent
felt was important, thus implying that united benefice services were of
secondary importance to regular parish services. Some clergy furnished
other details concerning these fifth Sunday services. In some cases the
united service was the only one to be held in the benefice on that day.
Often the service rotated around the parishes, and some respondents said
that they used the occasion to bring in an outside preacher.

Several of the clergy who did not hold united services gave reasons
for this. In some cases the decision was based on past experience in other
parishes, where united services had not worked. Others, while not
relating their decisions to past experience, still felt that such services were
inappropriate and likely to fail, because people would simply not attend.
Two incumbents, whose benefices included both small country town
and rural parishes, felt that united services were inappropriate because

of the size differential between the two congregations. One of these incumbents also commented on the practical difficulty of the smaller parish church ever being able to host a reciprocal service. Another incumbent simply said that he had no building large enough in his parishes to hold any united services.

Respondents were also asked to comment on how well their united benefice services worked. Opinion seemed to be fairly evenly divided. Eleven clergy said that they did not go very well, or commented that people did not attend. Ten said that they worked "alright" or that they were "OK", and nine respondents were fairly positive and said that group services worked well. Most of the comments came from those whose services did not go well, and in general related to the fact that people were not prepared to move to attend services at another church, either because of transport difficulties, or because of parish loyalties:

> They don't work well. People will not move. People at C... are older, and not many have cars, but largely it's because there's not the will to come here.

Again, as with the question of general attendance at other churches in the group, some parishes seemed more reluctant to join in united benefice services than others. In one benefice with five parishes, the incumbent explained that one parish would simply not join in with the united benefice service, demanding that it had its own separate service at the same time, in order not to break their routine. In order to overcome parish loyalties and a reluctance to move, two respondents said that they put people from the churches not hosting the service on the rota for reading and other duties, to ensure that they would turn up.

To summarise this section, there seems to be little evidence that multi-parish benefices are truly acting as "united" benefices in terms of people moving between parishes to attend services. Most respondents commented that attendance at other churches in the group was generally limited to a few people, and often to specific occasions. Moreover, although nearly two thirds held some sort of united benefice service, these were often infrequent and relatively few clergy were particularly enthusiastic about their success. Despite the efforts of some incumbents, the loyalty of parishioners would seem to be very much to the parish, and to the parish church, rather than to the wider benefice.

Small Congregations

One of the characteristics most closely associated with rural churches is the small congregation. Many of us will have experienced such services and we will all have our own views as to their success. Leslie Francis' book on rural Anglicanism provides a series of subjective and perhaps rather negative pen-portraits of a stranger's view of attending such services. But what are the clergy's views of small congregations? What is the effect, in practice, of small congregations on preaching styles and music? We first of all asked clergy whether they found small congregations difficult or dispiriting in any way. The interesting response is that most clergy (61%) did not find small congregations a problem in this respect. Moreover, only 15% of the clergy gave an unqualified 'yes' to this question, the remainder pointing out that although they sometimes found such services difficult, they tried to have a positive attitude to them or indeed that small services did have some advantages.

Why is it that most clergy are relatively happy with having some small congregations? The reasons offered by the clergy were many and varied. In some cases it was simply that they had got used to low numbers over time. One commented simply that "You've got to adjust to it, I don't get depressed by them." Another response was that there was no point in being dispirited by small congregations as clergy should not be concerned about attendance figures. One respondent felt that:

> The greatest crime a clergyman can commit is to be obsessed by numbers. You should have concern with individuals. It can be more spiritually productive to have a service with 12 people than a big rally of 200-300.

As an extension to this view, some respondents commented on the fact that it was important to meet the needs of those who were there, rather than being concerned about those who were not, and that the Spirit of God was just as much present among small, as among large, congregations. At least ten of the clergy considered that there were actually positive advantages in having small congregations. Several said that they actually preferred low numbers, and even some of those who found small congregations generally difficult were able to point to some benefits. In general these related to the more reflective atmosphere of the service, and the closer and more informal relationship which the priest was able to have with the people. One noted that he was "sometimes almost frightened of large congregations" and another commented on his dispiriting experiences of large urban civic services.

The findings of the survey suggest that there is no one threshold beyond which a congregation becomes small enough to be difficult, but rather that the critical size will vary according to a whole host of other factors. It was quite possible therefore for the same sized congregation to be viewed as encouraging in one context, and dispiriting in another. This is reflected in the fact that so many clergy added qualifications to their "yes" or "no" answers to the question concerning the effect of small congregations, or simply said that "it depends". It was also evident from the variety of responses from those who did attempt to put a figure on what constitutes a small congregation. Some felt that there was a definite minimum viable number, with estimates ranging from five to 15 people, but others felt that the only threshold was if nobody attended the service at all. These priests said they did not mind how low the numbers were, but that that they felt disheartened if nobody came: "It hits you when nobody turns up at all."

One of the important factors determining whether or not a small congregation was dispiriting was not the *absolute* size of the congregation, but what *proportion* of the local population it represented. Some respondents viewed their attendance more in proportional terms, and felt that if a good percentage of the parish attended, it did not matter when absolute numbers were low. This is a particularly interesting finding when we consider the relatively high proportions of people in rural benefices attending church indicated by our survey results.

Another key influence on whether or not a small congregation was perceived as dispiriting was the extent to which low numbers were expected, and could be explained. At least six of the clergy who did not find small congregations dispiriting commented that it was precisely because they *expected* variations in attendance, and could usually give a reason for any particular drop, such as people being away on holiday, poor weather, or a major local event. Several clergy mentioned that the size of congregation which was perceived as dispiriting varied between parishes and between different types of services, according to the expected attendance. For clergy conducting several services in a day, the timing of the service with poor attendance could be another important factor. One clergyman commented:

> This is very important to me. The early small congregation is OK. The 9.30 [main service] is OK. But if I then go on to a 11.00am small congregation then I find this very hard. Your own

spirit is very low and ten minutes in it's a real worry. You feel tired and spent.

For some clergy the *nature* of the congregation who did attend was a determining factor. More than one commented that the type of people present in a small congregation, and their attentiveness, could be very important, presumably because individual reactions and responses were more visible. Another problem for some clergy was that the few attenders tended to sit far down the nave. In order to counteract this, and to minimise the sense of being a small congregation, some clergy altered the seating arrangements or held services in side chapels. Moreover, it was obvious that the nature of the building itself could be a factor in determining the effect of a small congregation, as one priest with two very different churches explained:

> M ... is very helpful - it's a small church and people sit at the front. I feel more at home. The sermon can be more of a dialogue - we pass the peace there. At P... only 26 or so sitting in a long church at the back does seem odd.

Preaching and Music

Most of the respondents felt their manner of presentation differed with small congregations with many preaching more informally and not using the pulpit. One commented "When it's small I'm far more chatty and friendly. You cannot declaim". A few clergy also mentioned that their sermons would become shorter if numbers were low. Some replaced the traditional sermon with more informal addresses. One replaced it with:

> A chat-show. I ask a question and a reciprocal session occurs.
> I rarely use the pulpit. It's too embarrassing really preaching to six.
> We often have intercessions instead of the sermon.

At least eight incumbents said that they actually found it more difficult preaching to small congregations, either because they personally found it hard to adopt an informal style, or because of a sense of feeling more constrained: "It's much easier to preach to 250 than 25 - you notice what they're doing more, looking for the next hymn etc". In addition, some clergy commented on the problem of motivation when preaching to small congregations, or as one put it, the difficulty in getting "fired up". Some pointed to the fact that the congregation could experience a sense of unease if there were only a few of them, because they might feel more exposed and vulnerable:

> I find preaching to ten quite difficult- it doesn't feel quite right. You can't hide behind numbers. People see themselves in what you say more easily. It's more difficult to deal from the pulpit with issues. Personal problems I deal with one to one, and not via the pulpit as I would in a suburban church.

When asked about the effects of small congregations on music and worship well over half of the respondents thought that there was an effect. The most common effect was to make the singing of the psalms and canticles more difficult. In some cases the psalms and canticles were still sung despite the difficulty, in others they were said, and in some places low numbers resulted in their being cut out altogether. This needs to be put in the context of the findings earlier in this chapter on service types, which showed the continued strength of the Book of Common Prayer, especially for evensong. Despite the widespread use of such a service, the comments from clergy in this section show that there are some practical problems in attempting to continue with Prayer Book sung evensongs in some of these smaller rural churches.

The second main way in which small numbers had an effect on the worship was to limit the repertoire of music which could be used, and make changes harder to introduce. One noted that he had to choose well known hymns and another that if he found the congregation did not know a hymn, he would stop it and replace it with another. Despite these problems a few clergy remarked that their congregations preferred to sing everything anyway. One said "we do sing here even if there are small numbers", and another commented "people still like to sing, regardless of the number". One respondent actually felt that a small congregation was beneficial to the worship:

> On the whole I think that when you have a small group that you put more effort in. Perhaps it's more important to make a joyful noise before the Lord than to worry about being too precise. There's a certain charm - you shouldn't have too grandiose expectations.

Apart from the quality of singing from the congregation, two themes recurred most frequently - the presence and quality of organists, and whether or not there was a choir. It would be a misrepresentation to say that there were universal problems in obtaining the services of a good organist – a number of clergy said that organists were not in short supply, that they served loyally, and were willing to come out from nearby small towns. However, the more general tenor of the comments was that there were considerable problems in some rural areas getting a regular, and good, organist for small churches. One incumbent went so far as to say "A good organist is a rare animal. We need more organists than parish priests".

Some of these respondents remarked upon the effect of the lack of an organist on the music. In some churches alternative arrangements were made, such as using the harmonium. In a few instances incumbents had been able to introduce guitars to lead the worship instead, although other clergy reported opposition to this. At least three clergy said that they themselves sometimes had to play the organ as a substitute. Even if no alternative arrangements could be made, in some churches the singing carried on regardless. In others, however, the lack of an organist prevented any music, although this was not always felt to be a disadvantage:

> We don't have music because the organist resigned. Most of
> the services are said. People like this – the said service here has a
> quality of its own, and people are beginning to appreciate this.

The other main issue upon which incumbents commented was the presence or absence of a choir. As with the organists, there were clergy who felt they were fortunate in having a reasonable choir, but by and large more commented upon the problems they faced in trying to assemble a choir, and to sing without one. A rather depressing picture was painted by one respondent: "We used to have a choir, but now most children are not church-going."

In general our findings suggest that the majority of clergy do not find small congregations dispiriting. In many cases they had got used to small numbers, and in some instances, perhaps surprisingly, the incumbents actually preferred such congregations. Defining a small congregation in itself was difficult. There was no one threshold level at which a congregation became small enough to be disheartening; rather this varied according to other factors such as expectations of attendance, the proportion of the parish population represented, the type of service, and the nature of the congregation.

Ecumenism

Clergy Assessment of Ecumenical Cooperation

From our postal survey we discovered that more than four fifths (81%) of the incumbents of the five dioceses were involved in some form of ecumenical cooperation. Only five per cent said that there was a local ecumenical project (LEP) in the parishes for which they were responsible, but 79% said they were involved in other forms of cooperation. From the outset "ecumenism" was deliberately left undefined, in order that clergy could attach to it their own meaning. Hence the activities which clergy deemed to be ecumenical varied from the very informal – such as attendance by members of other denominations at Anglican churches, to more formal working arrangements.

TABLE 48. Denominations Involved in Ecumenical Cooperation

	No of clergy	%
Methodists	342	60
Roman Catholics	199	35
Baptists	89	16
URC/Congregationalist	79	14
Salvation Army	49	9
Pentecostals	39	7
Other specified	51	9
All/unspecified	69	12

Note: (i) "other specified" refers to any other specific denomination mentioned. These included, among others, Quakers, Independent Chapels, Free Evangelical churches, Brethren and house churches. (ii) "all/unspecified" refers to those who simply mentioned "all denominations in the parish" or "nonconformists generally" without giving specific denominations.

Six specific denominations were mentioned with particular frequency. These were Methodist, Baptist, Roman Catholic, URC/Congregational, Salvation Army, and Pentecostal. Contact with Methodists stood at a far higher level than any of the other individual denominations. This is interesting considering the failure of two schemes of unity between the Church of England and the Methodists since 1945. Despite the absence to date of any formal unity of the two churches, the survey shows that links at the level of the local church are nevertheless strong. Next came Roman Catholics, with more than a third (35%) of Anglican clergy having links with the Catholic church. Each of the other individual denominations was mentioned by less than one fifth of clergy; Baptists and URCs being the only ones to be cited by more than a tenth of incumbents.

The Nature of Ecumenical Cooperation

By far the most frequent form of cooperation, mentioned by more than a third (34%) of clergy, was holding regular united services, which may have been fortnightly or just two or three times a year. In addition, nearly a fifth (18%) of respondents said that they held united *seasonal* services, usually carol services, Good Friday services, harvest festivals and services of remembrance. The importance of other types of ecumenical cooperation are shown in Table 49.

TABLE 49. Nature of Ecumenical Cooperation

Cooperation	No of clergy	%
United services	197	34
Seasonal services	104	18
Church councils	94	16
Clergy fraternals	81	14
Yearly/occasional	62	11
Lent	55	10
Prayer/study groups	48	8
Children/youth	41	7
Shared buildings	29	5
Other specified	105	18
Other unspecified	52	9

The wide range of types of contact is shown by the fact that 18% of clergy specified other forms of co-operation. This included a very varied group of activities, of which the main types were speaking engagements or pulpit exchanges, cooperation at funerals, missions, joint magazines, visiting, social action in the community, fundraising and social events.

Variations in Ecumenical Cooperation by Rurality

If we consider the variations in the denominations involved in ecumenical cooperation by rurality (Table 50) the major finding is the considerable extent of ecumenical cooperation in small country towns. Small country town clergy were the most likely to have had ecumenical links with five out of the six main denominations. The only denomination with whom contact was not greatest in small country towns was the Pentecostals. Links with the Pentecostal church were greatest in partly urban and then urban benefices although the extent of Pentecostal cooperation was only slightly less in small country towns and partly rural areas.

TABLE 50. Denominations Involved in Ecumenical Cooperation by Rurality

Denomination	Totally rural %	Partly rural %	Small country town %	Part urban non rural %	Urban %
Methodist	63	61	69	65	47
Roman Catholic	25	24	55	37	43
Baptist	10	10	34	18	14
URC/Congregationalist	5	10	25	12	23
Salvation Army	2	7	16	7	15
Pentecostal	1	10	9	13	11
Other specified	5	10	12	12	11
All/unspecified	5	14	11	19	17

There appear to be three main reasons for the extensive ecumenical links reported by clergy in small country towns. The high incidence of LEPs is one factor, although this in itself calls for some explanation. Another reason is that the size and dynamics of such settlements makes them very conducive to joint working. The third, and possibly most important reason is that small country towns have more resident ministers than the totally rural benefices, and yet at the same time there is not the perhaps counter-productive profusion of other denominations of an urban community.

The difference in ecumenical contact between small country towns and other types of benefice was particularly marked with Baptist and Roman Catholic cooperation. More than a third of clergy (34%) in small country towns had links with Baptists, but less than a fifth in all other types of benefice. Similarly more than half (55%) had contact with the

Roman Catholic church in small country towns. Cooperation with Catholics was next most common in urban benefices (43% of clergy), but in totally rural and partly rural benefices only 25% and 24% respectively had such contacts. This is largely due to the strong urban and small country town bias in the location of Roman Catholic priests and churches.

Rural Ecumenical Cooperation

Some types of ecumenical cooperation are strongly influenced by the rurality of the area, being more likely, or more able, to take place in certain benefice types (Table 51). For example, clergy fraternals and Church Councils showed a marked urban bias, whereas work with children, and seasonal services were slightly more frequent in rural areas. The other types showed no clear trend except for the importance of small country towns in terms of frequency of occurrence.

Table 51. Nature of Ecumenical Cooperation by Rurality

Cooperation	Totally rural	Partly rural	Small country town	Part urban non rural	Urban
	%	%	%	%	%
United services	33	39	33	35	34
Seasonal services	22	10	22	19	14
Church council	5	14	27	27	21
Clergy fraternals	6	13	13	21	24
Yearly/occasional	5	14	17	12	12
Lent	6	13	11	13	11
Prayer/study groups	7	10	12	9	7
Children/youth	10	8	4	7	5
Shared buildings	4	4	9	7	5
Other specified	18	21	12	24	20
Other unspecified	7	13	8	9	12

The types of cooperation which occurred most frequently in small country towns were yearly/occasional co-operation, shared buildings and prayer/study groups. In addition, more than a fifth (22%) of both small country town and totally rural clergy were involved in seasonal united services, compared to only ten per cent in partly rural benefices.

Church council involvement was, in general, much more common in the urban benefices than in the two most rural benefice types, presumably because of the sheer presence of enough other denominations to make such groups viable.

Clergy in totally rural benefices were the least likely of all respondents to be involved in seven out of the nine specific types of ecumenical contact. This reflects the lack of potential clergy and lay people of other denominations with whom to work in the more sparsely populated rural areas where the Anglican church may be the only denomination represented. The only exceptions to this were seasonal services and work with children and youth. The frequency of co-operation for seasonal services in rural areas may reflect the continued central role of the major church festivals in these communities, and their importance as village events. In the case of children's or youth work it may demonstrate the sheer necessity of sharing scant resources in areas where there are too few children to make two separate Sunday schools viable, and probably a scarcity of people to act as Sunday school teachers, and more especially, youth workers.

The Effect of Rural Circumstances on Ecumenism

Overall, the two most frequently mentioned ways in which rural circumstances affected ecumenism were the lack of other denominations present, whether people, ministers or buildings, and the presence of small communities. Clergy were evenly divided as to whether they regarded the lack of other denominations as an encouraging or inhibiting factor. This to some extent depended on how they defined ecumenism. For those who saw ecumenism as a formal working relationship between two denominations, the fact that none of the structures of another denomination were present was obviously an inhibiting factor. However, other clergy viewed ecumenical cooperation as more informal, in the sense of members of other denominations worshipping at each other's churches. For these respondents, the lack of buildings of any other denominations in rural areas could be seen in a positive light:

> These are all country parishes with no other denominational buildings therefore we regularly have Methodists, United Reformed, Scottish Presbyterians and Roman Catholics and sometimes Jews as part of the congregation.
>
> Both Methodists and Baptists support all our functions. It isn't

really ecclesiastical; simply that in the Forest every activity is supported by local people.

The other factors which clergy mentioned were in general those which had an inhibiting effect on ecumenism in rural areas. The most common one was loyalty of the people either to their buildings or to their denomination to the extent that joint working was prevented. Other clergy found that loyalties were broader, and more linked with the denomination than the building *per se*. In some cases this loyalty was found to fly in the face of "common sense". One clergyman commented that in a nearby rural parish there was a Baptist chapel supported by three people, a Methodist congregation who met in the church hall, and only a small Anglican congregation. He remarked that "it is a situation where cooperation would be sensible, but there is no feeling that they are part of the same world at all".

Linked with this issue was the fact that in many rural areas there was a deeply historical sense in which different denominations were independent of, or even antagonistic towards, each other. Some clergy found a conservative attitude among rural people, and often among the older people in particular, which prevented the development of ecumenical cooperation. This was not necessarily an antagonism towards other denominations, but rather a desire to avoid change.

It was clear, however, from some of the general remarks from clergy that this strong denominational loyalty was by no means always prevalent, or that even if it was, there could still be a certain attachment to the Church of England from members of other denominations who looked upon the Anglican church as *the* parish church. As a result, some clergy explicitly stated that their responsibility was for all members of the parish, whatever denomination:

> An old Baptist lady who was dying said 'you are our parish priest'; so I take responsibility for all denominations. I take the whole village as my brief.

Six clergy mentioned that the relative strengths of the denominations involved in rural areas was the factor which determined whether or not ecumenism would take place. Four of these six clergy felt that where the two denominations were of unequal strength it would diminish the likelihood of their working together. The opposing view was that two churches of unequal strength would come together out of necessity, and that where they were equally strong neither was likely to give way. Finally, a large proportion of those who felt that rural circumstances in themselves neither encouraged or inhibited ecumenism commented that this was because ecumenical developments were so dependent on the personalities of the ministers and clergy involved.

Strength of Denominations

All the parishioners in the 25 sample parishes were asked to specify whether 'they belonged to any church, denomination or religion'. Their answers are shown in Table 52 which also provides comparative data from other surveys. The great majority (88%) of the respondents from the general sample gave Christianity as their religion. Only ten per cent of those interviewed specified no allegiance to any church, denomination or religion and as few as one per cent of this sample named a religion other than Christianity. Looking at the general sample in more detail it is immediately clear that the majority belong to the Church of England: the other specified denominations, when added together, represented only one fifth (21%) of the population. This low proportion of other denominations is particulary important for rural ecumenism as it means the actual numbers of people from the non–Anglican denominations living in rural parishes is very small indeed.

TABLE 52. Religious Allegiance - Comparison of Different Surveys

Religious allegiance	Rural Church Project No	%	Bible Society/Gallup Villages %	Cities %	Forster (Hull) No	%
Church of England	212	62	68	59	160	77
Roman Catholic	19	6	9	16	19	9
Methodist	28	8			10	5
Baptists	3	1	} 12	} 7	2	1
United Reformed	2	1			3	2
Other Denomination	15	5	6	9	1	0
Christianity	26	7	-	-	2	1
Other religions	2	1	-	-	1	0
Don't know	2	1	6	8	2	1
No allegiance	37	10	-	-	7	4
Total	341	100	101	99	207	100

The Bible Society (Harrison 1983) commissioned Gallup to carry out a study on a wide range of religious issues. As a basis for the study the interviewees were asked "which of the following, if any, is your religious denomination?". The sample was also asked if their home was in a city, suburbs, town or village and Table 52 shows the religious affiliation of those responding 'village' and 'city'. The figures from the Bible Society 'village' figures and those from our general sample are roughly comparable. When the figures for the 'city' respondents are considered the number of Anglicans drops and second place is taken by the Roman Catholics. Roman Catholics were also slightly more common in a recent study of religion on a Hull council estate (Forster 1989:28). The number of Anglicans was far higher at 77% but this difference is likely to be partly explained by the wording of the questions. In our survey the respondents were asked if they 'belonged to any church, denomination or religion'. The fact that they were brought up or even baptised in a certain church was not on its own categorised as a sense of 'belonging'. In Forster's work the sample were asked which denomination they would declare when they entered a hospital and thus a rather more nominal response may be expected.

The data show that the Church of England is dominant in rural areas whatever the gender or age of the parishioner. The strength of the other denominations tended to vary on a regional basis and was more common among the older members of the community. The ecumenical implications of this are that the Church of England will inevitably be at the centre of virtually all rural ecumenism. The denomination with which the contacts are made will vary depending largely on the relative strength of denominations in different parishes.

Parishioners' Knowledge of Ecumenical Services

As part of the interview all the respondents were asked if, to the best of their knowledge, there were joint or ecumenical services within the parish. Information gathered from the incumbent showed that ecumenical services only took place in eight of the 25 parishes included in the parishioners survey. Almost three-quarters of the Anglican attenders living in parishes where ecumenical services were held agreed that they did occur. This leaves, however, over a fifth of the Anglican attenders (21%) who were unaware that such services took place.

Rather surprisingly, over half (54%) of the Anglican attenders who lived in parishes where ecumenical services did not take place mistakenly believed that they were held. A partial explanation may be that the respondents were thinking on a benefice scale rather than a parish one. Further analysis showed that there would appear to be some truth in this, but even when the occurrence of such services in other parishes in the benefice was taken into account, over a third (36%) of the sample mistakenly thought ecumenical services were held.

One can only speculate why the figure is so high but perhaps the respondents were thinking of the past or have a wider view of ecumenism than the existence of joint services. The attendance of a Methodist or Roman Catholic family at some services may, for example, be reason enough to call these services ecumenical. Alternatively, the close links between the denominations in other events,such as village fetes, flower festivals or some charity occasions may be as important as joint services.

Conclusions

We have shown that although the level of attendance in rural benefices is relatively low, when the number of people living in the benefices is considered, the rates of attendance are high, especially in the smallest benefices. These rates of attendance relate to a relatively short slice of time: four Sundays in the autumn of 1988. Many people, of course, do not attend church every Sunday, and the extent of this less regular attendance was clearly shown by the results of our survey of parishioners. We found, for example, that a third of a random sample of residents had attended a normal Sunday service at least once over the previous year. This implies that the influence of the church in rural areas is rather stronger than might be deduced from attendance levels on particular Sundays. Moreover, higher proportions of the parish population attend special services associated with festivals such as Christmas and Harvest. The continued popularity of services on these occasions will be discussed further when we consider the patterns of popular religion in Chapter 9.

The survey of parishioners provided evidence which confirmed the views of many of the clergy that there are significant gaps in the make-up of rural congregations. If we had to draw a pen-portrait of the type of person most likely to be a regular attender, *she* would probably be aged over 45 and belong to one of the higher social classes. She would be a housewife who had not lived in the parish all her life, but had moved there at least ten years ago. Conversely, the person least likely to attend church regularly would be a young man. *He* would belong to one of the lower social classes and either have recently moved to the parish, or lived in the parish all his life. Many of the incumbents were clearly aware of the types of people who did not attend church but were finding difficulty in trying to attract a greater range of regular attenders.

When the services on offer were considered we found that communion services were dominant throughout the five dioceses, although there were considerable variations between dioceses. The frequency of communion services was shown to be closely related to the churchmanship of the incumbent. When the forms of service were considered, we found that BCP morning and evening prayer were held much more frequently in rural and small country town benefices than in urban ones. We also found that the range of services on offer in rural benefices is roughly in line with the preferences expressed by the parishioners, although there was still a strong tendency for rural residents to prefer BCP to ASB forms of service. This clear indication of conservatism seems to be reflected by the results of our review of the reasons for the present pattern of services in rural areas. This showed that there was little innovation from the clergy in terms of the services provided. The sense of conservatism amongst parishioners was reinforced by clergy's comments on the general lack of enthusiasm shown by congregations for united benefice services. Finally, our assessment of the issue of small congregations provided some particularly interesting insights into the nature of rural religion. It also had some important policy implications in terms of whether small rural churches should be encouraged to survive. There was certainly little evidence here of any desire by the clergy to close churches if the numbers attending became small. This provides additional backing for the conclusions reached in Chapter 7 where we dealt with the question of redundant churches.

By far the most common form of ecumenism cited was the holding of united services. Cooperation was least extensive in totally rural areas. Clergy in small country towns reported the most extensive cooperation and were also considerably more likely to be involved in LEPs. Clergy in totally rural benefices reported significantly less cooperation on virtually all counts and the overwhelming impression both from both postal and interview surveys was that rural circumstances have a considerable effect on the extent to which ecumenism takes place. The lack of other denominations in rural areas, whether in terms of people, ministers or buildings seemed to inhibit formal ecumenism, but could encourage informal links between the people. Other inhibiting influences were strong denominational loyalties – often built up over years – and the effect of the distances between communities. Finally, whatever other factors were present, these could be overridden by the personalities of the ministers involved, and their churchmanship.

9

Belief and Theology

One person's religion is another's superstition. This is true to some extent among equally devoted churchpeople let alone between active and relatively inactive churchgoers, or believers and non-believers. The distinction can be subtle or blunt. If, for example, we look at different theological styles of thought we will find that some Christians take the bible in a very literal way while others interpret it metaphorically. The literalists might regard others as liberals who have forsaken the true faith, while the latter might see the literalists as childish fundamentalists in need of maturity of thought. This example is a significant one in today's religious world, for example with the highly visible differences between evangelicals and fundamentalists in the United States of America over metaphorical or literalist approaches to scripture (Cox, 1984). Both biblical interpretation and spirituality offer areas where different religious styles exist and where various devotees label each other according to their own lights.

In this chapter we explore these and other varieties of religious belief and practice to gain some picture of rural religion today and how the pastoral ministry has responded to it. First we consider the issue of orthodoxy and its shadowlands of folk religion, then beliefs of the afterlife, and finally we present a pattern of religious themes which we discovered in the rural public.

Orthodoxy, Folk Religion and Popular Opinion

The case of biblical literalism mentioned above immediately raises the problem of defining orthodoxy in any realistic and practical sense since it would be perfectly possible for the literalist interpretation of the bible to be viewed as an example of unsophisticated folk-religion existing within the church. Thus in the case of the doctrine of Creation, some say that God made the world in six days while for others the same text refers to the divine responsibility for creative processes over millennia. Similarly with the doctrine of the Resurrection. For some the body of Jesus was transformed by God's power from being a dead human body to being a living body of the new age. For others the resurrection implies the power to live a transformed life in terms of attitudes and hope. Many other similar differences could be catalogued amongst people who are regular church members.

These and many other possible examples show that theology is not just about the history of the creeds and the writings of modern giants in the field. It also concerns style and mood in church life, individual life events, and those chance encounters with religious ideas, people, and insights which help make people what they are. Formal theology, including that sometimes taught to priests in training, stresses the academically historical aspect of doctrine to the detriment of personal constructions of belief within and outside the faith community. This is why we deal here both with central Christian doctrine and that other domain which has been variously labelled as common, folk or implicit religion, or as subterranean theology.

The Church of England does not in practice require its members to give an explicit and detailed account of their beliefs. Beliefs for the British are today part of private life. Religious belonging relates more to a practice of attendance rather than to the necessity of believing particular things. Clergy will, inevitably, be unhappy with such a situation since they see themselves as teachers of the gospel message of God's creative power and redemptive love in Jesus Christ. For them there are specific ideas which form the foundation of Christian religion. The practical problem of religion relates to precisely which issues are central and whether they need to be expressed in very particular ways. Many very active and committed church people may also have a firm version of the faith and wonder about those who are only occasionally involved in church life or who may be regulars but who seem to have but little by way of a clear formal grasp of doctrine.

The idea of folk religion turns on this view that there is a recognisable mainstream Christian tradition expressed in doctrine but that this central strand is perverted by popular opinions which alter the real sense of Christianity. These other views may predate Christianity, may come from non-Christian culture, or may simply be fond things vainly invented by unlettered or uninstructed people. Some are half-truths, or truths half understood. We will see later in this chapter what clergy think of folk religion but before that we explore some aspects of this belief in the general population. In our survey we singled out four issues for special attention. These were belief in ghosts, belief that Friday the Thirteenth is an unlucky day, ideas about life after death, and finally some aspects of life experience in relation to church services. These seemed to run the gamut from ideas that practically everyone would regard as outside the Christian doctrinal network to issues of central doctrinal concern. From a strictly theological perspective it would be easy to argue that true religion had but little to do with superstition connected with ghosts or Friday the Thirteenth. But for many people religion covers these issues even though to theologically trained people this might not be the case. We must even say 'might' here because within the Christian churches there are those for whom superstition is an aspect of religiosity albeit an evil dimension. The case of exorcism is classic in that within the Church of England there are exorcists appointed by ecclesiastical authorities to deal with objectively focused evil which some church people regard as a futile throwback and retrograde medievalism. Having sketched these bounds of propriety in generalizations we turn to a detailed study of particulars and begin with ghosts.

Ghost Belief

Of the total sample of the rural parishioners (489) 26% said they believed in ghosts, 16% did not know, while 58% clearly rejected the idea. A fifth of the church roll people (19%) believed in ghosts as against just under a third (29%) of the general sample. Comparing these results with Gorer's survey of the nineteen fifties we find that 58% rejected the idea of ghosts (1955). Gorer found that 17% believed in ghosts and a quarter were either unsure (23%) or made no reply (2%). It is interesting that both Gorer's study and the Rural Church Project found the same level of disbelief in ghosts and even more interesting that our more recent exploration found more people believing in ghosts in the nineteen eighties than in the nineteen fifties (29% from the general sample as against 17%). Our subjects were, of course, unlike Gorer's, specifically rural.

These findings give a general picture of attitudes to ghosts, phenomena which are not part and parcel of orthodox Christian religion and which are therefore suitable material for a folk religion label. Why they might

be significant aspects of life we shall consider below, for the moment we
need to look in more detail at our research findings where a complex
picture emerges as to the dynamics of ghost belief. Men and women
showed no difference of outlook on ghosts. Twenty six percent of each
gender believed in ghosts, and then practically the same proportions did
not believe (56% men, 53% women) and did not know (16% men, 16%
women). Differences began to emerge when age, and regional distribution
of the general population were taken into account. The full distribution
of ghost beliefs as far as age was concerned was as follows:-

TABLE 53. Belief in Ghosts in Relation to Age: General Sample (%)

	18-34	35-44	45-54	55-64	65+
Yes	33	44	31	19	15
No	45	45	53	64	71
Don't know	22	11	16	17	14
Total	100	100	100	100	100

So as to age there was a pattern in the fact that the young believed
in ghosts more than the old, indeed belief in ghosts seemed to decline
steadily throughout all the age groups studied. This is an interesting fact
and would seem to indicate that experience of life increasingly denies
ghost belief. Had the results been inverted with the older groups
believing more in ghosts than younger groups some notion of
secularization might have been admissible. We could have said that the
elderly were born in a world given to belief in ghosts while present day
youth were brought up in a more rational and scientific environment.
But this seems specifically not to be the case. Indeed some might argue
that younger generations have been far more subjected to cinema,
literary, and a broad media presentation of supernatural and paranormal
phenomena which foster ghost ideas. E.B.Tylor's extensive and germinal
study of ghosts in religion which was part of his theory of Animism is
still not without some interest in our modern times in connection with
these issues (1871), so too Finucane's description of cultural and
historical factors which typify apparitions in particular periods (1982).
Still the individual's life experience is not unimportant when it comes
to experiencing ghosts as also in the adjacent domain of sensing the
presence of one's dead kin as we shall discuss later in this chapter.

Turning to geographical issues for a moment we found interesting differences between the dioceses. Durham showed the lowest rate of ghost belief (15%) and Gloucester the highest (39%). Truro and Southwell were similarly placed (35% and 32%) with Lincoln being intermediately located (25%). The variation from lowest to highest is not easily explained. Indeed much more research would have to be done before a fully satisfactory explanation could be given. But then this is the case for a great deal connected with popular religion in Britain.

Friday the Thirteenth

Is this day unlucky? Answers to this question were clear with very few indeed not having a definite opinion. Fifteen per cent did think the day unlucky; 82% did not. Amongst the Anglicans, very few regular church attenders held the view (6%) while many more Anglican non-attenders did so (22%). This suggests that unlucky days are not the same category of idea as ghost belief as far as Anglican attenders are concerned, 27% of whom believed in ghosts. In fact the regular churchgoers believed in ghosts more often than did non-attending Anglicans, a point to which we will return when discussing ideas of the afterlife.

For the moment it is again worth comparing our findings with those of Gorer's 1955 exploration into English character even though the two studies are not strictly comparable in that Gorer asked people if they had lucky and unlucky days rather than focusing on Friday the Thirteenth as such. He also reported on two surveys, but the general outcome was that between eighty and ninety percent did not accept ideas about lucky or unlucky days while between nine and seventeen per cent did accept these ideas. These figures are also broadly similar to our own.

In terms of gender the general sample survey showed a slight difference with men being less keen on the idea than women (12% men, 18% women). There was a difference between the young and old with the under thirty five year olds standing at 21% and the over sixty five year olds at 11%. Perhaps old age induces a sense of realism. Regional variations were negligible and again suggest that this sort of category differs from that of ghost belief. It is worth stressing this difference between ghost beliefs and the influence of Friday the Thirteenth and to hint at the complexity of such ideas within human life. Jahoda (1969) has cogently argued the case for superstitions as potentially useful in human life as people seek to interpret experience and adapt to ever changing circumstances. It seems to us that some caution is needed to prevent the catch-all category of superstition obliterating differences between particular popular beliefs.

Life after Death

If ghosts and ill-omened Fridays may be far from Christian truth we are on surer ground when we come to the theme of life after death. Here is a central Christian belief, enshrined in the creeds, and foundational to liturgy. The risen Christ witnesses to the saving work of the Father, and expresses the future that awaits a transformed humanity.

But what do people actually believe? How has Christian teaching and the Christian hope been appropriated by individuals? The way in which people hear and receive and make teaching their own is a very complex business. It is subject to each individual's life experience, outlook, mental and emotional abilities. As might be expected we found a considerable variation in belief moving from firm ideas on the resurrection of the body through to ideas of reincarnation which are more typical of Indian religion. So here too we find orthodoxy and folk-religion rubbing shoulders.

Of the general sample 42% said they believed in life after death; 32% did not, while another 26% did not know or refused to answer. The difference between men and women in this sample was itself marked. Many more women (53%) believed in life after death than did men (30%). Similarly fewer women (22%) gave a definite 'no' than did men (30%). Those who did not know were similarly placed, (men 26%, women 25%). These differences are quite marked and they would certainly be worth exploring in future research. It would be worth investigating how important the element of after-life is as a motivation for church involvement given the general trend for congregations to possess more active women than men members.

TABLE 54. Belief in Life After Death (%)

Belief	General sample	Church roll sample
Yes	42	69
No	32	10
Don't know	26	21
Total	100	100

Table 54 shows that those with a formal association with the church are much more likely to believe in life after death, but even so 10% from the church roll sample did not, and a further 21% did not know whether they believed in it or not. When we analysed the material to single out those Anglicans who were more regular attenders than nominal we found much the same picture with a third of attenders not believing or not knowing what they believed about life after death. This must be an important issue for the clergy and for liturgical life at large given the fact that so much of what is said in church works on the broad assumption that people agree with it. Pastoral experience sometimes shows that this is not the case but, still, the point should be made that those who worship and listen to sermons may be somewhat at odds with the content of church talk. But even here some caution is necessary since it is not impossible that individuals tend to one view when in one context and to another view elsewhere. The significance of context upon religious belief has not been fully enough explored for popular Christianity for anything certain to be said (Lewis 1986).

Other factors affecting belief in an after-life are denominational affiliation and age. We found that non-Anglican attenders in the sample believed more strongly (82%) in an after-life than did Anglicans (69%) while non-Anglican non-attenders (41%) clearly disbelieved in it more than did Anglican non-attenders (33%). In terms of age in the general sample those who did not know what they believed remained moderately constant across all age groups (between 21% and 31%). In terms of regional variation the general population surveyed in Southwell, Lincoln, and Durham furnished the broad average response while Truro had most people believing in an afterlife (49%) with Gloucester having the fewest (29%).

Secularization and the Afterlife ?

It is interesting that these general responses to belief in life after death also match quite closely the findings of two British studies carried out in 1950 and 1963 by Geoffrey Gorer (1965). In 1963 he found that just under a half believed in an afterlife (in 1950 the figure was 47%). The gender division saw women (55% or 56% in 1950) believing more than did men (41% or 39% in 1950). Staying with the gender distinction the difference between 1950 and our study for men was small (39% and 30%), and for women was even less (56% and 53%). When it came to outright denial of life after death the greatest difference is amongst men:

whereas just over a quarter (28%) disbelieved in 1950 well over a third (44%) disbelieved in our 1988 study.

Types of Belief in Afterlife

These sorts of variation in belief in an afterlife can be explored further by examining the content of belief. Just what did people mean when they said they believed in a life after death? In terms of the sociology of religion this is an important point because subtlety of belief can easily be lost in a simple statistic about life after death. To achieve some insight into popular attitudes we sought people's responses to five statements about possible forms of life after death. Which were:-

i.   Nothing happens- we come to an end.
ii. Our souls pass to another world.
iii. Our bodies await a resurrection.
iv. We come back as something/someone else.
v.   Trust in God, all is in his hands.

We asked people whether they agreed, disagreed, or were unsure about each of these statements. An additional category of 'don't know' was used and included any who did not understand the meaning of a statement. Finally people were given opportunity to express any other view they might have about life after death. Though complicated by the fact that a few people gave different answers on the same subject when answering different questions, the results produce the following general picture.

Nothing Happens

A third of the general sample thought that nothing happened after death; while 23% did not know or were unsure about postmortality. This matches the earlier question where nearly a third (32%) said they did not believe in life after death.

Souls Passing and Bodies Resurrecting

The most popular view was that the soul passes to another world after death, some 43% supported that idea, while 27% disagreed with it and they largely were those who did not believe in a life after death at all. In terms of the propositions which had some definite notion of the future, the soul idea stood out as the clear favourite. More than twice as many people agreed with this as agreed with the idea of a bodily resurrection

(19%). A clearer picture of popular belief in the afterlife emerges when we supplement the rural church survey with work from the Cremation Research Project undertaken by D.J.Davies. This shows a similar level of belief in life after death (47%) and a similar stress on the passing of the soul. But in the dynamics of practical religion those who believed in the resurrection of the body also seemed to believe in what we might call the mobile soul. In other words practically all those who believed in life after death also believed that the soul passed on at death. About a half of all these believers also thought that something will happen to the body.

This is a most interesting and pastorally valuable fact. The theological distinction between the eternal soul and the resurrection is denied in popular belief where they are combined despite the fact that this runs counter to theological orthodoxy. The New Testament approaches the future through the idea of the resurrection and it is this motif which is central to the ritual form of burial and which underlies the idea and ritual practice of Easter. But for many individuals the vaguer yet apparently simpler notion of an eternal soul passing on its way is more readily accepted, perhaps especially for an immediate grasp of the nature of death following bereavement.

What is noteworthy is that more people on church electoral rolls believed in the eternal soul idea than the general public, (68% against 43%). This 68% acceptance of souls was far greater than the same church group's 24% acceptance of bodily resurrection. This raises some intriguing questions about recent church debates concerning the Resurrection of Jesus, on the assumption that it is not impossible for beliefs about self to be unrelated to beliefs about Jesus as far as Christians are concerned.

Our respondents were of course talking about their own future and not about the Resurrection of Jesus. They might well say one thing about a point of doctrine and another thing about their own eternity. But it is not too speculative perhaps to suggest that if a large proportion of the church-roll members questioned here were unsure (27%) of their own resurrection or definitely did not see their future in resurrection terms (41%) then it is possible that they might not be zealous supporters of a strict resurrection doctrine of Christ. More will be said on this later in our consideration of 'trust in God'. For the moment we turn to consider views on reincarnation.

Reincarnation and Spiritualism

Over half (56%) rejected outright the reincarnation idea that one might come back to this life as someone or something else. This was the clearest rejection of any specific scheme of the future given by those interviewed. Nonetheless 12% accepted it and a fifth were unsure. This could be interpreted to mean that nearly a third of those questioned thought there might be something in it. This is not surprising in one sense given the fact that at least half of all interviewed seemed to believe in the existence of souls as such. What seems to be the case is that this widespread belief in a 'souls' theory of human reality receives no cultural shaping in the direction of reincarnation. Increasingly throughout the twentieth century Eastern ideas of reincarnation have become familiar through literature, media, and the popular press, and even some theologians have discussed it in connection with life after death which indicates something of its potential significance (Badham, 1982). The ability of a culture to provide mythical and theological shape to people's vague soul or life-force beliefs cannot be overemphasised (Obeyesekere, 1981).

Christianity has no possible way of helping to formulate such notions of reincarnation or transmigration of souls. The idea can very legitimately be regarded as an aspect of heretical folk-religion as far as mainstream Christian orthodoxy is concerned. What then were the opinions of those who were on church electoral rolls compared with those of the general population? Some four per cent of the church roll sample, compared with 12% of the general sample accepted this idea. Approximately the same percentage were unsure (18% against 20%) while more church people disagreed with the notion than those from the general sample (69% against 56%). If the variations are not chance then it is likely that the absence of any doctrinal support or reinforcement for the idea would lead to its demise amongst those with church allegiance.

One associated aspect of reincarnation is spiritualism. Something must be said about our findings on this subject since it plays a significant part in Robert Towler's important study of British religiosity (1984). Towler constructed a type of religiosity which he called 'Gnosticism' following Bryan Wilson's earlier usage. This embraced people deeply concerned with the afterlife who believed it was possible to access that domain from this world. These certainly believed in souls, in their continuation, and in contact with them. Towler's intriguing book is based on letters written to the late Dr. John Robinson the author of *Honest to God* when he was Bishop of Woolwich. Towler stresses that he is not in any sense dealing with a random group of people but with those self-selected and wanting to express their views on Robinson's work. Towler also tells us that this Gnostic type was not 'over-represented in letters to Dr. Robinson' (1984:72).

Precisely because of Towler's 'Gnostic' type we included a question which sought to elicit thoughts of this kind. We asked if they thought *the other world was near to this one* as perhaps the best way of summarizing Towler's description of this outlook. In the general sample we found a one per cent response. Since this was a random sample and not self-selected we think Gnosticism ought not to be overemphasised in any pattern of contemporary British religion. Following the detailed work of Vieda Skultans (1974) on spiritualist groups in South Wales we might suggest that therapeutic aspects of contact between spiritualist mediums and their largely female congregation attenders might be as important as any commitment to a soul theory. Gorer's two studies in 1950 and 1963 resemble our own in having found very few reincarnation beliefs among the general public with no more than some two per cent holding them (1965:167).

Trust in God

When asked about trusting in God in the context of life after death many people gave positive assent. Yes, agreed 60% of the general sample, we must trust in God because everything is in his hands. Some 17% were unsure of this and a fifth disagreed. In the church sample the percentage of those 'trusting to God' rose to a large majority (85%). Five per cent were unsure even of this, while seven per cent actively disagreed, and two per cent did not know.

This category of response was an important element in reflecting on eternity since it seemed to embrace those with a variety of more specific views. It only attracted a 20% disagreement amongst the general population whereas nearly a third of the same sample did not believe in life after death in any shape or form. It is also an important idea as a framework for faith. We mentioned above that even church roll members are not all staunch advocates of their own resurrection and we speculated that because of this they might not be dedicated protagonists of the resurrection of Jesus. If some theologian raises aspects of the future hope of faith in terms of a broad trust in God rather than a specific resurrection doctrine we might expect a fair number of church people to agree, or at least to find that kind of thought helpful.

Holy Communion, Religiosity, and the Dead

When some clergy spoke of folk-religion as an ill-conceived or unthought out scheme they did not perhaps have their own more immediate church members in mind. Yet it is to be expected that the faithful present in church vary in their thoughts and emotions and may not totally reflect in their spirituality the expectations of liturgical theology.

The Parish and People movement beginning in 1949 influenced eucharistic life throughout the Church of England to a marked extent. By the nineteen seventies very many evangelical churches had joined those of anglo-catholic and central traditions in a commitment to the Holy Communion as a central Sunday service for parishioners. The Church of England may now, more uniformly than ever before, be said to be a eucharistic church as far as frequency of public services is concerned. The publication and wide use of the *Alternative Service Book* from 1980 saw to it that this eucharistic stress could be implemented with ease. Yet the uniformity of eucharistic worship was matched by options within that worship which may themselves denote a pluralist society where a number of choices may be equally acceptable (Fenn, 1987:85).

What of the actual consequences of eucharistic spirituality as far as practitioners are concerned? While it is easy enough to spell out theological meanings of the eucharist in relation to the life of faith it is also useful to be more empirical and ask people about their experience. This is what we did, and these are some of the responses from those who said they were active communicant church members, made up of people from both the general and church roll samples and numbering one hundred and sixty eight individuals.

Five statements about the Holy Communion service were formulated and put to these communicants. They sought to explore five potential dimensions of religious belief and are largely self evident. They suggested that Communion:-

    i.   Makes you feel at one with God.
    ii.   Makes you feel at one with other people.
    iii. Gives you a sense of the presence of dead loved ones.
    iv.   Makes you realise what Jesus did for you on the Cross.
    v.   Makes you feel at one with yourself.

The first two dealt with the 'vertical and horizontal' aspects of religion. The fourth touches on a central aspect of the doctrine explicit in the eucharist. The fifth was included to explore aspects of ritual and symbolic behaviour which may be thought to have an integrative function for participants (d'Aquili, 1979), while the third requires some explanation. Because in cognate research by D.J.Davies on cremation it was clear that some people attended church in association with bereavement and also, though not necessarily in contexts of worship, experienced a sense of dead loved ones, we thought it worth exploring people's experience in the eucharistic context.

Practical Eucharistic Spirituality

The results were dramatically similar for men and women:-

On being One with Self (72% and 75%),
Jesus and the Cross (84% and 86%),
Sense of dead loved ones (36% and 38%).

Even the slight numerical differences on One with God (90% and 86%) and One with Others (66% and 71%) were not statistically significant. In the light of these particular questions which were, we must stress, our questions put to people rather than their own unsolicited comments, we might offer a cameo of practical eucharistic spirituality. At its centre is a sense of being at one with God (87%) with a realisation of what Jesus did for the believer on the Cross (85%). This is surrounded by a sense of unity within the self (74%) and just beyond that of unity with others (69%). Finally for a substantial minority there lies the sense of the presence of dead loved ones (37%).

Faithful Departed as Presence

The percentage figures provided above refer to the number of people who mentioned these items. As we see most of the characteristics stand close together except for the sense of presence of dead loved ones which takes a subsidiary place. But perhaps the surprising thing is that over a third of those questioned answered this in the affirmative. That 37% could agree that such a sense or awareness was part of their eucharistic experience might be regarded as a notable finding. Some similar research by Hay and Morisy (1985:217) on a smaller sample showed 22% of an industrial city saying they had 'experienced the presence of or help from the deceased'. How might such findings be evaluated in terms of expected orthodoxy or of a folk religiosity ?

This is an interesting issue which brings to the fore the interaction of formal doctrine and liturgical practice. The eucharist has a very definite place in it for the faithful departed, built as they are into its formal structure of prayer and intercession. But if asked whether they thought that members of the congregation 'ought' to have a sense of their dead during the eucharist many priests might even be astonished by the question. There is, of course, a problem over the meaning of 'sense of the presence of dead loved ones', yet it was a question which a large minority of those interviewed found it easy to understand and answer.

Regional differences were marked on this topic with Lincoln having over half its people mention the dead (56%) while in Gloucester just over a quarter did so (28%). One explanation for this might have been that Lincoln residents were more static in their parishes and have more long standing emotional associations with their parish churches than was the case in Gloucester. But the facts do not bear this out since duration of residence in the Lincoln and Gloucester samples were very similar.

In the cremation project, individuals were interviewed at length on aspects of bereavement and their relationship with the dead (Davies, 1990). It was found that just under a half (45%) had experienced a sense of contact with the dead relative or friend. The actual mode of encounter varied with the most usual being a general sense of the presence of the person concerned (27%), the next group (11%) reckoned to see the person, while a few (5%) heard a voice speaking to them. This sort of information is important for clergy and friends as part of their pastoral outlook on bereaved people. Of those interviewed the majority did not say that they read any particular significance into the event, yet some 11% thought it was specifically aimed at them and most felt such encounters fostered the wellbeing of the living.

In terms of pastoral theology these experiences speak of the complexity of human relationships and of the way in which an individual's identity shares in the identity of others, including those who are dead. Thus, the dead may themselves continue to possess a social identity within the psychology of the living. The pastor can help the bereaved in reorganizing life in relation to those who have died and now have their own identity as dead people. It is interesting that experiences of this sort are not as isolated as might be expected. One modern author even includes an encounter between a pragmatic Oxford Don and his recently dead brother in a story of everyday events (Aldiss 1989:238).

Broadly speaking, then, in this experience of the dead we see

Christian ritual and doctrine giving shape to people's experience as the doctrine of the Communion of Saints and the practice of prayers for the dead focus personal experience. Age did seem to make a difference to this experience with the under thirty five year old group having the highest incidence of 50% which then gradually dropped through all the age groups becoming 27% for the fifty five to sixty four year olds. Then with the over sixty fives it rises again to (47%) nearer the youngest group's experience. It is as though the older and younger relate to the dead more than middle aged groups seem to do.

By contrast with experiencing the dead, the central eucharistic theme of the work of Christ in and through his crucifixion presented an interesting difference between the under and over forty five year olds. There seemed to be a natural break at this middle age point. About 70% of the younger group mentioned the importance of this Christological feature compared with 90% of the older group. One other notable feature connected with age is the sense of being at one with others. This sense was reported by half the under thirty four year olds and then rises steadily throughout the age bands until with the over sixty five year olds it stood at 80%.

Having now looked in some detail at particular aspects of popular religious belief we turn to consider the attitudes of the clergy towards this whole realm of received Christian tradition and its interaction with popular pieties.

Clerical Views on Folk Religion

It is only in recent decades that it has become usual for ecclesiastical commentators to use the phrase 'folk religion' when seeking to draw some distinction between officially orthodox styles of Christian belief and unofficial forms of popular thought, feeling and practice. This trend has tended to follow the approach of social scientists who have, for some time, been concerned with diversity of religious adherence. E.B.Tylor (1871), Max Weber (1922), A.M. Hocart (1935), and Edmund Leach (1968) all addressed themselves to the relation between formal orthodoxy and popular religiosity .

More generally influential was David Martin's pinpointing of 'superstition and subterranean theology' as an important theoretical area for future research in his stimulating *Sociology of English Religion* of 1967. Less well known but important for rural church contexts is James Obelkevich's rich study of rural Lincolnshire (1976). This provides one good account of the way in which Christian superstition and pagan superstition interact within what he calls popular religion. David Clark's *Between Pulpit and Pew* (1982) has done something similar for a Yorkshire fishing village. Many other scholars have touched on the same area with their own preferred terms. Edward Bailey (1990) has done much to foster an interest in the whole field through study days with clergy, teachers, and others and he prefers 'implicit religion' to define popular attitudes to religiosity and life affirmation. John Habgood as Archbishop of York devoted a chapter of his *Church and Nation in a Secular Age* to his sympathetic and pastorally minded concern over what he calls folk religion (1983).

It is not our intention in this book to argue the merit of one term over another. We prefer to seek the views of clergy themselves and to try and document a broad sweep of attitudes, moods, and practices of varying official status in the lives of some ordinary churchgoing and non-churchgoing individuals. This is a field of some obvious importance to the clergy because of the way popular religious beliefs interact with professional clerical interests (Davies 1985). Yet it is also of interest to many others whose faith, however orthodox, is likely to be coloured by regional, denominational, or psychological factors.

This area of folk religion has come to prominence largely because Christianity possesses a theologically trained priesthood and a long history of debate over orthodoxy, heresy, and popular opinion. As an explicit and formal discipline theology interprets this tradition of faith and helps control the life of established churches. Theology comes to life through professional theologians, ministers and others trained in it. Bearing in mind the importance of clerical control, we asked the interviewed clergy whether or not they made any distinction between mainline Christian tradition and folk religion (Table 55).

TABLE 55. Folk-Religion and Christian Tradition: Is There a Distinction to be Drawn ?

	All clergy	
	No	%
Yes	64	63
No	18	18
Unsure	19	19
	101	100

We found that 63% of these clergy did distinguish between folk religion and mainline Christian tradition while 18% did not and a further 19% were unsure. This information is important in forming judgements on the outlook of priests as far as the openness of the Church of England is concerned.

We then asked clergy how they themselves would define folk religion and followed this up by asking specifically which aspects of folk religion they encountered in the course of their ministry. The responses were far from simple and not always easy to interpret.

For simplicity's sake and after extensive content analysis we suggest that two emphases emerged from the replies and these may be typified in terms of ritual practices on the one hand and items of belief on the other. By ritual we refer to the performance of formalized behaviour usually in church or in connection with church, while by belief we indicate ideas and opinions which people are prepared to express with some degree of explicitness. Both these features may be made clearer in the following table which presents in the form of percentages some 137 responses from the 64 clergy who distinguished between folk religion and the mainline tradition. Some stressed more than one feature and we have included these multiple comments below.

TABLE 56. What Aspects of Folk Religion do you Encounter? All Dioceses.

Praxis:	Baptism	20%
	Funerals	17%
	Harvest	13%
	Weddings	10%
	Witchcraft	6%
	Remembrance	4%
	Christmas	3%
	Churching	3%
	Contacting dead	1%
Belief:	Unthinking	7%
	Superstition	6%
	Sincerity	4%
	Fate and luck	3%
	A higher power	3%

Miscellaneous responses not included in the above list were also provided by some 25 different clergy. We present these as a prose cameo of the variety of things which struck these clergy as problematic or as not part and parcel of what Christian faith ought to entertain. This list also serves to show how wide the idea of folk religion can be in clerical minds embracing as it does:-

Smoking in church.

The British Legion coming to hold a service in church.

Sankey Hymn Singing Evenings in the Methodist Church have the same sentiment that Christmas and Easter have in the Church of England.

Flower Festivals and Songs of Praise.

Elderly people say they used to go to church while others say they don't go to church but still lead a Christian life. Some say they are nice people but don't realise they need Jesus' help.

Some like to hear the baby cry at baptism so that the devil can get out, and others think the baby grows better after baptism.

If these seem to address the issue in a negative way almost as many spoke more positively of popular strands of religiosity.

In God's eyes there is no folk religion but there is in the eyes of the church.

People are honestly trying to find God but we are so insensitive to that. I am appalled by the difference between what's said at General Synod and what it's like on the ground.

All religion is natural, and there is some folk religion in all of us.

Trying to understand what lies behind this great variety of clerical opinion we have drawn some distinctions between what we have called practical and creedal elements of folk religion, and also between strong and weak forms of each.

Strong and Weak Forms of Practical Folk Religion

A weak form of practical folk religion is exemplified in the single reference to smoking in church. It is an interesting case for while it hardly involves any doctrinal issue it touches on convention and the respect felt to be due to a church building. The mention of it indicates a sense that only unchurched people would behave in this disrespectful manner. The eight references to witchcraft: two from Durham and six from Truro, fall into a more immediately recognisable form of irreligious belief because of the historical place of witchcraft in European Christianity and in contemporary paganism. They referred to events that had taken place or people who were known to be associated with witchcraft. Clergy from the other three dioceses did not mention witchcraft while there were three items of superstition in Gloucester. There seems to be a distinction between certain very obvious and specific folk-religion items of a clear non-Christian type such as witchcraft and vaguer areas which lie partly or largely within the church domain.

As far as this latter group is concerned the basic question seems to be that of attitude towards official church rites. So it seems that folk religion moves from one end of a continuum of outlawed behaviour to the other end of suspect motivation of otherwise established practices, and it is this group which comprises the great majority of folk religion references. They cover the gamut of church focused rites viz., baptisms, funerals, weddings, and harvests. This raises a critical theoretical point of interpretation and intention underlying the more belief focused aspects of folk religion.

Strong and Weak Forms of Creedal Folk Religion

In its 'strong' version folk faith speaks of ideas like that of baptism as making a child grow better, while at its 'weakest' it involves a vague and ill-conceived bundle of ideas on themes such as luck or just simply having baptism 'done' for some vaguer notion of welfare. Thoughts like these were said by the clergy to be, 'not thought through',or the result of people with an 'inability to express anything abstract'. So clarity, explicitness, and logical fit of beliefs into traditional doctrine seem to be the implicit qualification of orthodoxy while the alternative world of unorthodoxy shares deeply in vagueness.

The fact that the church itself has in the past and to a degree still fosters many rites that people practise but cannot fully or rationally explain underlies some clerical opinion. One individual even saw a congregation's insistence on singing the canticles at Matins as an expression of folk religion in the sense of wanting to perpetuate traditional practice. This shows in one of the clearest ways how varied the perception of folk religion can be, one moment representing antique attitudes of regular churchgoers and the next witchcraft outside the church. Because we anticipated such variation we asked clergy to offer us their own definitions of folk religion to enable us to get away from what have tended to become rather conventional ways of talking about folk-religion as the semi-superstitious opinions of relatively unchurched people. In the past church discussions about folk religion have, perhaps, told us more about the church than about the people who are supposed to be folk-religionists.

The following three lists have been arranged in a very particular way and on the assumption that the items are really telling us more about the informants than about their congregations and people. The concept underlying the organisation of these groups is the sociological distinction between exclusive and inclusive principles of membership in religious groups. The three groups represent bands on a continuum from exclusivist to inclusivist forms of religion. The choice of this distinction arises from many comments in recent years on the Church of England becoming rather sectarian in outlook, since it is customary in the sociology of religion to distinguish between an exclusive membership principle which exacts a relatively high levels of commitment from sect members, and an inclusive membership principle which works on much laxer levels of commitment and clarity of faith amongst members of more established churches. Group One marks the exclusivist and Group Three the inclusivist ends of the continuum.

Folk Religion (F-R) and Mainstream Christian Tradition
Some Clerical Distinctions.

Group 1

Totally different, black and white.
F-R is anti-Christian: seeks protection against evil.
Revealed Religion vs. F-R.
Sacramental Basis of Christianity vs F-R.
Worshipping Community vs F-R.
Church Structures vs FR lying outside church.
Converted vs F-R.
Commitment vs Residual Religion.
Real Christianity vs F-R.
Lively Spirituality vs F-R.
Needing Jesus' help vs being a nice person.

Group 2

Real old mixture of integrity and God's presence.

Honestly trying to find God.
Sense of something beyond without a detailed theology.
As meaningful as intellectual religion but lacks expression.
Not thought through.
Residual Christianity on the fringe of church.
F-R involves ministry to people.
Church Ministry involves ministry with people.
We have New Testament Christianity, Traditional Anglicanism and the Church of England: the church they stay away from.

Group 3

No boundaries to evil.
In God's eyes there is no F-R only in eyes of Church.
All religion is natural.
All have their own religion. But revealed vs natural contradict

These clerical opinions add more depth to our analysis of pastoral perspectives as detailed in Chapter 5 and should be read alongside that material. Of course it would be perfectly possible to interpret the clergy's views in other ways if we chose alternative perspectives. While staying close to the idea of membership principles we can exemplify this by broadening our concern to include three particular emphases which seemed to emerge in the clerical opinions each of which could have been used as the basic criterion for interpreting the material. One focuses on spirituality and commitment, another on orthodoxy of doctrine, and the third on institutional involvement. A rapid sketch of the significance of each will indicate something of the dimensions they add to what has already been said.

Spirituality focuses on issues of religious commitment and insight. It surfaced both for those within and those on the margin of formal church activity and stressed men and women as religious beings whose instinctive humanity was sensitive to faith. This outlook tended to be more inclusive in attitude.

Doctrine emphasizes the degree to which orthodoxy involves clear articulation of belief in contrast to the unformed and vague clusters of folk belief. A more mixed attitude underlay this position perhaps because of the recognition that even regular church attenders may have a relatively unformed theological understanding in any systematic sense.

Overall those who thought in this way adopted a positive attitude and a sense of welcome to people irrespective of their level of knowledge. Organization dwells on active participation in church worship and sacramental activity. If anything this tended to be more exclusive in nature, but that is quite intelligible since attending church is a clear activity. Visible behaviour is obvious, even measurable, while thought, opinion, and belief, are less so. We might expect that participation and clarity of expression would be correlated by some clergy though others would not see attendance and formal understanding of doctrine as necessarily related. Another aspect of the relation between motivation and church attendance emerged in the clergy interviews when we asked whether they thought that people made use of the Church for their own convenience? The answers which have already been explored in Chapter 5 show that pastoral work is the primary touchstone for clerical outlook. That same concern influenced the choice of the membership principle as the basis for discussing folk religion and mainstream Christian tradition in this chapter so far. But now the emphasis shifts as we turn to look in some detail at the content of people's outlook on life, though it will certainly be the case that many ministers will find the emerging picture of some pastoral interest.

Attitudes to Religion

The question of religious beliefs among the population at large and among churchgoing people in particular is obviously important in any study of religion in contemporary Britain. With this in mind the Rural Church Project set about discovering popular attitudes to religion. Questions were constructed in such a way as to increase options rather than to limit responses in simple yes–no answers. An important reason for this was to explore patterns of religious belief rather than simple percentage agreement with particular and isolated beliefs.

To focus our work we took Robert Towler's scheme for what he called conventional religion in his book *The Need for Certainty* (1984). He constructed five types of religion which he called: Exemplarism, Conversionism, Theism, Gnosticism, and Traditionalism. Each was associated with what he called a particular 'cognitive style'. In one sense this is a misnomer because he uses the phrase to express distinctive emotions rather than central logical features of faith, but it was a sound theoretical move because it emphasized the importance of the emotional dimension of religion. Exemplarism had the cognitive style of hope, Conversionism of assurance, Theism of trust, Gnosticism a scientific view or, better perhaps a matter of factness, while Traditionalism possessed an unquestioned acceptance of religion.

His work was not derived from survey methods but, as noted earlier, from a content analysis of letters written to John Robinson the former Bishop of Woolwich following the publication of Robinson's popular book *Honest To God* (1963). He proceeded with caution, as we do ourselves, in the following analysis of results. We show that Towler's types are reflected in our findings but that we have found it necessary to go beyond them in specific cases. We included questions to extend the possible variety of answers and to tease out some broader attitudes to life which might not normally be regarded as religious.

People were first asked whether they agreed, disagreed, or were unsure, of their response to these twelve questions:

1. God is the Creator of everything.
2. We must keep the faith handed down to us.
3. Each person must receive Christ into their lives.
4. Everything will be alright in the end.
5. We must follow Jesus as an example of how to live.
6. The other world is near to this one.
7. We must search for the Truth throughout our lives.
8. Science explains everything we need to know.
9. We only live once so let's make the most of it.
10. Nearly all religious people are hypocrites or fanatics.
11. We need renewing by the Holy Spirt.
12. Each person must be 'Born Again'.

Every respondent was able to comment on each item enabling us to obtain a profile on all items for each person interviewed. They were then asked which of these statements best fitted their outlook on life. This 'best fit' answer was subsequently related to the earlier profile to produce a religious 'theme' for each individual. We shall use the word 'theme' throughout the remainder of this chapter preferring it to 'type' or 'pattern' since it is easier to think, for example, of a congregation composed of people with different religious themes in mind than with types or patterns. Each theme was arranged in such a way that the profile began with the most and ended with the least emphasized attitude.

The twelve questions moved from standard ideas of God as creator, of the need to Keep the Faith handed down to us, through ideas of Christ as Example, of the Holy Spirit and Renewal, to the generalized hope that Everything will be alright in the End, and that Science Explains all we Need to Know. The relationship of the 'Other World' to this world was included to touch on Towler's concern for 'Gnostic' forms of religion which touch on Spiritualist views. The ideas that we Only Live Once and also that we must Search for Truth throughout our lives were included to seek a broader frame of possible response of a less traditional religious focus. The question that Religious People are Hypocrites was included to see how that might relate to the other factors. The following table shows the full list of questions asked and the 'best fit' responses from both Civil and Church Registers.

TABLE 57. *Chosen Outlook on Religion*

Chosen outlook	General sample (n=341)	Church roll sample (n=148)
'Best fit'	%	%
Only live once	22	9
Jesus as example	13	22
Search for truth	17	14
God is creator	10	8
Faith handed down	9	15
Receive Christ	4	6
Alright in end	5	3
Other world near	1	1
Science explains	1	2
Renew by spirit	1	3
Born again	1	1
Hypocrites	2	0
Combination	3	11
None of these	4	1
Refused answer	5	2
Don't know	2	2
Total	100	100

One interesting feature here lies in the fact that on three of the five categories which we may identify as the most popular overall forms of response there is a difference between the church roll and the general population.

The 'Only Live Once' preference heads the general population response (22%), but comes much lower on the church roll list (9%). Similarly the second overall category 'Jesus as Example' differs markedly between church roll (22%) and general samples (13%). On the idea that we must 'Keep the Faith' handed down to us, we find church roll members placing a higher stress (15%) than did the general population (9%).

For the other two popular categories there is less of a distinction between the two samples. On 'Search for the Truth' the general sample has a higher rate (17%) than the church roll sample (14%). With the idea of 'God as Creator' there is very little difference between the groups.

From among the other responses it is worth noting that the view of Science as Explanation gained a very small preference. Similarly low preferences were expressed for the 'Born Again' response, the 'Other World is Near', and for the idea that most religious people are either Hypocrites or Fanatics.

Preferred Religious Themes

Seven of the themes together account for the first preferences of more than three quarters of respondents in both samples and these we now examine by exploring the detailed profile of each. Using the 'best fit' statement to head each theme we *look at the order in which people selected additional beliefs to go with their main choice.* Additional beliefs mentioned by more than 40% of those choosing the dominant theme are included. In the following discussion the focus is on all respondents taken together since we have already considered some of the differences between those from the church roll and general samples.

The variation in level of response is itself an interesting feature of the survey. It seems that when the best-fit theme is explicitly religious the respondent gives higher positive value to many statements about life than when the dominant theme is more general. This variation is such that in the 'Only Live Once', 'Search for Truth', and 'Alright in End' themes there is a lower general rate of response than in the two themes of 'Keeping the Faith' and 'God is Creator'. The 'Jesus as Example' and 'Receive Christ' themes have the highest percentage of agreement with all other statements offered. This might be expected in that distinctive ideas are likely to attract aligned concepts whereas vaguer notions are more likely to stand alone. Of course, other factors are doubtless involved and require further research. Our task now is to give an account of popular religion as found in our five diocese sample and expressed under each theme heading.

Theme One: We only live once so let's make the most of it
    For each theme, those interviewed were shown a statement and asked whether they agreed, disagreed, or were unsure about it as far as their 'own outlook on religion' was concerned. Of those individuals who chose 'Only Live Once' as their dominant outlook (89–18%), 67% also agreed that one should Search for the Truth, and 48% that one should Keep the Faith handed down to us (Table 58).

TABLE 58. Only Live Once (n=89, 18% of Total respondents)

	% Selecting additional beliefs
We must search for the truth . . .	67
We must keep the faith . . .	48
Everything will be alright . . .	45
We must follow Jesus as example . . .	43

The idea that we Only Live Once was included to try to identify a general attitude to life that did not specifically involve a religious conviction or belief in a life after death. It is interesting that while just about half of the total population in the entire survey did not believe in an after-life only eighteen per cent actually chose this theme as their major perspective. There was a huge difference here between the general (22%) and church roll (9%) samples which is likely to indicate an underlying divergence between more existentialist and more theistic perspectives.
    The Search for Truth theme is the main partner to Only Live Once, followed by the Faith Handed Down and the sense of all being well in the end. The only explicitly religious idea that passes the forty per cent mark, is the acceptance that Jesus is an example to follow. Science is given its highest rating of any type (33%) while the Born Again feature is at its lowest (10%)

Theme Two: We must search for the Truth throughout our lives
The response to the idea that one should 'Search for Truth' throughout one's life was placed first by seventy seven individuals, 16% of the total number of respondents. These Search for Truth individuals responded to the other themes as shown Table 59.

TABLE 59. *Search for Truth* (n=77; 16% of Total Respondents)

	% Selecting additional beliefs
We only live once . . .	65
We must follow Jesus as example . . .	62
God is the Creator of everything . . .	52
We must keep the Faith . . .	49
We need renewing by the Holy Spirit . . .	46

The pattern that emerges here is of people who see the Search for Truth as important in a life only lived once. In addition these individuals are likely to cite Jesus as a good example to follow and just over half (52%) of the group believed that God was Creator. Thus some people were happy to see Jesus as an example for life whilst not accepting God as Creator. Though not shown in the table, support for the idea that science explains all we need to know about life stood at 12%, the same level as the perceived necessity to be Born Again. Thus the search for Truth seems to be associated far more with religious ideas than with science. Interestingly there was little difference between general (17%) and church roll samples (14%) on this theme, unlike the situation found in theme one.

Theme Three: Everything will be Alright in the End
As in the case of the Only Live Once theme, this option was included to cover an open and generalised optimism towards life which did not invest any special significance in doctrinally formulated perspectives. Table 60 shows the pattern that emerged.

TABLE 60. *Everything will be Alright in the End* (n=21, 4% of Total Respondents)

	% Selecting additional beliefs
We only live once . . .	71
We must search for the truth . . .	67
We must follow Jesus as example . . .	52
We must keep the Faith . . .	48
(God is the creator of everything . . .	38)

Only 21 individuals, four per cent of all respondents, went for this option. They very largely also agreed with the idea that we only Live Once (71%), and that it is important to Search for the Truth (67%). Just over a half of them (52%) thought that Jesus was an Example to Follow. Just under a half (48%) thought it was important to Keep the Faith handed down to us, with fewer still (38%) agreeing with the idea that God was Creator. This shows again that the place of Jesus as Example can be stressed by people who do not stress the notion of a Creator, although theologically trained people might implicitly assume that Christ related statements were dependent upon prior belief in God as Creator.

Theme Four: We must keep the Faith handed down to us

Before we look in detail at the nature of this theme it is worth making a general observation on the element of tradition in all of the themes. The other six themes can be divided into two broad categories of low and high emphasis on the keeping of tradition. The three we have so far covered all had Keeping the Faith at about the same level at just under fifty per cent. The final three themes all recorded high support for Keeping the Faith: theme five (57%), theme six (70%), and theme seven (70%). Perhaps certain ideas associated with tradition are more intimately linked with religious aspects of life than with more individualistic and possibly humanistic tendencies.

If we look at the theme of Keeping the Faith in its own right we find a group of 51 people (Table 61). They show a high emphasis on the Search for Truth (84%), and Jesus as Example (73%), followed by similar and moderately high agreement with God as Creator (69%), Receiving Christ (67%) and Only Living Once (67%).

TABLE 61. *Keeping the Faith* (n=51, 10% of Total Respondents)

	% Selecting additional beliefs
We must search for the truth . . .	84
We must follow Jesus as example . . .	73
God is the creator of everything . . .	69
Each person must receive Christ . . .	67
We only live once . . .	67
We need renewing by the Holy Spirit . . .	55
Everything will be alright . . .	51

The stress on Receiving Christ (67%) into the individual's life shows a conversionist element higher than in any other type save that devoted to Receiving Christ. The idea of renewal by the Holy Spirit was also affirmed to by more than half of the respondents (55%). Towler's Traditionalist type does not entirely resemble the profile presented here. The high rate of Search for Truth (84%) does not seem entirely consonant with unquestioning acceptance which Towler takes as the 'cognitive style' typical of the traditionalist but, equally, it might be possible to interpret Search for Truth in terms of Towler's insistence that the British traditionalist has a firm empirical outlook.

Theme Five: God is the Creator of Everything

Ten per cent of all respondents made this their first choice. As with the previous theme of Keeping the Faith the first two supportive items are Search for Truth (81%), and Jesus as Example (77%). Interestingly the Search for Truth, Jesus as Example, Keep the Faith, and God as Creator items are very closely related in themes four and five. As far as the first two of these items are concerned they are practically parallel for both themes. The scheme for the Creator respondents is shown in Table 62.

Another similarity with Keeping the Faith theme lies in the Need for Renewal, both being in the fifty per cent range. It might be that these types are versions of one form of piety. There is only one small difference between them and it is that while the two issues of Receiving Christ and Only Living Once lie close together in each type the position of the pair varies. The Traditionalists place both at sixty seven per cent while the Creationists give them forty and forty three per cent respectively.

Belief and Theology

Belief and Theology 277

TABLE 62. God is Creator of Everything (n=47; 10% of Total Respondents)

	% Selecting additional beliefs
We must search for the truth . . .	81
We must follow Jesus as example . . .	77
We must keep the faith . . .	75
We each need renewing by the Holy Spirit . . .	57
The other world is near to this one . . .	53
We only live once . . .	43
Each person must receive Christ . . .	40

Theme Six: We must follow Jesus as an example of how to live

Sixteen per cent of all surveyed elected this as their central theme. Here the ninety per cent level is reached in a supporting statement, viz Search for Truth. The full pattern of responses above 40% is shown in Table 63.

TABLE 63. Jesus Example to Follow (n=76; 16% of Total Respondents)

	% Selecting additional beliefs
We must search for the truth . . .	90
God is the creator of everything . . .	75
We must keep the faith . . .	70
We need renewing by the Holy Spirit . . .	63
Each person must receive Christ . . .	62
We only live once . . .	59
Everything will be alright in the end . . .	48

Once more we see that to take Jesus as Example does not necessarily involve acceptance of belief in God as Creator, though three quarters did so believe. The dual themes of Receiving Christ and Renewing by the Spirit stand close together (62% and 63%). These items raise an important point of discrepancy with Towler's discussion of his Exemplarism type. He saw Exemplarism as an important aspect of popular religion in Britain. For him it is a 'Christian form of humanism'

(1984:28), and is largely private in its operation but, above all, he thought that questions about God were 'profoundly irrelevant' to this way of being religious. Because of this Towler thought that the "don't know" response should be treated with particular care.

It was with this caution in mind that we presented people with a wide variety of belief and value statements and asked if they agreed, disagreed, or were unsure of their attitude towards particular items. Having included a statement specifically aimed at attracting Exemplarists and also having given them an opportunity to comment on the other beliefs we are in a position to see the range of response that they accepted. The two items of Receiving Christ and Renewal by the Spirit stand out, as we have already suggested, as having some distinctive characteristics that might suggest more of an element of personal piety than an incipient atheism might anticipate. Similarly the high level of agreement on God as Creator suggests that at least some questions about God were not "profoundly irrelevant" for many of a Traditionalist perspective.

Theme Seven: Each person must receive Christ into their lives

This group of respondents was small, numbering only twenty three individuals (5%). But it was a group of intense responses. Those choosing the Receive Christ Theme as that which best fitted their outlook on religion were those who also had the highest level of overall agreement with many other items as Table 64 demonstrates.

TABLE 64. Receive Christ (n=23; 5% of Total Respondents)

	% Selecting additional beliefs
We must search for the truth . . .	96
God is the creator of everything . . .	96
We must follow Jesus as example . . .	91
We need renewing by the Holy Spirit . . .	78
We must keep the faith . . .	70
Everything will be alright in the end . . .	70
The other world is near to this one . . .	61
We only live once . . .	57
(Each person must be born again . . .	30)

Three items stand together as agreed by over 90% of the respondents. Topping these at 96% we have both the Search for Truth and God as Creator items. Jesus as Example is also very high (91%). Tradition too is relatively high (70%) as is the optimistic view that everything will be alright in the end (70%).

The stress on Renewal by the Holy Spirit (78%) is even higher than in theme six Jesus as Example (63%). An interesting feature of this theme is that although seventy eight per cent assert the need for Renewal by the Spirit, only thirty per cent assent to the need to be Born Again. In the first five themes the Born Again entry lies below twenty per cent (varying from 10% to 19%). This suggests the need for further research in that the term may not have been fully intelligible to many respondents. To some extent it might be that the idea of Renewal by the Spirit has come to assume priority over ideas of rebirth in the traditional evangelical form of discourse.

Emergent Patterns of Types

Relatively little is known about the dynamics and nature of popular religion in contemporary Britain, and what we have shown is that it is a complex field. The themes dealt with here must be viewed with caution. We have erred in the direction of allowing for complexity within a dominant form of response rather than paring down to a single defining feature. The Born Again theme exemplifies this complexity and shows some of the problems involved in asking people about their religiosity. Terms used for questions are particularly prone to variation of understanding, meaning, and significance.

The seven themes presented may stand on their own as offering distinctive trends in world view. The first three emphasise philosophical or existential features over and above more orthodox doctrinal issues. The last three are more specifically religious, in the ordinary church use of that word, while the fourth seems to share in features present in the other two major groupings.

In terms of Robert Towler's sociological types his Exemplarist and Conversionist correspond with Jesus as Example and Receiving Christ; his Theism with our God as Creator, and his Traditionalist with our Keep the Faith. As far as our data are concerned it would be reasonable to unite the first three into a category not represented by Towler but which seems important from our study. This represents a pragmatism with only a relatively low preponderance of explicit doctrinal ideas.

The Traditional type could be merged with God as Creator to give a Traditionalist Theme, while Jesus as Example and Receiving Christ seem to belong together as a more explicit type of Christian piety which might be called a theme of commitment.

Gnostic Type as Trend

The only type which is clear in Towler but which finds relatively little support in our study is his Gnostic type. Our question on the 'Other World being near to this one' was intended to elicit the 'gnostic' response. Perhaps it failed to do this and was a poor question. Only four people in the entire sample gave this as the best fit with their attitude to life. However it was a response that found a place within other types, with a similar representation in the first four themes (22%, 22%, 24% and 28%). In the remaining three themes its presence varies most interestingly. In God as Creator (theme six) it is high (53%) and may represent something of Towler's notion of transcendence rather than a spiritualist-like significance. In the Receiving Christ type (theme seven) it is extremely high (61%) where it is likely to refer to the reality of Christ in people with a sense of spiritual renewal. This is a good example of a phrase, 'the other world', with a wide band of meaning.

Themes, Types and Orientations

As we conclude this section on patterns of religion we stress once more the theoretical nature of the exercise. The idea of 'orientation to the world' of a person or group has been a theoretically fruitful issue ever since Max Weber's (1922) explicit study of the sociology of religion in the first two decades of this century. The use of themes in this Chapter is intended to express such a picture. Each theme is an orientation to the world, or as we rather bluntly expressed it earlier, each is a 'best fit' of idea and individual outlook.

In everyday life people possess a combination of belief, attitudes, and values which may vary throughout life. But the different contexts in which people find themselves may also affect which aspect of belief or non-belief they draw upon. The anthropologist Ioan Lewis has done much to encourage a concern with context as a means of grasping the way people select and use their beliefs (1986).

The results presented in this survey are the result of interviews and do not accurately reflect a person's chosen belief in the face of trial or leisure. With that theoretical caution in mind, we think we have shown that, in the interview context, people make a broad choice of belief so that some sort of thematic construction is demanded to do them justice and to show how thematic material is woven into the complexity of practical belief. Such insight is very needful for pastoral work and will be important as a background analysis for the following final reflections in the more doctrinal aspects of pastoral theology.

10

Theological Reflections

This book emerged from intensive collaboration in research and fieldwork. Using social survey methods in an interdisciplinary way we have sought to rise above the local and anecdotal whilst being fully aware that particular parish factors are often dramatically important for parishioners and clergy. The material we have presented is offered as much to stimulate discussion as to contribute to our stock of knowledge of the rural Church of England. We end with some very particular theological reflections to make it clear that as far as we are concerned social scientific analysis can usefully enter into theology. Pastoral theology in particular stands in need of this sort of dialogue because as a form of theology it has tended to languish in England despite the fact that across the land many devoted pastors are dedicatedly at work.

Church and Religion in Rural England has not been a book of theology. It has been largely about measurable religious behaviour approached from the perspectives of social science and geography. Nonetheless we believe its contents have important theological implications. Therefore this final chapter, by way of conclusion, is devoted to theological reflection. At its best theology is creativity of a particular type sparked by an imagination excited by God. In worship it becomes wonder, in service it yields ethics, and in duty demands social comment.

This is important for those readers who have had theological and pastoral interests in mind while reading earlier chapters and because we, too, want this book to express the benefit gained from interdisciplinary collaboration. For many readers theological and pastoral concerns are ultimately one as doctrinal issues spark among the concerns of daily life. This very interaction of theology with ordinary lives, day in and day out, is itself a resource that can never be ignored as Liberation Theology has taught us. People and clergy take the everydayness of life, the tradition of bible and comment, and the power of joint worship to engage in theology together. This has been apparent to us in talking to many clergy over the course of the Rural Church Project. The collaboration of experts and 'lay' amateurs is a feature of theology which marks it out from many other academic disciplines whose proponents only have their colleagues and peers as partners in their venture.

Theology, by contrast has a wide public. People inside and outside the churches show an interest in theology because it involves life, reality, and destiny. They have a right to be interested, they also have a right to be involved. Theologians too have a duty to mutual involvement and education. This conclusion is one small contribution along these lines. Our concern at this closing point is with theological ideas which have been prompted by our many conversations and other findings, a concern focused through the doctrines of Creation and Salvation in relation to images and contexts of Christian living and ministry in rural areas.

Creation and Salvation

If Christian religion is about anything it is about depth. Depth in humanity, depth in God, and depth in divine-human relationships. Depth is a most appropriate word, at once open to poetry and available for metaphor. In our culture it also catches the sense of a life we value and praise. So too with its opposite. None of us would be shallow, devoid of the humanity that makes persons real. Depth embraces the sense of the sacred as it does a sense of purpose in existence. It reaches into the power of mood in religious life as it fills out the explorations of intellect (Tillich,1953:88 ff.)

Theology describes and fosters that depth in human beings which arises from the depth of God. In the Christian doctrine of creation we learn that God wills a world of extensive complexity, varied and interactive. A world of material depth. But, biblically speaking, social life and human institutions are also part and parcel of the natural world: in biblical Israel at least good social order mirrored the orderliness of nature which in turn reflected the perfection of God. As such society too is deep in significance.

The idea of covenant in the Old Testament extends both into nature and society. God is committed to both domains and calls the chosen people into a similar mutual bond. So it is that in Christian theological terms humanity becomes responsible both for natural and social phenomena. The biblical idea of this human responsibility has tended more recently to be interpreted as 'rights', the rights of natural things to survive and of society to express itself.

In the Bible Israel is seen as the focus of God's commitment, love, and purpose. Israel is as much a creation as is nature itself. Indeed the distinction between nature and culture which has increasingly established itself in European thought is very hard to read from the Old Testament. The theological ideas of creation and salvation are united in the theme of covenant. It is the God who wills a world into being who also wills a nation into existence and who is committed to its flourishing. Salvation becomes national wellbeing rooted firmly in agricultural, economic, and political solidarity.

When we shift our focus to New Testament theology we find these natural and social perspectives of creation and salvation taking a different turn and coming to a personified focus in Jesus as Messiah and subsequently as Divinity. In Christian theology human nature and the purpose of Israel are joined together in God's chosen one. Here depth extends in humanity, a divine depth which generates depth both in the believer, and in the community of those who believe. The church has come to be the formal expression of that group belief and a critical means of fostering faith.

It is perhaps because the Jewish notion of Messiah only made sense in the social framework of Israel that Christology demands a church. Be that as it may, the historical fact is that Christian theology begins with Jesus and is framed by the church that holds and reflects upon Him. In this, Christian theology is intrinsically person focused and group located. Historically speaking too the church is an urban religion which in origin involved voluntary membership. The relationship between the urban and the rural was, initially, the relationship between the civilized and the pagan. And civilization soon carried Christian identity with it. The expansion of Christianity throughout Europe is more a history of cities and monarchs than of fields and peasants (Frend, 1979; Mann, 1986). Some Celtic and other monastic traditions to the contrary, Christianity has tended to come to a theology of the rural from a theology of the social. The nomadic and pastoral motifs of the Old Testament and the rural threads of Gospel stories should not obliterate the urban substratum of much of the New Testament.

This is especially important for theology in Britain where for historical and cultural reasons rural situations have not only come to represent a particularly intense sense of the divine (Fuller, 1988), but have also served as a background framework for 'the life and times' of Jesus. The more recent ideal of the rural village as a commuter haven finds precedents in both eighteenth and nineteenth century views of landscape and society in Britain (Cosgrove and Daniels, 1988). Such a rural ideal has also supported ecclesiastical views of the rural parish as the typical model of and for Anglican pastoral practice as we argued in Chapter 2.

Salvation in Town and Country

The city came into its own in twentieth century theology not as an expression of St. Augustine's City of God nor of the Heavenly Jerusalem of The Apocalypse but as a radical challenge to traditional faith. Freed from the shadowy constraints of Babel and divine disapproval it flourished as Harvey Cox's *Secular City* (1965). Here, for a while, the modern individual tasted freedom from traditional and kinship constraints and experienced the relativising of religious beliefs within cosmopolitan neighbourhoods. But not for long. Soon the pressured life spent in economic gain or in the abandonment of poverty and displacement made the city into a poor place for human depth.

Idyllic country retreats or domiciles were desirable for those able to afford them, otherwise the church or other agencies had to seek to create communities or refuges within cities. In other words depth had to be organized by one means or other to preserve humanity. The Church of England's report *Faith in the City* (1985) is, in a sense, a timely partner to Harvey Cox's latter day reflection significantly entitled *Religion in the Secular City* (1984), urging a rethink of religious awareness within social responsibility in contemporary city life. For Cox the American surprise is that secularization has not triumphed, for the Church of England there is less surprise than pragmatic concern to foster social and ethical concerns.

Salvation here lies in transformed human relationships where a sense of worth emerges between human beings. Worth is one aspect of depth, worth is the moral and personal form of depth within Christian theology. Ministry seeks to foster relationships in such a way as to aid the sense of identity grounded in self-respect and self-worth. In many respects this is the Christian church returning to its earliest Mediterranean context of providing a fellowship for the disinherited or the intellectually disoriented.

Rural Theology

At a simple level this urban emphasis might seem a false start given that the bible opens with the Genesis stories of creation stressing the natural order and taking its time before ending with the Apocalyptic City of God and its transformed urbanization of humankind. But dates of books apart priority is with humankind and not with the beasts, with society and not with the animals. Indeed Christianity's theology of nature is secondary, vitally important but secondary, to its theology of humanity. Consequently one of the implicit problems of rural theology lies in a lack of clear perspective. This easily leads to a sense of awkwardness as thoughts about nature and the stewardship of nature seem to edge against ideas of Christ and salvation. Since there has never been any formal theological distinction between church doctrine for towns and for the countryside this is not surprising. Christian doctrine has emerged without particular regard for rural life, which means that rural theology, like any applied aspect of theological analysis, has to be worked out for the purpose in hand. But, as we showed in Chapter 2, in England the church had established itself historically as a rural presence with the implied assumption that there was an inevitable link between church, rurality, and theological truth. This situation is a challenge and one which people in their own contexts need to take up. In the points which now follow we simply make some suggestions on but a few possible theological perspectives.

Two basically different models underlie much thinking on rural religion and if they are not distinguished from each other they tend to produce a logical clash at some point in discussing the application of the Christian message within rural parishes. The one focuses on nature and creation, the other on Jesus and redemption. We consider each in turn before looking at rites of passage, as a pastoral issue which itself needs to be related to each of the two basic theological models.

It is important to stress that the two models or schemes to which we draw attention here are specifically theological. In this we differ from Anthony Russell, whose study *The Country Parish* has a fundamentally sociological focus on the twofold understanding of the church in rural areas, (1986:259). He places special importance on the committed gathered congregation on the one hand and the geographical parish residents on the other. We have fully explored this sociological theme in Chapter 5 but now an explicitly theological discussion is required. Sociological models are helpful and sometimes even vital when considering church life but they should not determine the theological endeavour which needs a life of its own in relation to the social facts. Having said that we should also add that while the two theological schemes of creation and salvation may be associated with the two sociological notions of geographical community and committed congregation they are certainly not matching and identical pairs.

The history of religion teaches us that humankind has ever tended to be religious. Myths of creation abound the world over, as do divinely sanctioned laws touching the natural world. Ideas of God as Creator are natural to the human species and a sense of dependence upon God has often been associated with dependence upon the raw materials of the world and the seasons controlling them. Being 'close to nature' somehow involves a sense of proximity to God. The expression, 'nearer God's heart in a garden than anywhere else on earth', is for some people a great truth while for others it is a sentimental untruth of ill-tutored minds or religiously uncommitted hearts.

The biblical lessons associated with Harvest Festivals do not need a great degree of translation and application to modern congregations whether rural or urban. They speak of God as ultimately responsible for all things and of humankind as benefitting from the divine bounty and as desirous of giving thanks for it. Humanity's stewardship of creation is recognized as of fundamental importance and is easily accepted as reasonable. 'Green theology' flows from this creation religion. In more traditional terms this outlook lies close to natural theology in which reason itself speaks to us of an idea of God as Creative Father who providentially orders the seasons aright and is, if anything, somewhat remote from individuals. Even so the recognition of sacred places where access to deity is relatively easy is important and feeds into some views of the parish church.

Salvation in this type of religion involves the sustaining capacity of deity within an ordered framework of moral responsibility. Salvation means harvest, damnation means drought, famine, and plague. Formal religious leadership often takes the form of priests who act on behalf of the people and also speak for God when occasion demands it. A central feature of this kind of spirituality links merit with reward (Davies 1986:11). God should treat people according to their actions. Merit is rewarded and punishment may well be expected. All this fits with the sense of Covenant explicit in the Old Testament picture sketched earlier. To a degree it also fits the social world of related kin set in a network of obligation and duty to each other.

In some respects this stereotyped view of natural religion fits images of rural religion which some of the priests we interviewed thought might be in the minds of their rural congregations. If the Harvest Festival Service is one ritual expression of this outlook then it is interesting to see that for the general sample or parish residents more people attended Harvest Festivals (31%) than attended at Easter (24%). For those on church electoral rolls the attendance was practically identical (71% and 72% respectively).

Christ and Re-creation

Easter services immediately raise the second type of religious outlook, that which is more specifically Christ focused and moves from creation as a nature linked perspective to salvation which is person focused. While the religion of the general sample may be more concerned with a Creator God, this was not the case for regular church attenders. What Jesus did on the Cross for believers was said to be an important aspect of the Holy Communion service by 85% of church attenders interviewed in this study. Almost exactly the same number mentioned the sense of being at one with God as an important part of their eucharistic experience. This strikes the note of a style of religion which is concerned with salvation as a more personal and intimate awareness of God. Indeed even the awareness of being at one with oneself (73%) came lower in priority than the issues just mentioned. The external world and its relationships, important as they are, take second place to the sense of God as personally related to the individual. If to this outlook is added the style of religion which sees Jesus as an example to follow then the Christ centred focus of faith is even greater in the sample of people we surveyed. We have already discussed these types of faith and here we simply make the point that a Christ related faith differs to a degree from that of the Creator God style.

Easter is the festival of Christ centred faith, for those for whom God is more directly involved in life through the life of Jesus rather than through nature. Salvation here is more personal and less related to the elements of nature as such. The style of ministry appropriate to this form of religion focuses on the priest's concern with the spiritual development of individuals rather than the broad welfare of a geographically located association of people.

Rites of Passage in Nature and Salvation

If Harvest exemplifies God in Creation, and Easter God in Redemption then rites of passage show God in providential concern with the social life of individuals. As such, rites of passage touch both the domains of creation and redemption. All these areas show the scale over which ministers of the church have to operate in a variety of pastoral involvement which influences their religious outlook. We can see something of this influence in the fact that just under a half (43%) of the clergy interviewed reckoned to have experienced a shift in their own churchmanship.

Central to this change was the daily experience of pastoral concerns both with individuals and with specific parishes each with their own tradition. The power of practical experience to influence theology was reckoned to be important by many clergy, and is not unconnected with those people served through the occasional offices. Despite the large number coming for weddings, funerals, and baptisms, it is still easy for theological discussion to focus on the eucharist and the major festivals while ignoring those rites which touch the largest number of people. In the survey we found that 70% of the general sample had attended church in the previous year for weddings, or baptisms, or funerals. As far as the church roll people were concerned more of them (86%) had attended for these rites of passage than had even attended church at Christmas (80%) which was itself the most popular feast in terms of attendance. Pastoral theology needs to take account of this mass presence which, though it can be interpreted in a number of ways, is at least indicative of moments of contact between personal lives and formal religion.

The theological motif that demands attention in the context of rites of passage is best expressed in the Greek idea of koinonia or fellowship (Davies, 1986). It is here that theological understanding cross fertilizes with the insights of social anthropology to a marked extent. The anthropologist Arnold Van Gennep first wrote about rites of passage in 1909. He spoke of society as taking its members in hand as they moved from one social status to another in a threefold rite. Separation from former identity led into a period apart before a final reintegration into the new status. A generation after Van Gennep the British anthropologist Victor Turner returned to the scheme of rites of passage and focused in particular on that central phase (1969). This 'liminal' or threshold period was seen as one possessing very particular social and psychological dynamics. It seemed to represent moments when individuals passed out of ordinary social life with its formal hierarchies and statuses and entered a period of shared identity and unity with others undergoing the same experience. So it was that Turner described this liminal period as one in which people experienced what he called *communitas*. Communitas involved a gut-sense of shared humanity, of being in the same boat together, and very often of sharing hardship. Turner later coined the word 'liminoid' to describe some modern western social situations which only partly resembled the full blown liminality of traditional societies normally studied by anthropologists. His analysis of Christian pilgrimages was a good example of such liminoid behaviour (1978). Turner's caution needs bearing in mind since some have too readily adopted the rites of passage model and applied it too hastily to modern situations.

But the idea of communitas is one which can, perhaps, also be employed to describe the way in which priests enter into the joys and sorrows of those served through the occasional offices as also through some pastoral moments associated with both suffering and success. There is a sense in which the priest is continually liminal. In this the minister is, in a sense, more in touch with the guts of humanity more often than are many congregation members. In theological terms rites of passage draw on ideas of God's support and strength for the move in hand and also on the hope that comes from faith for what lies ahead. It is what might be called God's covenant of care of which the priest is a minister (Atkinson, 1984).

Creation in Religion

We can go further than this and set rites of passage in the two contexts of creation and salvation. In the one the rite of care is subsumed into creation's continuity, in the other into a personally focused salvation. A clear understanding of the relationship between rites of passage and the dominant mode of either creation or salvation religion might help overcome the contradictions and conflicts which some clergy seem to experience as they reflect upon their professional and Christian duties.

The merit of creation theology is that it can be grounded in a common sense view of the world. Almost in terms of the argument from design it lays its foundation in the assumption that the world is not accidental and that God is its creator. As such creation is a dynamic and complex process which continues to this day. Not only is it dynamic but its complexity presents to our minds an aspect of God's mystery. The universe is not transparent, its significance is not displayed for all to see, yet it is there for all to perceive.

Not only does God make the world but God also owns responsibility for it. This responsibility is shared to a degree with humankind, God's self-conscious creatures. Stewardship within the world falls to humanity and this enhances human identity and status. Human freedom is aligned with profound responsibility. Following the Genesis insights humankind is of the same substance as the world, dust from dust and dust to dust. Yet throughout life people have a duty to creativity both in exploration of the world and in transforming aspects of it, and in that capacity demonstrate the divine breath which activates life and allows the image of God to engage with the world of matter.

A vital feature of this perspective involves society. Society, the organization of ways of cooperative human endeavour, is not separate from nature. Society is a natural product because humankind is a natural entity. Not only so but religion itself is natural. As part of social life it expresses a dimension of human nature. Priesthood too is natural. Most religions have priests and holy people who assist others in their dealings with deity. And as with priests so with sacred places. Churches are centres where human spirituality comes to a focus and where religious leaders help form and articulate the experience of people. The historical background of Christian religion in Britain stands as that tradition which moulds religious identity. The state church is part and parcel of space and time. Its ancient buildings are rooted in the landscape and it is intimately linked with society in a similar way having buried and housed the British dead for more than a millennium.

This sense of tradition makes it easy for religion to be seen as a growing understanding of God attained through the ages. It is here that the person of Jesus enters as God's special revelation of truth, building upon the Old Testament foundation. A long established church is itself a readily available model of ancient Israel. Truths are held and are periodically reformed and revived. The Church of England in rural areas is a good medium for the message of progressive revelation. On this line of thought the special revelation through Jesus is only recognisable because of the revelation of God that has already been seen in and through nature and human life. The task that falls to the Christian community is to take up the truth of Jesus and to seek to foster a world in which Christ's values predominate. The rationale for such an evangelistic thrust is grounded in the prior acceptance of the existence of God as Creator. Redemption follows creation.

But both creation and redemption have firm local roots in this form of religion. The parish and the parish priest are basic to this scheme of things. The Church of England has, if anything, become more rather than less devoted to the idea of parish ministry for its priests during the twentieth century. In part this is probably due to the extraordinary power of the creation model of religion, of church, of land, and of priests, that has grown in Britain. As we mention elsewhere in this book the occasional rise of sector ministries whether in the armed forces, hospitals, or the attempt at ministers in secular employment, has not led to any significant changes in theory of ministry or practice. The ambivalence which many detect towards ministers in secular employment may be connected with its theological uncertainty.

So it is that creation and parish hang together. Clergy in our survey who were of a central churchmanship had the highest degree of interest in 'people' in a general sense and were twice as interested in the idea of being a priest to a community than were the evangelicals. They too had the greatest interest in general pastoral work and in this we again see the strength of the parochial focus on ministry. As a means of developing this it becomes obvious that pastoral theology needs to be seen as a shared concern, shared between theologically instructed and relatively uninstructed people. Shared too between formal pastors and those who assist them. Liberation theology in several parts of the world is an example to the church everywhere of how believers may be mobilized into Christian action as they are encouraged to think themselves into the work of God. Theology in this sense is knowledge for the people of God, by the people of God. The parish is the place where theological thinking is focused, where it is stimulated or depressed. The local context is the focus where the biblical tradition relives and where streams of theological argument can be energized for today's use. If we wanted to be theoretical we could say that the parish guarantees that traditional theories are localized and realized.

There is much intellectual discussion today about ideas of postmodernity and the end of all embracing theories of life (Harvey 1989). This interesting line of thought may possibly have an impact on more popular theology sooner or later but if and when it does the parish as a local centre of Christian thought and action will be seen as a vital resource. It will throw into sharp contrast the dual, and perhaps ambivalent, strand of Anglican operation which theoretically stresses the historical flow of creeds, church councils, and episcopacy, but which practically depends upon local action and necessity. Having said that we now move from the creation model of God the Father, of tradition, land and people to a theology of Salvation focused on the divine Son, on a church, and on individual believers.

Salvation in Religion

Salvation in Christian theology depends on God's activity focused in Jesus of Nazareth. In one sense this outlook is immediately more complex than that of creation because it demands a re-evaluation of the individual. In creation there can be a simple acceptance of the way things are. Creation is world affirming in a straightforward way. Salvation presupposes a negation. The way things are is not the way things should be. There is, in this great tradition of Christian theology, a sense of the flawedness of life and the world.

Salvation involves judgement. Both a judgement on self and on the world. The believer moves from a simple acceptance of the status quo through a radical criticism of it to a new position of being saved from its consequences. In terms of Christian theology this process is focused in Jesus as the Son of God. A new life, a higher order analysis, indeed a new creation is entailed in salvation. If the focus is on Jesus, the medium of the message is the church as a community of the redeemed. The way salvation is understood and the pattern prescribed for the church takes one of two forms, either that of incarnational-sacramental religion, or else of a more prophetic and biblically based religion addressing itself to the inward heart of each believer.

The first is enshrined in what is technically called sacramental and incarnational theology. This means that God became human in Jesus of Nazareth. This act of assuming human nature is the basis of the Incarnation. Through this Incarnation God places a stamp of approval not only on human flesh and blood, but on material things in general. By the Incarnation God acknowledges that all things have value. Things may be flawed and fallen but they still have value and are in the process of being renewed and restored through the saving work of Christ. Christ's resurrection is the great symbol of salvation as He becomes the first example of the new creation.

The church universal is now seen as the central focus where these great truths are known and where men and women, boys and girls, become caught up in the transforming process of salvation. They have their part to play in the coming Kingdom of God. The eucharist is, above all else, the window into the new age and the source from which its power and inspiration flow. It is the symbol which gives meaning to other symbols and speaks of an entire symbolic world.Creation is taken up into the redemptive scheme as becomes very obvious when Harvest Festival services become eucharists. A typical index of religion is whether Harvest Festivals take the form of evensong or eucharist. In the Church of England creation outlook evensong serves as the vehicle for an inclusive thanksgiving for regular and occasional churchgoers. The salvation perspective with a sacramental focus prefers the eucharistic stance. The sacramental perspective just mentioned is not limited to the formal sacraments of baptism and eucharist but assumes that God makes use of material things as symbols of spiritual and ultimate realities. Bread and wine along with water are but clear examples of the power of God to press mater into spiritual service. This aspect of the Church of England has, traditionally, been typified by the catholic and anglo-catholic outlook.

When we consider salvation as biblical prophecy and faith, the evangelical and protestant aspect of the Church of England comes to the fore. Salvation is through Christ and by faith in Christ. God's grace makes faith possible and it is through the bible, its preaching and teaching, that the truth about sin and salvation comes across to the believer. The Holy Spirit enlightens the heart and salvation comes through the forgiveness of sins. Truthfulness to the biblical message far outweighs any church tradition, and the material world of symbolism is said to be largely bypassed.

In accord with the protestant outlook each individual is responsible for deciding to repent and follow Christ. The idea of personal rebirth and renewal of life takes the central position away from an emerging Kingdom of God. Because individuals experience a sense of 'before' and 'after' in their spiritual lives they place additional weight on the idea that the world of creation is flawed, albeit through human sin, and on the necessity for a new start.

When taken to extremes this kind of religion reflects the sectarian 'conversionist' type of religion and can easily lead to the notion of certain Christians being genuine while others are more nominal. The pastoral attitude demanded from ministers in this scheme emphasizes the spiritual growth of each member of the congregation. In the survey of clergy we did, in fact, find that evangelical clergy mentioned their involvement with the individual growth of people three times more often than their catholic colleagues. Similarly the catholic clergy mentioned the eucharist and worship twice as often as did evangelicals when it came to rewarding aspects of their ministry.

Some clergy, including a few avowed evangelicals, said that this kind of religious outlook was difficult to maintain in rural parishes. The reason for it seemed to be that evangelical clergy who saw conversion as the prime goal of pastoral work found it difficult to sustain ongoing relationships with parishioners who had not and did not look as though they were going to be converted. In one sense this kind of radical conversionist outlook on salvation is better adapted for an urban and suburban religion where congregations can be recruited from those who are converted and where ongoing relationships between a conversion minded pastor and a non-conversion minded congregation do not have to be sustained over long periods of time. The question of commitment involved in this situation is also important in the third and final type of religion which is important in rural parishes, that of the occasional attender.

Rites of Passage, Theology, and Occasional Religion
In both creation and salvation styles of religion there is a clarity of theological focus which both clergy and people can use as a basis for understanding their faith and what they do in church. In this third case there is no simple focus. Because of that it is often ignored or simply handled as folk religion or even nominal religion. But ignoring it or labelling it into marginality is a mistake because it touches many lives inside as outside the church. The idea of nominal religion is perhaps one useful way of tackling this problem.

The distinction between nominal and committed believers is an interesting product of world religions where revealed truth involves a call to live a dedicated life in a prescribed manner. Even so not all branches of the Christian church press the idea in the same way. For more catholic traditions commitment might involve ritual participation while some protestants emphasize the need for a distinctive form of conversion. Whichever is the case it is likely that actual attendance at specified services will be a requirement for those wishing to live dedicated religious lives. This is inevitable given the existence of church buildings and established priesthoods. Although some forms of Christian theology might stress the need for an inward love of God expressed outwardly in ethical living it would be exceptional for church-based Christians to say that church attendance was optional in the life of faith. In some cultures, as in some Roman Catholic and many Greek Orthodox settings, actual attendance is expected more of women than men in a form of sexual division of religious labour.

In Britain today attendance is often seen as a sign of religious commitment. Christianity is very often equated with regularity of church attendance and even though many believers would agree that attendance is no guarantee of sincerity the rule of thumb on religion is that attendance is a fair index of religious commitment. This is, of course, something of a circular argument as commitment and attendance become marks of each other. Surveys of religion often fasten on to frequency of attendance because it is observable whereas belief and the inwardness of religion are hard to assess. Priests too often talk of laity as either involved or only occasionally caught up in church events. We have already explored this dimension fairly thoroughly as far as priests are concerned in Chapter 5 in connection with people taking advantage of the church for their various rites of passage. Similarly in Chapter 6 we explored people's attitudes to church involvement.

In this conclusion our purpose is more theological as we try to depict a religion in which the personal beliefs of people may not be very closely linked to formal church attendance. This is an important issue since some church leaders tend to devalue the religion of infrequent attenders. This may not be intentional or explicit but it often underlies what they say: what is an occasional office for a priest is also 'occasional religion' for many of those in attendance.

If religion is about 'ultimate concern' as Paul Tillich so clearly suggested then these moments of ritual involvement are perhaps vital in the articulation of ultimate concern. We have already discussed theological aspects of rites of passage and as we intimated above much attention has been given to them by church leaders. In the *Alternative Service Book* of the Church of England there is a section entitled Initiation Services including thanksgiving for the birth or adoption of a child, baptism, and confirmation. Interestingly both marriage and ordination, two absolute classic forms of rites of passage in anthropological terms, have separate entries of their own.

So it is that the idea of rites of passage has become part of everyday language. But there are other forms of rite which are equally important for an understanding of public ritual and which have attracted very little attention. In particular we think of rites of intensification. These occur when people repeat rites performed on previous occasions through which beliefs or values are publically rehearsed and stressed anew. In some senses they involve a rededication and challenge, and to an extent can also involve a sense of common purpose as well as personal commitment to the task in hand.

The weekly eucharist is, in one sense a ritual of intensification. Basic Christian truths and standards are expressed and actions undertaken to renew the life of discipleship. The service of Renewal of Baptismal Vows which is included in the *Alternative Service Book* among the Initiation Services is, properly speaking, a rite of intensification. The eucharist and renewal of baptismal or indeed of ordination vows would generally presuppose a congregation of regular and committed church members. But intensification may also occur among those infrequent attenders present at occasional services and for whom religious experience is a fact of life. In other words it would be wrong for religious leaders to assume that only frequent attendance guarantees authenticity of religion.

In a wedding as in a baptism or funeral there are at least two processes underlying the ritual performed. One changes the status of the central figures undergoing the rite of passage with repercussions on the status of others especially parents, but also family and friends. But for many of those friends, family, and parents, another process, one of intensification, occurs. Old memories, hopes, and failures, are recalled through the process of ritual and its symbolism. The emotion and subtle mood changes of these occasions are vehicles for such embodied memories. Clergy in particular need to be aware of these things to enable them to foster faith and life. As one of us has argued elsewhere the public ritual of the Church of England is likely to involve what we have called 'dual purpose ritual' where the priest intends one goal and the people another, especially when their private circumstances are evoked by events (Davies, 1986:53). The priest has an attitude grounded in the doctrine of the church which he believes is expressed through the ritual and which he wants the people to enter into through their participation. Preparation classes before the event aim to serve this end. But people are not always so easily taught, and in any case there are many present who have not undergone any training. So it is that people bring to the occasion their own way of interpreting what is going on. To acknowledge this is to take the first step in preparing an outlook which can stimulate the wide variety of interpretations present through prayers, silence, and sermons, with inclusive language serving to foster the varied faith insights present. All this requires a degree of self-conscious concern on the part of ministers of the gospel and underlines the fact that we have tended to stress this clerically focused activity. Others might want to lay the stress elsewhere. Robin Gill (1989:78) whose recent work also genuinely seeks to relate sociological and theological issues, took the theme of corporate worship and the facilities available for it as his prime concern and that is perfectly justifiable. Both pastoral ministry and the worshipping church, are obviously important as far as the rural Church of England is concerned. We have attempted an integration of both.

Appendix

Research Methodology

In this appendix we provide the basic details of the surveys undertaken for the Rural Church Project which provide the data for this book. Additional details are available in the four volumes (Davies et al 1990) available from the Centre for Rural Studies, Royal Agricultural College, Cirencester or the Department of Theology, University of Nottingham.

1) CLERGY POSTAL SURVEY METHODOLOGY

A complete census of incumbents within the dioceses of Durham, Gloucester, Lincoln, Southwell and Truro was undertaken. It included all vicars, rectors, priests-in-charge, team rectors and team vicars. In total, 871 questionnaires were dispatched. (See Table A1)

TABLE A1. The Number of Postal Questionnaires Distributed

Gloucester	158
Truro	140
Southwell	152
Lincoln	213
Durham	208
Total	871

The postal survey collected information on a wide range of topics pertaining to the clergy's working life and ministry.

The main topics covered were as follows:

1) Details of Benefice. The numbers of parishes and churches, type of ministry, status of incumbent, details of staff (full and part time, paid and

non–stipendiary), description by clergy of type of benefice (rural, urban etc.).

2) Services. The number and types of Sunday services (including liturgy used) held on four specified Sundays in the period preceding the survey (October, 1988).

3) Attendance by Sunday for each of the four specified Sundays prior to the survey. By parish, and by age (16+ and under 16).

4) Details of Ecumenical Involvement.

5) Clergy Work. The time spent on certain activities in a prescribed week, and positions of responsibility in the community.

7) Sociography of the Clergy: age, ordination and training, marital status, past appointments, future plans, and churchmanship.

8) Ministry. Problems, rewards, attitudes to lay ministry.

9) An opportunity for other comments.

In total, 572 useful returns were received, which represents an overall response rate of 66%. There was little variation in response rate by diocese. In order to establish whether there was any bias in the response towards the more rural clergy (because urban clergy might have felt the survey to be irrelevant), the response rate was analysed by size of population under the care of one priest, and also by number of parishes held. These were felt to be relevant indicators since "rural" benefices are likely to contain fewer people than "urban" ones, and because the majority of urban clergy hold single parish benefices, whereas most of the large groupings are in rural areas. The following tables show little evidence of rural bias, beyond a slightly higher response from likely 'rural' parishes.

TABLE A2. Response Rates by Population of Benefice

Population	% Response rate
Under 1,000	70
1,000–1,999	64
2,000–4,999	66
5,000–9,999	64
10,000 and over	66

TABLE A3. *Response Rates by Number of Parishes Held*

Number of parishes	% Response rate
One	65
Two	60
Three	72
Four or more	73
Teams	66

PARISH POPULATIONS

A preliminary to the sampling procedure for the interview survey was the identification of all ecclesiastical parishes in the five dioceses, and the calculation of their 1988 population sizes. We felt it was important to base our sample on the population of ecclesiastical parishes rather than civil parishes, but these were not easily available. The mismatch between ecclesiastical and civil parish boundaries in all our dioceses meant that this exercise required a considerable amount of work. Maps of ecclesiastical parishes were constructed for each of the five dioceses by reference to the maps held by the Church Commissioners in London which represent the up-to-date legal state of the Church of England parochial network. Ecclesiastical parish boundaries were transferred from the Church Commissioner's six inch to one mile maps onto 1:100,000 county series maps, showing *civil* boundaries at the county, district and parish levels, correct to the 1st of June 1988. This process was necessary because the boundaries of civil parishes and ecclesiastical parishes are in certain areas significantly different, and because the dioceses themselves did not have copies of small-scale maps of their parishes. The dioceses did hold copies of the six inch to one mile Church Commissioners' maps but these had sometimes *not* been updated since they were originally sent out.

The areal units mapped in this way were identified as particular parishes by reference to the most recent Diocesan Directories or Handbooks that were available, and the settlement names on the civil parish maps. The dates of the Handbooks or Directories used were as follows:

Gloucester: Oct. 1987 (for parish identification) and July 1989 (for urban populations)

Truro: 1989 (correct at Oct. 1988)

Southwell: 1989
Lincoln: 1989
Durham: 1987/88.

Problems arose with this system when extra-parochial areas or detached parish parcels existed. These had to be checked against the Church Commissioners' original maps for identification. Extra-parochial areas include castles or their sites, religious establishments or their sites, semi-religious establishments or their sites, Royal forests, some islands, and some reclaimed land (General Register Office 1955). They are still commonly found in the five dioceses.

Although all of the Diocesan Handbooks contained some sort of parish list, this was found in practice to be more of a collection of village or settlement names, rather than a comprehensive and exclusive list of legally-constituted parishes. Another attempt to identify parishes from the Diocesan Handbooks was made by listing places with Parochial Church Councils. As each parish is legally required to have a PCC, we thought that this method would separate out legal parishes, but we were not successful in defining parishes accurately by this method.

In the postal questionnaire, priests were asked to note the number of parishes in the benefice(s) for which they held main responsibility. The replies given were not always consistent with the parish structures calculated from the Church Commissioner's maps, even when informal arrangements were allowed for. Therefore, numbers of ecclesiastical parishes looked after by a single priest were adjusted to correspond with the parish network derived from the mapping process. One implication of this discrepancy is that some priests are unclear as to the legal status of the areas under their charge. The confusion over the term 'parish' and the PCC listings in the Diocesan Handbooks suggests that this problem extends to the diocesan level.

A variety of methods was utilised to estimate the population of each ecclesiastical parish in the five dioceses. Where possible the estimates were made using the most up-to-date figures for civil parish populations available from County Council Planning Departments. It was not, however, possible to use County Council estimates for Durham as population figures were available only at the ward level and not for civil parishes. Therefore, the 1987/88 Diocesan Handbook estimates were used for the whole of Durham. The County Councils covering the five dioceses and the dates of their population estimates are listed below:

Gloucester:	Gloucestershire (mid-1987)	
	Avon (1986)	
	Hereford and Worcester (1987)	
	Warwickshire (1986)	
	Wiltshire (1988)	
Truro:	Cornwall (1987)	
	Devon (mid-1987)	
Southwell:	Nottinghamshire (mid-1987)	
	South Yorkshire (1987)	
Lincoln:	Lincolnshire (1988)	
	South Humberside (mid-1987)	
Durham:	Co.Durham	
	South Tyneside	Diocesan Handbook information
	Cleveland	used, based on clergy estimates
		(1987)

These figures were adjusted according to the different areas of settlement covered by the civil and the ecclesiastical parishes. In the case of rural areas and areas of less dense population, where an ecclesiastical parish did not correspond exactly to a civil parish, the population was adjusted by reference to the number of houses and average household size for the civil district, calculated from the 1981 Census. (Usually resident population in private households, divided by the number of private households with usual residents, permanent buildings only.) Where the difference was only small, a count was made of the number of houses by which the civil and ecclesiastical parishes varied. When the difference was greater, for example where two ecclesiastical parishes constituted a single civil parish, the total number of houses was estimated and the population split according to the weighting derived. This was the method used for the vast majority of non-urban parishes in the dioceses of Gloucester, Truro, Southwell and Lincoln.

2) CLERGY INTERVIEW SURVEY

Rural benefices from which the interview sample was to be drawn were identified as those with a low population density and with a low absolute population relative to other benefices in the diocese. We did not place an absolute ceiling on rural benefice population size because of the larger nature of rural benefice populations in Truro and Durham, and because we particularly wanted to include some small country towns and team ministries in our sample. In fact, the benefice sizes in the interview sample varied from one of 135 people in Southwell to one of around 7,660 in Durham. Once a set of rural benefices had been drawn up for each diocese, three main sampling criteria were applied:

1) The first step was to group the rural benefices within each diocese into a number of contrasting regions. We aimed for four in each diocese but this was not appropriate in every case. The factors considered in making these choices were type of agriculture, settlement structure, proximity to urban centres, economic base and so forth. The rural regions used are listed below:

Gloucester:	Forest of Dean (5)
	Severn Vale (5)
	North Cotswolds (5)
	South Cotswolds (5)
Truro:	East Truro (8)
	Central Truro (6)
	West Truro (6)
Southwell:	North Nottinghamshire Clays (7)
	South Nottinghamshire Clays (7)
	West Nottinghamshire Mining (4)
Lincoln:	Central Lincoln (1)
	Fens (4)
	Isle of Axholme (3)
	Marsh (3)
	West Lincoln (3)
	Wolds (4)
Durham:	Central Durham (5)
	Durham Dales (6)
	East Durham (5)
	South Durham (5)

2) The second step was to select 20 benefices in each diocese, as equally divided amongst the regions as possible. The number of interview benefices in each region are in brackets in the list above. Interview benefices were chosen according to a mixture of benefice population and parochial structure criteria appropriate to the composition of the rural areas in each individual diocese. However, we did attempt to include the following:

(1) At least four single parish benefices per diocese ideally one per rural region.
(2) At least two small country towns per diocese.
(3) Rural teams where present.
(4) United parishes where present.

The following tables show the nature of the sample according to the important criteria of population and parochial structure.

TABLE A4. Parochial Structure of Interview Benefices

Number of Parishes	Number of Clergy					
	ALL	Gloucester	Truro	Southwell	Lincoln	Durham
One	33	4	7	4	6	12
Two	23	6	7	4	1	5
Three	20	5	3	5	4	3
Four	6	1	1	1	2	1
Five	7	4	–	3	–	–
Six	2	–	–	1	1	–
Seven	1	–	–	–	1	–
Ten	1	–	–	–	1	–
Eleven	1	–	–	–	1	–
Teams	7	–	5	–	2	–
TOTAL	101	20	23	18	19	21

TABLE A5. Population Size of Interview Benefices

Number of People per Priest	Number of Clergy					
	ALL	Gloucester	Truro	Southwell	Lincoln	Durham
< 500	2	–	–	2	–	–
500–999	17	7	2	3	3	2
1,000–1,499	18	2	7	4	–	5
1,500–1,999	26	6	6	5	4	5
2,000–2,999	16	3	6	–	4	3
3,000–3,999	12	1	1	2	5	3
4,000–4,999	2	–	–	2	–	–
5,000+	8	1	1	–	3	3
TOTAL	101	20	23	18	19	21

TABLE A6. *Parish Sizes Covered in Interview Sample*

Number of people in parish	ALL	Gloucester	Number of clergy Truro	Southwell	Lincoln	Durham
< 200	73	25	10	17	27	4
200-499	78	23	14	17	18	6
500-999	38	6	11	10	3	8
1,000-1,499	21	6	7	2	1	5
1,500-1,999	17	1	5	3	6	2
2,000+	28	4	4	3	7	10
TOTAL	255	55	51	52	62	35

THE INTERVIEWS

The response rate was high: only three refused in Gloucester, one in Truro, one in Southwell, two in Lincoln, and one in Durham. In the case of refusals a replacement benefice was selected. The main aim of the interviews was to obtain qualitative data as a means of deepening and enriching our interpretation of the statistical findings of the postal survey. Accordingly the interview schedule was developed as a 'guide' to the conduct of the interview. For most topics precise questions were not formulated – instead subject and section headings were given. There were seventy-five main sections (although not each was applicable to every interviewee). Each of the sections was sub-divided into two, three or even up to nine or ten specific topics for investigation. In a few instances specific carefully worded questions were employed as an aid to subsequent comparative and quantitative analysis. There were thirteen of these specific questions in the interview. Most of the interviews lasted between two and three hours with some taking four or five hours to complete.

In contrast to the postal survey the findings of the interviews were not computerised. They do not, in the main, lend themselves to sophisticated statistical analysis. In some instances numeric findings have been presented and these have been calculated by hand. The main analysis of the interviews has been interpretive and illustrative. The interviews allow a more detailed assessment of the views of the clergy, particularly as they pertain to issues already highlighted in the postal survey.

3) PARISHIONERS SURVEY

The sample areas for the general population survey were chosen from the 100 benefices selected for the clergy interviews. The aim was to interview a total of 500 people, divided equally amongst the five dioceses (ie. a hundred interviews in each diocese). We decided to interview these 500 people by sampling from *ecclesiatical parish units*. To overcome problems of regional or localised bias, the parishes were dispersed throughout the dioceses according to the regional divisions indicated above. One parish was chosen from each of the rural regions in a diocese, with any remaining parishes being drawn from the largest or most diverse of the regions.

Bearing in mind the wish to sample considerable proportions of a community or parish, we decided to interview *20 people per parish in five ecclesiastical parishes* within each diocese. None of the parishes was drawn from the same benefice. The structuring of the sample in this way was advantageous in the following respects. Firstly, it enabled us to cover all of our rural regions (except in Lincoln). Secondly, the parish sample size allowed us to cover the very small parish, and at the same time to interview a significant proportion of people in the smaller of the country towns. Thirdly, it enabled us to select a range of parishes differing in parochial structure, population and type of incumbent.

The guidelines within which the selection of the parishes took place were that at least one single parish benefice should be chosen in each diocese. There should be a representative spread among the multi-parish benefices to reflect the diocese as a whole. Lastly, team ministries should be selected as and when they occurred within the rural regions. The principal features of the parishes selected are reported in detail in Davies et al (1990).

THE SAMPLE

It was decided to interview a sample of twenty in each of the parishes. In order to guarantee a reasonably high proportion of church attenders a 'quota' sampling system was adopted with the sample being taken from two sources: from the Register of Electors (described as the General Sample) and from the church electoral roll for the Anglican church (described as the Church Roll Sample) in each of the selected parishes with a ratio of 70:30. The church sample of 30% would give 150 responses overall and this was considered large enough especially as a number of respondents from the parish sub-sample were also expected to be church attenders. The survey response rate is given below.

TABLE A7. *Total Sample: Type of Response*

Type of response	General Sample		Church Sample		Total Sample	
	No	%	No	%	No	%
Refused	52	10	6	3	58	8
Left parish	37	7	5	3	42	5
Disabled/too old	18	3	7	4	25	3
Deceased	9	2	1	–	10	1
Away/not in	59	11	13	7	72	10
On holiday	26	4	6	3	32	4
COMPLETED	341	63	148	80	489	67
Total	542	100	186	100	728	100

TABLE A8. *General Sample: Type of Response by Gender*

Type of response	Male		Female		Total	
	No	%	No	%	No	%
Refused	27	10	25	10	52	10
Left parish	19	7	18	7	37	7
Disabled/too old	6	2	12	4	18	3
Deceased	8	3	1	–	9	2
Away/not in	33	12	26	10	59	11
On holiday	15	6	11	3	26	4
COMPLETED	159	60	182	66	341	63
Total	267	100	275	100	542	100

TABLE A9. *Church Sample: Type of Response by Gender*

Type of response	Male		Female		Total	
	No	%	No	%	No	%
Refused	1	2	5	4	6	3
Left parish	1	2	4	3	5	3
Disabled/too old	2	3	5	4	7	4
Deceased	–	–	1	1	1	–
Away/not in	6	9	7	6	13	7
On holiday	4	6	2	2	6	3
COMPLETED	51	78	97	80	148	80
Total	65	100	121	100	186	100

CHURCH ATTENDANCE

All respondents were asked how often, on average, they attended a regular Sunday service at church. As well as being of interest in itself, the answers to this question were used to divide the respondents into two groups: *Attenders* and *non-Attenders*. These were defined as follows:

1) *Attenders*: all respondents who attended a regular Sunday service on average at least three times a year. It is important to note that weddings, funerals and baptisms and services at Christmas, Easter, Harvest and Remembrance were *not* classified as regular church services.

2) *Non-attenders*: all respondents who attended a regular Sunday service on average less than three times a year.

The variable was modified by considering non–Anglican denominations as folows:

1) *Anglican Attenders*: respondents who described themselves as Anglicans and who attended Anglican services.
2) *Anglican non-Attenders*: respondents who described themselves as Anglicans who did not attend church services.
3) *Non-Anglican Attenders*: respondents who did not describe themselves as Anglicans and who attended non–Anglican services.
4) *Non-Anglican non-Attenders*: respondents who did not describe themselves as Anglicans and who did not attend church services.
5) *Other*: this category consists of two small sub-groups. First, those who described themselves as Anglicans, but attended services of another denomination and second, those who did not describe themselves as Anglicans, but who did attend Anglican services.

Bibliography

Abbott, P. and Sapsford, R. 1987. WOMEN AND SOCIAL CLASS. London: Tavistock.

ACORA. 1990. FAITH IN THE COUNTRYSIDE. London: Churchman.

ACUPA. 1986. FAITH IN THE CITY. London: Church House.

Advisory Council for the Church's Ministry. 1989. CALL TO ORDER. London: Church House.

Aldiss, B. 1989. FORGOTTEN LIFE. London: Mandarin.

d' Aquili, E. et.al. 1979. THE SPECTRUM OF RITUAL. New York: Columbia University Press.

Advisory Council for the Church's Ministry. 1989. CALL TO ORDER: VOCATION AND MINISTRY IN THE CHURCH OF ENGLAND.

Anon. 1940. THE CHURCH IN COUNTRY PARISHES. London: S.P.C.K.

Atkinson, D. 1984. Covenant and counselling, ANVIL Vol.1, No.2, 121-138.

Badham, P 1982. CHRISTIAN BELIEFS ABOUT LIFE AFTER DEATH, London, S.P.C.K.

Badham, P and Badham, L. 1984. IMMORTALITY OR EXTINCTION? London: S.P.C.K.

Bailey, E. 1990. The implicit religion of contemporary society. SOCIAL COMPASS. December.

Bell, C. and Newby, H. 1971. COMMUNITY STUDIES. London: George, Allen and Unwin.

Bennett, E.N. c1914. PROBLEMS OF VILLAGE LIFE. London: Williams and Norgate.

Bennett, W.J. 1949. The origins and development of the tourist industry in Cornwall, ROYAL CORNWALL POLYTECHNIC SOCIETY ANNUAL REPORT, 3-23.

Blacksell, M. Economides, K. and Watkins, C. 1991. JUSTICE OUTSIDE THE CITY: ACCESS TO LEGAL SERVICES IN RURAL AREAS. London: Longman.

Blizzard, S. 1956. The minster's dilemma, THE CHRISTIAN CENTURY, 73, 508-509.

Bolton, N. and Chalkley, B. 1990. The rural population turnround: a case-study of North Devon, JOURNAL OF RURAL STUDIES, 6, 29-43.

Bradley, T. 1984. Segmentation in local labour markets, In LOCALITY AND RURALITY. (ed.) T. Bradley and P. Lowe. Norwich: Geo Books.

Bradley, T. 1985. Reworking the quiet revolution: industrial and labour market restructuring in village England, SOCIOLOGIA RURALIS, 25, 40-60.

Bradley, T. 1987. Poverty and dependency in village England. In DEPRIVATION AND WELFARE IN RURAL AREAS. (ed.) P. Lowe. T. Bradley and S. Wright. Norwich: Geo Books.

Brown, H.M. 1977. A CENTURY FOR CORNWALL: THE DIOCESE OF TRURO 1877-1977. Truro: Oscar Blackford.

Bulmer, M. (ed.) 1978. MINING AND SOCIAL CHANGE: DURHAM COUNTY IN THE TWENTIETH CENTURY. London: Croom Helm.

Champion, A.G. (ed.) 1989. COUNTERURBANISATION: THE CHANGING FACE OF POPULATION DECONCENTRATION. London: Edward Arnold.

Champion, T. and Watkins, C. (eds.) 1991. PEOPLE IN THE COUNTRYSIDE: STUDIES OF SOCIAL CHANGE IN RURAL BRITAIN. London: Paul Chapman.

Christaller, W. 1966. CENTRAL PLACES IN SOUTHERN GERMANY. Englewood Cliffs: Prentice-Hall.

Church of England. 1937. MEN, MONEY AND MINISTRY.

Church of England. 1940. THE CHURCH IN COUNTRY PARISHES.

Church of England. 1941. PUTTING OUR HOUSE IN ORDER.

Church of England. 1944. TRAINING FOR THE MINISTRY.

Clark, D. 1982. BETWEEN PULPIT AND PEW. Cambridge: Cambridge University Press.

Cloke, P. 1977. An index of rurality for England and Wales, REGIONAL STUDIES, 11, 313-346.

Cloke, P. 1979. KEY SETTLEMENTS IN RURAL AREAS. London: Methuen.

Cloke, P. and Edwards, G. 1986. Rurality in England and Wales 1981: a replication of the 1971 Index, REGIONAL STUDIES, 20, 289-306.

Cloke, P. and Little, J. 1987. Rural policies in the Gloucestershire structure plan, parts 1 & 2, ENVIRONMENT AND PLANNING, 19, 959-981 and 1027-1050.

Cohen, A.P. 1985. THE SYMBOLIC CONSTRUCTION OF COMMUNITY. London: Ellis Horwood and Tavistock.

Collinson, P. 1982. THE RELIGION OF PROTESTANTS. Oxford, Clarendon Press.

Cooke, P. 1989. LOCALITIES: A COMPARITIVE ANALYSIS OF URBAN CHANGE. London: Unwin and Hyman.

Cornish, M. Jackson, C. Urdsell, G. and Walker, R. 1977. Regional culture and identity in industrialised societies: a critical comment, REGIONAL STUDIES, 11, 113-116.

Cosgrove, D. and Daniels, S. (eds) 1988. THE ICONOGRAPHY OF LANDSCAPE. Cambridge, Cambridge University Press.

Court, G. and Boddy, M. 1989. THE FUTURE OF THE SOUTH WEST ECONOMY: REVIEW AND PROSPECTS. University of Bristol.

Cox, H. 1965. THE SECULAR CITY. New York: Methuen.

Cox, H. 1984. RELIGION IN THE SECULAR CITY. New York: Simon and Schuster.

Damesick, P.J. 1986. Service industries, employment and regional development in Britain: a review of recent trends and issues. TRANSACTIONS OF THE INSTITUTE OF BRITISH GEOGRAPHERS, 11, 212-226.

Davies, D.J. 1984a. MEANING AND SALVATION IN RELIGIOUS STUDIES. Leiden: Brill.

Davies, D.J. 1984b. The Charismatic Ethic and the Spirit of Post-Industrialism. IN STRANGE GIFTS. (ed) D. Martin and P. Mullen. Oxford: Basil Blackwell.

Davies, D.J. 1985. Natural and Christian priesthood in folk religiosity. ANVIL, 43-54.

Davies, D.J. 1986. STUDIES IN PASTORAL THEOLOGY AND SOCIAL ANTHROPOLOGY. (2nd. Ed. 1990). Birmingham University: Institute for Worship and Religious Architecture.

Davies, D.J. 1990. CREMATION TODAY AND TOMMORROW. Nottingham: Grove Books.

Davies, D.J. Pack, C. Seymour, S. Short, C. Watkins, C. and Winter, M. 1990. THE RURAL CHURCH: STAFF AND BUILDINGS. Cirencester and Nottingham: Rural Church Project.

Davies, D.J. Pack, C. Seymour, S. Short, C. Watkins, C. and Winter, M. 1990. THE CLERGY LIFE. Cirencester and Nottingham: Rural Church Project.

Davies, D.J. Pack, C. Seymour, S. Short, C. Watkins, C. and Winter, M. 1990. PARISH LIFE AND RURAL RELIGION. Cirencester and Nottingham: Rural Church Project.

Davies, D.J. Pack, C. Seymour, S. Short, C. Watkins, C. and Winter, M. 1990. THE VIEWS OF RURAL PARISHIONERS. Cirencester and Nottingham: Rural Church Project.

Deacon, B. 1987. POVERTY AND DEPRIVATION IN THE SOUTH WEST: A PRELIMINARY SURVEY. London: Child Poverty Action Group.

Deacon, B. George, A. and Perry, R. 1988. CORNWALL AT THE CROSSROADS? Redruth: CoSERG.

Dean, K. Brown, B. and Perry, R. 1984. Counterurbanisation and the characteristics of persons migrating to West Cornwall, GEOFORUM, 15, 177-190.

Dewey, C.J. 1974. The rehabilitation of the peasant proprietor in nineteenth century economic thought, HISTORY OF POLITICAL ECONOMY, 6, 17-47.

Dunstan, G. R. 1967. The sacred ministry as a learned profession, THEOLOGY, 52, 433-442.

Edwards, J.A. 1971. The viability of lower size-order settlements in rural areas: the case of north-east England, SOCIOLOGIA RURALIS, 11, 247-276.

Everitt, A. 1972. Nonconformity in country parishes, AGRICULTURAL HISTORY REVIEW, (Special Supplement)

Fenn, R. 1987. THE DREAM OF THE PERFECT ACT. London: Tavistock.

314 *Church and Religion in Rural England*

Finucane, R.C. 1982. APPEARANCES OF THE DEAD. London: Junction Books.

Forder, C. 1947. THE PARISH PRIEST AT WORK. London: S.P.C.K.

Forster, P.G. 1989. CHURCH AND PEOPLE ON LONGHILL ESTATE. University of Hull, Department of Sociology and Social Anthropology, Occasional Paper No.5.

Francis. L.J. 1985. RURAL ANGLICANISM. London: Collins.

Frend. W. 1979. Town and countryside in early Christianity. In Baker, D. (ed) THE CHURCH IN TOWN AND COUNTRYSIDE. Oxford: Blackwell, 25-42.

Fuller, P. 1988. The Geography of Mother Nature. In Cosgrove, D. and Daniels, S. (ed) 1988. THE ICONOGRAPHY OF LANDSCAPE. Cambridge University Press 11-31.

General Register Office 1955. CENSUS 1951: POPULATIONS OF ECCLESIASTICAL AREAS (ENGLAND). London: H.M.S.O.

Giddens. A, 1979. CENTRAL PROBLEMS IN SOCIAL THEORY. London: Macmillan.

Gill, R. 1989. COMPETING CONVICTIONS. London: S.C.M. Press.

Gilligan, H. 1987. Visitors, tourists and outsiders in a Cornish town. In WHO FROM THEIR LABOURS REST? CONFLICT AND PRACTICE IN RURAL TOURISM (ed.) M. Bouquet. and M. Winter. Norwich: Geo Books.

Goldthorpe, J.H. 1980. SOCIAL MOBILITY AND CLASS STRUCTURE IN MODERN BRITAIN. Oxford: Clarendon Press.

Golner, F.H, Terence, T. and Ritti, R. 1973. Priests and laity; a profession in transition, SOCIOLOGICAL REVIEW MONOGRAPHS, 20, pp. 119-137.

Gorer, G. 1955. EXPLORING ENGLISH CHARACTER. London: Cresset Press.

Gorer, G. 1965. DEATH, GRIEF, AND MOURNING. London: Cresset Press.

Gott, J. 1906. THE PARISH PRIEST OF THE TOWN. London: S.P.C.K. 1st.ed. 1888.

Green, A.E. 1988. The north-south divide in Great Britain: an examination of the evidence, TRANSACTIONS OF THE INSTITUTE OF BRITISH GEOGRAPHERS, 13, 179-198.

Gregory, D. 1978. IDEOLOGY, SCIENCE AND HUMAN GEOGRAPHY. London: Hutchinson.

Habgood, J. 1983. CHURCH AND NATION IN A SECULAR AGE. London: Darton, Longman and Todd.

Hamilton Jenkin, A.K. 1945. CORNWALL AND ITS PEOPLE. London: Dent & Sons.

Hanson, A.T. and Hanson, R.P.C. 1987. THE IDENTITY OF THE CHURCH. London: S.C.M. Press.

Harloe, M. Pickvance, C.G. and Urry, J. 1990. PLACE, POLICY AND POLITICS: DO LOCALITIES MATTER? London: Unwin and Hyman.

Harper, S. 1987a. A humanistic approach to the study of rural populations, JOURNAL OF RURAL STUDIES, 3, 309-319.

Harper, S. 1987b. The rural–urban interface in England: a framework of analysis, TRANSACTIONS OF THE INSTITUTE OF BRITISH GEOGRAPHERS, 12, 284-302.

Harper, S. 1989. The British rural community: an overview of perspectives, JOURNAL OF RURAL STUDIES, 5, 161-184.

Harrison, J. 1983. ATTITUDES TO BIBLE, GOD, CHURCH. London: Bible Society.

Harvey, D. 1989. THE CONDITION OF POSTMODERNITY. Oxford: Blackwell.

Hastings, A. 1986. A HISTORY OF ENGLISH CHRISTIANITY. London: Collins.

Hay, D. and Morisy A. 1985. Settler society, religious meanings: a contemporary paradox. REVIEW OF RELIGIOUS STUDIES. 26 (3) 213.

Hebert, A.G. 1935. LITURGY AND SOCIETY. London, Faber and Faber.

Hebert, A.G. 1937. THE PARISH COMMUNION. London: S.P.C.K.

Herbert, G. 1652. A PRIEST TO THE TEMPLE OR THE COUNTRY PARSON. Oxford: Oxford University Press 1843 ed.

Hinings, C. R. and Foster, B. D. 1973. The organisation structure of churches: a preliminary model, SOCIOLOGY, 7, 93-106.

Hobsbawm, E.J. 1983. Introduction: inventing traditions. In THE INVENTION OF TRADITION. (ed.) Hobsbawm, E.J. and Ranger, T. Cambridge: Cambridge University Press.

Hocart, A.M. 1935. The Purpose of Ritual. In Hocart, A.M. 1969. THE LIFE GIVING MYTH. London: Methuen.

Hodge, M. 1987. PATTERNS OF MINISTERIAL TRAINING. London, Advisory Council for the Church's Ministry.

Hoggart, K. 1988. Not a definition of rural. AREA, 20, 35-40.

Hooker, R. 1865. Ecclesiastical Polity in J. Keble (ed) THE WORKS OF RICHARD HOOKER. Oxford, Clarendon Press (5th ed).

Hopkins, G. 1974. MINISTRY. London: Advisory Council for the Church's Ministry.

Hornsby-Smith, M.P. 1989. THE CHANGING PARISH. London: Routledge.

House, J.W. and Knight, E.M. 1967. Pit closure and the community, PAPERS ON MIGRATION AND MOBILITY IN NORTHERN ENGLAND. University of Newcastle-upon-Tyne.

Isard, W. 1956. LOCATION AND SPACE-ECONOMY. Cambridge, Mass: MIT Press.

Jackson, V.J. 1968. POPULATION IN THE COUNTRYSIDE: GROWTH AND STAGNATION IN THE COTSWOLDS. London: Frank Cass.

Jahoda, G. 1969. THE PSYCHOLOGY OF SUPERSTITION. London: Allen Lane Press.

Jarvis, P. 1975. The parish ministry as a semi-profession, SOCIOLOGICAL REVIEW, 23, 911-922.

Jarvis, P. 1976. A profession in process: a theoretical model for the ministry, SOCIOLOGICAL REVIEW, 24, 351-364.

Jud, G.J. Mills, Jr. E.W. and Burch, G.W. 1970. EX-PASTORS. Philadelphia: Pilgrim Press.

Lauer, R.H. 1973. Organisational punishment: punitive relations in a voluntary association, HUMAN RELATIONS, 26, 189-202.

Leach, E. (ed) 1968. DIALECTIC IN PRACTICAL RELIGION. Cambridge: Cambridge University Press.

Lewis, I. M. 1986. ECSTATIC RELIGION, Harmondsworth: Penguin.

Lloyd, A.L. 1969. FOLK SONG IN ENGLAND. London.

Lloyd, R. 1946. THE CHURCH OF ENGLAND IN THE TWENTIETH CENTURY Vol. 1. London: Longmans.

Lloyd, R. 1950. THE CHURCH OF ENGLAND IN THE TWENTIETH CENTURY Vol. 2. London: Longmans.

Lowe, P. and Goyder, J. 1983. ENVIRONMENTAL GROUPS IN POLITICS. London: Allen and Unwin.

Lowe, P. Bradley, T. and Wright, S. 1987. DEPRIVATION AND WELFARE IN RURAL AREAS. Norwich: Geo Books.

Mann, M. 1986. THE SOURCES OF SOCIAL POWER (VOL I). Cambridge: Cambridge University Press.

Marsh, J. 1982. BACK TO THE LAND: THE PASTORAL IMPULSE IN VICTORIAN ENGLAND FROM 1880 TO 1914. London: Quartet Books.

Martin, D. 1967. A SOCIOLOGY OF ENGLISH RELIGION. London: Heinemann.

Martin, D. 1978. A GENERAL THEORY OF SECULARISATION. Oxford: Basil Blackwell.

Martin, D. & P. Mullen. 1984. STRANGE GIFTS. Oxford: Basil Blackwell.

Massey, D. 1983. Industrial restructuring as class restructuring: production decentralization and local uniqueness, REGIONAL STUDIES, 17, 73-89.

Massey, D. 1984. SPATIAL DIVISIONS OF LABOUR: SOCIAL STRUCTURES AND THE GEOGRAPHY OF PRODUCTION. Basingstoke: Macmillan.

Mayfield, G. 1958. THE CHURCH OF ENGLAND. Oxford: Oxford University Press.

Middleton, B. 1988. Community needs housing. 61-68. in Winter, M. and Rogers, A. Eds. WHO CAN AFFORD TO LIVE IN THE COUNTRYSIDE? Cirencester: CRS Occasional Paper No 2.

Mills, D.R. 1980. LORD AND PEASANT IN NINETEENTH CENTURY BRITAIN. London: Croom Helm.

Moore, R. 1974. PITMEN, PREACHERS AND POLITICS: THE EFFECT OF METHODISM IN THE DURHAM MINING COMMUNITY. Cambridge: Cambridge University Press.

Newby, H. 1977. THE DEFERENTIAL WORKER. London: Allen Lane.

Newby, H. Bell, C. Rose, D. and Saunders, P. 1978. PROPERTY, PATERNALISM AND POWER. London: Hutchinson.

Newby, H. 1979. GREEN AND PLEASANT LAND? SOCIAL CHANGE IN RURAL ENGLAND. London: Hutchinson.

Newby, H. 1990. Revitalising the countryside: the opportunities and pitfalls of counter-urban trends, JOURNAL OF THE ROYAL SOCIETY OF ARTS, 138, 630-636.

Obelkevich, J. 1976. RELIGION AND RURAL SOCIETY, SOUTH LINDSEY 1825-1875. Oxford: Clarendon Press.

Obeyesekere, G. 1981. MEDUSA'S HAIR. Chicago: University of Chicago Press.

O'Day, R. 1988. The clerical renaissance in Victorian Enlgand. In RELIGION IN VICTORIAN ENGLAND. 1 TRADITIONS. (ed.) Parsons, G. Manchester: Manchester University Press.

Orwin, C.S. 1944 (ed). COUNTRY PLANNING: A STUDY OF RURAL PROBLEMS. London: Oxford University Press.

Osborne, C.E. 1933. THE CHRISTIAN PRIEST OF TODAY. London: Mowbray.

Pahl, R.E. 1965a. Class and commuting in English commuter villages, SOCIOLOGIA RURALIS, 5, 5-23.

Pahl, R.E. 1965b. URBS IN RURE. London: Weidenfield and Nicholson.

Pahl, R.E. 1968. The rural-urban continuum. In Pahl, R.E. (ed.) READINGS IN URBAN SOCIOLOGY. London: Pergamon 263-305.

Parsons, D.J. c1978. Rural gentrification: the influence of rural settlement planning policies, UNIVERSITY OF SUSSEX RESEARCH PAPERS IN GEOGRAPHY. University of Sussex.

Paul, L. 1964. THE DEPLOYMENT AND PAYMENT OF THE CLERGY. London: C.I.O.

Perry, R. 1978. THE SMALL FIRM MANUFACTURING SECTOR IN CORNWALL. Camborne: Cornwall Industrial Development Association.

Perry, R. 1987. Population turnaround in Cornwall and Finistere, SOUTH WEST PAPERS IN GEOGRAPHY, 11.

Perry, R. Dean, K. and Brown, B. 1986. COUNTERURBANISATION. Norwich: Geobooks.

Phillips, D. and Williams, A. 1984. RURAL BRITAIN: A SOCIAL GEOGRAPHY. Oxford: Basil Blackwell.

Ranson, S. Bryman, A. and Hinings, B. 1977. CLERGY, MINISTERS AND PRIESTS. London: Routledge and Kegan Paul.

Reed, M. 1986. Nineteenth-century rural England: a case for 'peasant studies'?, JOURNAL OF PEASANT STUDIES, 14, 78-99.

Robinson, J. 1963. HONEST TO GOD. London, S.C.M. Press.

Rogers, C. 1912. AN INTRODUCTION TO THE STUDY OF PASTORAL THEOLOGY. Oxford: Clarendon Press.

Russell, A. 1986. THE COUNTRY PARISH. London: S.P.C.K.

Saville, J. 1957. RURAL DEPOPULATION IN ENGLAND AND WALES, 1851-1951. London: Routledge and Kegan Paul.

Shaw, G. and Williams, A. 1988. Tourism and employment: reflections on a pilot study of Looe Cornwall, AREA, 20, 23-34.

Sheffield Report. 1974. DEPLOYMENT OF THE CLERGY. Report of the House of Bishops' Working Group. GS205.

Shucksmith, M. 1981. NO HOMES FOR LOCALS? Aldershot: Gower.

Skultans, V. 1974. INTIMACY AND RITUAL. London: Routledge and Kegan Paul.

Strathern, M. 1981. KINSHIP AT THE CORE. Cambridge University Press.

Thorns, D.C. 1968. The changing system of rural stratification. SOCIOLOGIA RURALIS, 8. 161-178.

Thornton, M. 1964. PASTORAL THEOLOGY: A REORIENTATION London, S.P.C.K., (First ed 1956).

Tiller, J. 1983. A STRATEGY FOR THE CHURCH'S MINISTRY. London: CIO.

Tillich, P. 1953. SYSTEMATIC THEOLOGY. London, Nisbet.

Toennies, F. 1955. COMMUNITY AND ASSOCIATION. Trans. C.P.Loomis. London: Routledge.

Tonkin, E. McDonald, M. and M.Chapman. 1989. HISTORY AND ETHNICITY. London: Routledge.

Towler, R. and Coxon, A.P.M. 1979. THE FATE OF THE ANGLICAN CLERGY: A SOCIOLOGICAL STUDY. London: Macmillan.

Towler, R. 1984. THE NEED FOR CERTAINTY. London: Routledge and Kegan Paul.

Townsend, A.R. and Taylor, C.C. 1975. Regional culture and identity in industrialised societies: the case of north-east England, REGIONAL STUDIES, 9, 379-393.

Troeltsch, E. 1931. THE SOCIAL TEACHING OF THE CHRISTIAN CHURCHES. London, Allen and Unwin.

Turner, B.S. 1983. RELIGION AND SOCIAL THEORY: A MATERIALIST PERSPECTIVE. London: Heinemann.

Turner, V. 1969. THE RITUAL PROCESS. London, Routledge Kegan Paul.

Turner, V. and Turner, E. 1978. IMAGE AND PILGRIMAGE IN CHRISTIAN CULTURE. Oxford: Basil Blackwell.

Tylor, E.B. 1958. PRIMITIVE CULTURE. New York: Harper.

Urry, J. 1984. Capitalist restructuring, recomposition and the regions. In LOCALITY AND RURALITY. (ed.) T. Bradley and P. Lowe. Norwich: Geo Books.

Waller, R.J. 1983. THE DUKERIES TRANSFORMED: THE SOCIAL AND POLITICAL DEVELOPMENT OF A TWENTIETH CENTURY COALFIELD. Oxford: Clarendon Press.

Walker, A. 1985. RESTORING THE KINGDOM: THE RADICAL CHRISTIANITY OF THE HOUSE CHURCH MOVEMENT. London: Hodder and Stoughton.

Watkins, C. (ed.) 1989. TELEWORKING AND TELECOTTAGES. Cirencester: ACRE and Centre for Rural Studies.

Watkins, C. Blacksell, M. and Economides, K. 1988. The distribution of solicitors in England and Wales, TRANSACTIONS OF THE INSTITUTE OF BRITISH GEOGRAPHERS, 13, 39-56

Weber, M. 1963. THE SOCIOLOGY OF RELIGION. Trans Fischoff, E. London: Methuen. First Edition 1922.

Weekley, I. 1988 Rural depopulation and counterurbanisation: a paradox, AREA, 20, 127-134.

Wibberley, G.P. 1972. Conflicts in the countryside, TOWN AND COUNTRY PLANNING, 40, 259-265.

Wiener, M.J. 1981. ENGLISH CULTURE AND THE DECLINE OF THE INDUSTRIAL SPIRIT 1850-1980. Cambridge: Cambridge University Press.

Wilson, B. 1969. RELIGION IN SECULAR SOCIETY. London: Pelican. First Edition 1966.

Wilson, B. 1973. MAGIC AND THE MILLENIUM. London: Methuen.

Wilson, B. 1976. CONTEMPORARY TRANSFORMATIONS OF RELIGIONS. Oxford: Oxford University Pres.

Wilson, B. 1982. RELIGION IN SOCIOLOGICAL PERSPECTIVE. Oxford: Oxford University Press.

Winter, M. 1991. Contrasting traditions: the church in twentieth century Cornwall. In UNITY AND VARIETY: A HISTORY OF THE CHURCH IN DEVON AND CORNWALL. (ed.) N. Orme. University of Exeter.

Wright, S. 1983. Pigeon-holed policies: agriculture, employment and industrial development in a Lincolnshire case study, SOCIOLOGIA RURALIS, 23, 242-260.

Index